Miriam Lohr (ed.)

A life for L.O.V.E.

*Michael Jackson stories
you should have heard before*

tredition

© 2013 Brigitte Bloemen, Marina Dobler, Miriam Lohr

Verlag: tredition GmbH, Hamburg
Printed in Germany
ISBN: 978-3-8424-5196-4

Das Werk, einschließlich seiner Teile, ist urheberrechtlich ge-schützt. Jede Verwertung ist ohne Zustimmung des Verlages und des Autors unzulässig. Dies gilt insbesondere für die elek-tronische oder sonstige Vervielfältigung, Übersetzung, Verbrei-tung und öffentliche Zugänglichmachung.

Bibliografische Information der Deutschen Nationalbibliothek: Die Deutsche Nationalbibliothek verzeichnet diese Publikation in der Deutschen Nationalbibliografie; detaillierte bibliograf-ische Daten sind im Internet über http://dnb.d-nb.de abrufbar.

Visit us at mjjbook.com.

Contents

On what he would like to be remembered for:

$\mathcal{H}$elping - especially children

Preface

by Brigitte Bloemen, Marina Dobler & Miriam Lohr

The idea for this project started about a year after our first book "It's all about L.O.V.E." was released. The book, that contained stories by fans about their relationship and experiences with Michael Jackson, was well received in the fan community. We were happy about a lot of positive comments and especially about the fact that we were able to donate much more money resulting from the book's revenues to charity than we had initially expected. Apart from general comments on the book, we had also been contacted by enthusiastic readers asking if we would consider doing a "volume two" with more fan stories. While we believe that it had been important to publish a book showing the relationship between Michael and his fans, and while there are, no doubt, still thousands of incredible fan stories out there, we hesitated to put our energy and time into another book like that.

During that time we noticed the many stories about Michael's humanitarian efforts that started to emerge on the internet. As long-time fans we were familiar with a lot of Michael's humanitarian work, however, we were deeply touched by every new story we read and the big difference Michael had made in the lives of so many people.

The contrast to the stories published about Michael in the media at the same time, with the "Conrad Murray trial" unfolding, could not have been more blatant. As they have done for so many years, the media yet again put out outrageous and twisted stories about Michael. We all had witnessed and experienced first hand how misunderstood Michael was for so many years of his too short life. Too many times we had seen his pain caused by the cruel sensationalism of the media, too many times he was crucified for greed and money. And even now, after his death, the slander didn't stop. Untrustworthy sensationalized stories were preferred to beautiful accounts full of love and positive emotions.

The portrayal the world is currently given of Michael and his life is far from being complete and has rather been heavily manipulated during his living years and underwent further modifications after his death. Somehow the public picture of him is like looking into a "distorting mirror": Certain aspects of his life have been pointed out whereas other rather important parts strangely never found the attention they deserve. People talk about his "legacy", but we feel that this legacy is so much more than just that of his musical career achievements and so much different than that promoted in the media. Once asked in an interview what he would like to be remembered for, Michael himself said: "Helping, especially children!". So he himself left no doubt that he wanted his efforts to heal the world to be at least part of his legacy. Could we just sit back and watch how this was overlooked?

Suddenly it was crystal clear that if we would ever take on the burden to work on another book in our spare time again, it needed to be a project collecting stories about Michael's efforts to help, to be a source of support and positive energy for people, to be a good example as a human being, to spread love. It became a concern for us to create a record of Michael's small and big achievements - not his musical and artistical successes, which are well documented and recognized around the world, but his humanitarian accomplishments.

Only few people know that Michael Jackson not only broke records in the field of music and entertainment, but he also used his influence and success to break records with his humanitarian achievements. The Millennium Edition of the "Guinness Book of World Records" lists him for breaking the record of "Most Charities Supported By a Pop Star "; until the year 2000, Michael had given to 39 different charity organizations. Estimated amounts speak of more than 300 million dollars that were donated by Michael during his lifetime. And in 1992 he even set up his own charity organization called "Heal the World". He used his extraordinary level of fame to change things for the better and make people aware of problems long before it was popular to do so.

Recognizing his countless efforts to help and give, Michael has also received some awards during his lifetime, as well as after his death. Organizations like the NAACP, the UNCF or the "Boy Scouts of America", to name just a few, have honored him for his humanitarian work. Presidents Ronald Reagan and George Bush Senior have awarded him with acknowledgements for his commitment against drugs and his care for disadvantaged children at his Neverland Ranch. Rumour has it that he was even nominated for the Nobel Peace Prize twice, in 1997 and 2003 - the Committee only releases the names of the nominees officially 50 years later. Considering this public appreciation of Michael's charity work by well-known and recognized organizations and even presidents, it seems all the more strange that large parts of the public are not aware of Michael Jackson's humanitarian efforts.

We know that already much information on Michael and his humanitarian work is available on the internet, various beautifully designed sites are dedicated to this topic, however we believe that in our fast moving times, books become more important on the long run, as internet sites can easily be erased and valuable information can get lost. Books might spread much slower but they are here to stay.

Actually, both of our books started with the question: "Why isn't there a book that shows...?" We are no writers, no publishers, no professionals in the area of editing, and no native speakers of English – so maybe we are not the ideal people to take on a project like this. Although we worked hard on both books, we can never accomplish anything near perfection, but what we realized working on both projects is: If nobody else does it, then you have to do it yourself – if you really feel it is the right thing to do! Just as Michael said, "It's us, or else it will never be done". So we did it!

However, we knew from the start that this project would not be an easy task and, no doubt, there were times when we thought about giving up. Only our love and dedication for Michael helped us to keep the faith and not throw in the towel on the way.

Several factors made this project a challenge. First of all, we had to find people we could contact. Luckily the internet is a great source for that matter and it did not take long until we had an impressive list of people whom Michael had worked or been friends with. Our next step, however, was already more tricky, as it was to find out names of people whom Michael had helped directly. Those names were rarely publicly known as Michael tried his best to keep his help secret, so not many names could be found via the internet. After a lot of research, we at least managed to find some.

Naively we believed that contacting charity organizations that Michael had closely worked with would be easy game. But to our great surprise, we learned that almost all organizations had some kind of policy not to disclose any names or information about projects they had done or people who received help through them. Others could not even locate such information in their archives anymore, too much time had passed already. Not even our close contact to "Make-A-Wish Deutschland e.V. (Germany)", who receive ALL revenues from both books, was able to help us getting information from some of their sister organizations who had worked with Michael on several occasions. It was frustrating.

On top of that, many of those people we could get in contact with, were not easy to handle either. The work on this book was like a roller-coaster ride. Great excitement and joy about amazing people who contributed, were willing to help us and even tried to find others who could tell stories, went hand in hand with rather disillusioning experiences, when people who call themselves Michael's friends, would only contribute to our charity project if they were paid, would not bother to react on our countless efforts to reach them at all or simply declined for one reason or the other, mostly because they felt it was too much time and effort for them. Still others were reluctant to participate because they were bound by some contract and didn't know whether they could or simply were not allowed to contribute. And then there were those who said "yes" initially, but of some we never heard back again, even after countless reminders.

Although the request of money from people who call themselves Michael's friends was probably most outrageous in our opinion, we were actually more frustrated about the majority of people that did not even bother to react to our multiple requests at all.

To cut a long story short: After the first year of hard work, our outcome was only a small booklet of stories and we were rather disappointed. Michael deserves so much better and knowing that there are thousands of stories out there that only need to be found, we pulled ourselves together and continued the work.

During the second year, we decided to travel to California, hoping to personally find, and more importantly, convince people to tell us about their experiences with Michael. Our journey brought us from Los Angeles to the beautiful Santa Ynez Valley, the community where Michael once owned his famous "Neverland Valley Ranch". Having last been there during Michael's trial in 2005, it was a heartbreaking journey for us in many ways.

Looking out for stories, we literally walked into every shop and talked to every person that crossed our way. Every evening our heads were full of anecdotes which mirrored the people's affection and confirmed our view of Michael. For them, he was not the reclusive superstar the media wanted us to see, but a real member of their community, a real person. They convinced us that Michael was and still is loved and appreciated by a huge majority of citizens, who all remember and honor his charitable work and willingness to help their community. On the day he died, the flag in Los Olivos, the little town closest to his former home, was half-masted as a sign of the deep admiration and thankfulness people still have for him. We were told this ritual is only done for very respected members of this community, which he indeed was.

However, finding people that were willing to tell stories to be printed in our book was like a "Sherlock Holmes"-mission. Not because there were so few things Michael did to help, but rather the experiences people had with him were often very special to them and they wanted to keep them private, whereas others felt embarrassed about needing help at a certain time in their life and some did not feel that their story was spectacular enough to be printed in a book. Michael's way of giving also gave us a hard time, as he had mostly tried to help secretly, so a lot of people who received help never knew that it had come from him. We heard that he would often send money or made for things to be delivered to a needy family via a third person who was not allowed to disclose where the help came from. This was due to Michael's religious beliefs, but more importantly because he did not want to embarrass people. He simply loved to give - and that came from his heart.

The "time factor" was another underestimated barrier. Many years had passed since Michael left the Santa Ynez Valley and quite a few citizens who knew stories about him and his achievements moved away, sadly some even passed away in the meantime.

The fact that so many stories portraying Michael's humanitarian efforts will forever be unheard of, made us aware of how important it is to collect as many stories now, while the contemporary witnesses, the people who had first-hand contact, the ones who can truly portray Michael and his humanitarian work, are still alive! Only they can bear witness for the next generations to come, so they will know who Michael Jackson really was.

So against all odds we finally found them, personally and through the internet: Amazing people who took the time out of their hectic schedules to tell about their experiences with Michael and their feelings about him, who let us be a part of their dear memories and to whom it was a real concern to portray the Michael Jackson they had got to know. It took us two years, but in the end it was worth it and you are able to hold the evidence in your hands right now.

Through all this work on the book, hearing all these stories and anecdotes by people from around the world, we felt that we got to know Michael even better. We had learned all over again how special and unique a human being he was. All our admiration for him and reasons why we love him have been confirmed or even got ahead of our expectations.

Experiencing the emotions of some of the authors of these true stories in this book during personal interviews we did with them or via telephone or email, to see them laugh or cry while talking about Michael was simply amazing. Many times we cried with them. Michael touched people so deeply, that even for those who met several of the biggest stars in their lifetime, Michael Jackson was always very special and left a mark forever.

It was incredible to see that Michael not only seemed to have touched those people, he had also changed them. Often we had the feeling that meeting or working with him must have rubbed off on people. A lot of them had some Michael-like qualities - they were extremely nice, very open and compassionate. Even though they did not know us before, they talked honestly and very respectful to us. Most of them hugged us, telling us that this is what Michael would have done and thanked us for doing this. This impressed us immensely and left us changed forever.

The sad part of it all is that we are left with the intense feeling that the world has been stolen one of its most precious treasures and we can only assume how much more good Michael Jackson could have done if he were still alive. However it was Michael who always looked into the future with optimism, who always saw the brighter days and had great hope for the future of our human race and our planet.

With his songs and his deeds he consistently spread positive messages of global unity, healing and love. "Heal the World", "Earth Song", "We are the World", "Man in the Mirror", "What More can I Give", "We've had Enough" or "They don't Care About Us" were songs with which Michael tried to wake people up from their indifference and make them aware of everyone's responsibility for our world and that every one of us can change the world by doing his or her own little share.

Michael was never afraid to spread his message which is rooted in compassion, kindness and helping one another. In almost every speech or interview he spoke about what was most important to him and closest to his heart - to help and to give whenever he could. So, to get to know Michael Jackson's overlooked legacy, one must listen to his own words. That is why we want to let him speak in this book, too. You will find many quotes by him all over the book telling you what Michael truly believed in and what he wanted to achieve.

He was - and still is - a positive role model for millions of people that understand his message and try to follow his mantra of making the world a better place. Michael recognized and encouraged these efforts when, during a concert in Oslo in 1997, Michael called his fans "his messengers to heal the world". Especially now, with Michael gone, it is important that his fans carry on his message. Therefore we have decided to not only collect stories in this book showing Michael Jackson helping people all over the world, but also to include some accounts of his "messengers": Stories of people whom Michael inspired and who came up with their own projects to continue and spread the message of love and giving as good as they can to continue what he started.

This book can of course only offer a small excerpt of what Michael did in his 50 years of living on this planet. He touched millions more people and helped them without even meeting or knowing them personally all over the world, through his music, the values he shared, the example he set through his deeds and the inspiration he was.

So there is plenty of opportunity for anybody else out there determined to bring out more of the thousands of wonderful stories about Michael Jackson and his humanitarian work on this planet. There can be many more volumes of a book like this - and we truly want to encourage everyone reading this book to collect them!

At the same time we also hope that this book inspires its readers to go out and do something themselves! It doesn't matter whether you support a charity organization by donating money, join one of the initiatives introduced in this book, give your time to voluntary work or just make a homeless person smile by providing them with a good meal. We can all do something, just as Michael sang as a child already, "in our small way".

We are happy that we learned a lesson by following Michael for so many years. He made us aware of the importance of giving and the significance of caring for our planet at a very young age and we try to do our best to continue his message. This book is supposed to be our present to him for his 55th birthday to say "Thank you for the inspiration!" and "Your love will live on forever!".

We hope that you, our readers, will agree with us after reading this book that Michael's life was, no doubt, a life for L.O.V.E.!

THE WAY HE MADE ME FEEL

by Christine Dowling, Ireland

I will never forget the 19th of July 1997. I went to see my hero Michael Jackson in concert! It was my second MJ concert and I was so excited and happy that he had come back to Dublin. When I was picked to go onstage with Michael, I was in shock and will forever be grateful to my sister, who pointed me out to his security. When he picked me, my whole body started shaking, not because I was going to be in front of 35.000 screaming MJ fans, but because I was about to come face-to-face with my all-time hero.

While I was waiting just offstage, Michael ran past me and I let out such a scream, I thought he might have heard me. But thankfully, with all the noise, he didn't! Finally, the music for "Heal The World" began. When I was wheeled onto the stage, Michael held my hand. Normally I couldn't feel anything in my right hand as I had lost the power in it a few years before, but that night I could actually feel Michael's hand. He also turned to me as we headed offstage and told me he loved me - and I knew that he meant it.

A few hours after the concert, I could feel a burning sensation up and down my right arm. The next day I had power back in my right hand. I truly believe I got my power back from simply

20

Picture of Christine on stage with Michael, that he sent her signed afterwards

Portrait of Christine today

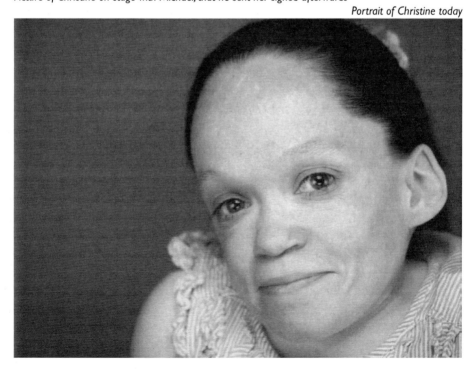

holding Michael's hand. My Ma said: "With 35.000 people singing such a positive song as 'Heal The World', you were bound to get a miracle".

I thought I would share this with you as only true MJ fans would truly understand what happened to me that night, and even though I am in a wheelchair, that night I felt like I was walking on air... I was 18 then and now, 15 years later, I can still honestly say that meeting Michael was THE BEST DAY OF MY LIFE and I am so blessed and thankful that my dream came true.

When Michael passed on I felt as though I had lost a member of my family. He had been a major part of my entire life, way before we had met he had been the biggest influence on me for as long as I can remember, getting me through so many bad experiences that I had as a child. I took his death badly and I felt so lost and confused that I needed to do something for him. I took it upon myself to organise a tree planting for him. I felt that wasn't enough though, so on the 8th of August 2009, alongside the tree planting, I organised a Michael Jackson Memorial / Funday, with all proceeds going to a children's hospital that I myself had attended throughout my childhood. I also did the same in June 2010, the day after his first anniversary, and I will continue to do so every single year for as long as I can. It's my way of giving back and saying thank you to Michael for all that he has done for me and millions of others worldwide. Michael's tree stands proudly in a park in Dublin, surrounded by a children's play-area. I think he would have liked it...

If I could have one last conversation with Michael, it would simply be to thank him for everything he has done for me personally, even though we just met one time, he has made such an impact on my life that nobody has or ever will come close. He opened my eyes in so many ways, not just because of his unique

by Christine Dowling

talent and genius but also for his ongoing kindness, not for one specific person but for the entire human race. He wanted to heal the world and I strongly believe that he did in his own special, unique way. This world is a better place simply because he was in it and I am so honoured and blessed that I got to witness this kindness firsthand.

There will never be another human like you, Michael, but then again I always thought of you as an Earth Angel and I thank God for allowing me to be on this planet at the same time as you. I know I will see you again one day my friend. THANK YOU!

SO THOUGHTFUL OF OTHERS

by Teddy Lakis, Germany

Already when I was pretty young, I knew what I wanted from life: I wanted to see the world and I wanted to work in show-business. I became a disc jockey, presented concerts and fashion shows around the world and finally became an assistant to Marcel Avram, who is one of the world's most renowned personalities in the international concert business. Marcel's agency, "Mama Concerts", has organized tours of world stars like Madonna, Tina Turner, the Rolling Stones, Pink Floyd – and of course Michael Jackson.

I was working for "Mama Concerts" during the "Bad"-Tour 1988 already, but I first met Michael during his "Dangerous"-Tour. I had arranged Michael's hotel in Bangkok and as both Marcel and Michael were very pleased with it, I was soon put in charge of Michael's accommodation worldwide. It also helped that I spoke several languages and so was able to translate for Michael while he was shopping or sightseeing. Over the years a friendship developed between us. We respected each other, Michael liked having me around and I enjoyed working for Michael. He was a guy whom the smallest things could make happy. He was the nicest man, he never yelled at me but was always friendly and very polite. He never complained about any arrangements I had made in the more than one hundred cities

24

First picture of Teddy and Michael, Munich, 1992   Teddy and Michael during the Dangerous Tour

Shopping in a record store in Budapest, Hungary, before the window burst

we visited together, as was often the case with other celebrities. Actually, the first thing he ever told me was "Thank you!" for doing my job and that he wanted me to look after his fans. So consequently, I became his fan co-ordinator. My task was to make the interaction between Michael and his fans an enjoyable one for both sides. So I organized barriers to ensure safety and kept the fans up to date about Michael's plans. I never once lied to them.

Michael was always concerned about his fans. I remember one occasion in Budapest when Michael visited a record store. There were hundreds of fans pressing against the shop window to get a glimpse of Michael. Suddenly the window burst under the pressure. We all started to worry about Michael's safety, and security started to hurry him back to his car. But instead of getting in and fleeing from the chaos, Michael kept asking if anybody was injured. When nobody answered him, he finally climbed up onto his car to see for himself. He shouted "Is anyone hurt?" and we were only able to get him into the car after he assured himself that everyone was alright.

Michael was always caring for others! During the HIStory tour, he also wanted to visit a lot of orphanages and hospitals. So we arranged with the local promoters to select a facility that we could visit for each stop. I also called toy stores in each respective city and asked them if they would donate 5000€ of goods to a hospital or orphanage. Usually they were hesitant. But as soon as I told them that Michael Jackson would distribute their toys and that they would get a "Meet & Greet" with him as well as VIP tickets for the concert, they quickly agreed. Of course this additionally was good advertising for them, but it was also a good deal for us, as the toys were brought to the place we would visit and were ready for Michael to hand out to the kids. Apart from the toys, Michael sometimes also brought other people with him to cheer the children up, for example Michu, a circus midget, with whom he developed a friendship.

Each visit was very emotional. We only arranged these on days where Michael did not have to perform in the evening because he had to be fresh and fit for that. After these visits, on the other hand, he was understandably sad. I often accompanied Michael and we usually fell into each others arms crying after spending a day in a hospital or orphanage. And Michael used to say things like: "Have you seen this cute baby? The doctor said it will only live for another week or so!" or "Did you see this beautiful girl? I can't believe she's going to die!"

Michael was very involved in his charity work and took great care to help where he could. I remember one occasion where he had promised a donation to an organization and his "Heal the world Foundation" somehow had not sent the money. He was very angry and took it to himself to see that the money was delivered as fast as possible.

During his concerts, Michael always dedicated a part of the show to children. While singing "Heal the world", he invited kids on stage with him, children of all ages and nationalities, handicapped, sick or healthy, they were all welcome. Although he mostly did not know his little extras because the local promoters had selected them, it was always wonderful to watch his interaction with them. And it was amazing to see how the kids beamed after their performance. I usually worked at the mixing tower to attend to the VIPs during the concerts and sometimes their children were allowed on stage with Michael. They were always completely hyped when they returned to their parents.

He also loved the company of children when he was at his ho-

by Teddy Lakis

Teddy's and Michael's wedding - fooling around in South Africa

With Michael and his mom Katherine in South Africa

tel. Once when we were in Sydney, there was a crowd of kids playing in the lobby and Michael asked me to get them up to his room. So Wayne Nagin, his bodyguard, and myself brought them up. Michael ordered some ice cream and they had a lot of fun. But they also got a little nosy and started to roam through Michael's closets. Just for fun they started to try on his clothes and of course loved all his sparkling, tailor-costumed outfits. So what did Michael do? He just told them to keep the clothes if they like them. He said they were a gift. That was so typical: He freely gave from the heart and whenever he realized that someone liked something that he had, he had no problem to give it away. Even when he had just bought something for himself, he just gave it away as a present in the next minute. Still in this occasion, when the children left, I had to play the killjoy, follow them to the elevator and ask them to give the clothes back, as there were some stage outfits among them. Michael Bush, MJ's costume designer, otherwise would have made real good business that day.

I witnessed Michael with children so often and I saw how he went out of his way to make them happy and help them however he could. He also helped Gavin Arvizo, although I don't know him personally. I once spoke to Michael about the press, how they twisted and turned things and how he continued to do his charity work, especially for children. Michael told me: "Teddy, I have nothing to hide! I love kids and the kids love me! I would never hurt a child!" He said it emphatically and it really got stuck in my mind.

By seeing Michael's example, I was inspired to do charity as well. I think it's especially important to know where your money goes. And that can be controlled best if you help locally. There are so many needy children in your neighborhood or city as well. I also take my time each year to invite handicapped children to the Oktoberfest in my hometown Munich, Germany. I know many of the vendors myself and arrange for the children to try the wildest rides, if they want to. I buy them some ice cream, sweets and the typical gingerbread hearts. To see their happy faces is all the "thank you!" I need.

My last conversation with Michael was on February 28th, 2009. I was in Las Vegas with my friends, the magicians Siegfried & Roy, who wanted to invite Michael to a gala of theirs. So I tried to reach him but he was unavailable, so I left my number. He called back and was, first of all, perplexed that he had dialed a German number but now reached me in Las Vegas. "How did you do that?", he asked me. And: "Can I do this with my phone as well when I'm in London?" He was already preparing for his upcoming concerts in London, that's why he also could not attend the Siegfried & Roy Gala unfortunately. But we talked for about two hours (which cost me a fortune), he told me about his plans and that he was very excited about the concerts. He even said that, if all went well, he'd come over to Germany to do a concert.

A few days after our conversation, I had a letter from Michael in my mailbox with two tickets for his London concerts for my 90-year-old aunt, whom he had met before, and myself including flights and accommodation. That's just how he was: ever thoughtful of others!

I'm just a person who wants to be honest and do good, make people happy and give them the greatest sense of escapism through the talent God has given me. That's where my heart is, that's all I want to do. Just let me share and give, put a smile on people's faces and make their hearts feel happy.

Do not say Anything!

by Firpo Carr, USA
best-selling author and Jackson family friend

Michael Jackson's humanitarian efforts were enormous. One of the reasons why he wanted to keep what he did secret was because some of the people he helped were at one time rich and famous, and to reveal that he helped would embarrass them, which he would never do! Fathom that. He helped EVERYBODY, and didn't want to toot his horn.

The fact that he passed, which he anticipated, did not void our private agreements. He trusted me, which means a lot to me. I cannot overstate it. Michael and I had a deal, and I take pride in being a man of my word. He may not be here with us today, but he is alive as ever in my heart. I can still see him pointing his finger at me and saying, "Don't say anything." During the trial, the entire nature of the relationship between Michael and me was not for public consumption. It is for this reason that I have not written a book on our friendship covering that time period.

The fact is, few people have ever been as generous as Michael Jackson. If it is true that actions speak louder than words, then Michael's magnanimous actions would gracefully reverberate for a long time to come down the eternal corridors of time.

...TAKE A LOOK AT YOURSELF...

Messenger

by Stephen Simpson, UK

What do I think when I hear the name Michael Jackson? "The biggest heart that had ever lived!" I first heard Michael through my parents who were listeners and ultimately the "Bad" album was played a lot in my dad's car. Ever since then I've loved him. But why does Michael inspire me to do what I do for charity? Growing up I was teased at school a lot for various reasons from the age of about 7-18. They'd tease about my dad being disabled as he'd had a stroke and heart attack when I was 6 which paralysed the left side of his body. They would tease me about my weight. They would also tease me about my Psoriasis (which would flake off from my scalp from time to time). When I'd get home I'd always borrow my mum's "Bad" album cassette and play it to feel better. Whenever bad stuff happened or I was feeling low I would listen to Michael. A lot. I even wore out my parents "HIStory" double cassette! Haha! See, that's the thing: Michael's music has the ability to heal those hearts who are open enough to receive it. I'd do this throughout my early to teen years, through the eras of Michael from "Bad" all the way to "HIStory" and on. To fight back against the bullies I'd make myself stronger emotionally inside through his music and through other interests that I had. I also took up Karate which helped discipline me and helped me out mentally.

33

by Stephen Simpson

Stephen during his bike ride to Paris

Finally at the Eiffel Tower

Stephen also took part in other charity bike rides

When I first heard "Heal The World" I absolutely loved the song! The song was positive, uplifting and had a soft touch to it. It wasn't until later that I first heard of the things that Michael did for children and the needy. Watching the "Dangerous"-Tour on TV and seeing Michael on stage with all those children asking everyone to make a better place for you and for me gave me a wonderful feeling inside. I am not a violent person and I really disliked confrontation growing up. I would ask why do bad things happen and why would people be so horrible towards each other. I would hear Michael sing about these subjects and I grew attached to the notion that we have the power within ourselves to make this world a better place. I wanted to do my bit. I'd help my mum and dad out with anything to take the burden away from her looking after my dad with his disability.

Fast forward a few years: my then local gym appealed for members to join their team to take part in a charity bike ride from London to Brighton on the south coast of England. We raised a lot of money for the charity organising the event, "The British Heart Foundation". As it always fell on Father's Day it was my nod towards and my way of saying to my dad "I care". I did this bike ride a few years in a row with the gym as well as taking part in various other bike rides for wonderful charities who dealt with Cancer, Children's Hospitals, Elderly care giving and health. I also took part in a few walks raising hundreds of pounds for charity through my role within the wonderful fan community. I have made great friends on the online Michael Jackson community "MJJC" and their "MJJC Legacy Project", for which I am a team member.

My biggest challenge was to come last year in the shape of the "London to Paris Bike Ride 2011". This ride was 300 miles over 4 days going from London through northern France to the capital Paris. I initially wanted to do the ride on the date June 1st to

June 4th but I missed the registration deadline. So the next date was June 22 to June 25…the anniversary of Michael's passing. At first I wasn't so sure about taking that date as I dread that day each June, as we all do. But after thinking it through I decided I would dedicate the ride to Michael and ride in his name for the "Make-A-Wish Foundation" UK, a cause close to Michael's heart which grants wishes of terminally ill children all over the world. The ride was challenging and I had a big problem on day one when my bike broke which meant I had to use the organisers spare bike to complete the ride. On the 4th and final day all of the riders in the bike ride were gathered at a central point in Paris and we were escorted by convoy by the organisers through the streets of Paris, passed the "Arc de Triomphe" and finally finishing in front of the Eiffel Tower. That convoy of hundreds of riders is an experience I will keep with me for the rest of my life! It was a huge achievement by all involved. I was filled with so many emotions when I finished and almost broke down as I got off my bike next to the tower. I had completed my greatest bike ride in Michael's name and on such an already emotional day for a Michael Jackson fan. He got me through every difficult mile of it!

I don't plan to stop giving. I am planning a ride next year on Father's Day in memory of my dad, who passed away before Christmas, 16th December 2011. I will once again be doing the London to Brighton bike ride. For you dad. RIP.

36

Hope in Humanity

by Adriana Lucas, Denmark

Way back in 1996, I worked at an animal (mostly dogs) shelter just outside London/UK. I worked there till 2007. At that time Michael Jackson stayed in London, too. One day, when Michael and his entourage were about to leave their hotel through the underground-garage, they found a little dog hiding under their car. After getting the dog out, they didn´t know what to do with it. They called for someone who worked at the hotel and that person contacted my friend who worked in the lobby. She knew about our shelter and was a doggie walker at the time, so she called us and asked if we could pick up the dog. Our shelter was overcrowded already, therefore we could not accept more dogs. They came with it anyway and I took it home with me for a couple of days.

Michael, being his usual self, didn´t just let some other people take care of it, he wanted to know exactly where the dog would be taken and what would happen to it. He kept asking about the dog and those who talked to him said that if no one claims it, it will be put down since there is no room left. Michael was very sad and upset to hear that and wondered why we did not have more room available for so many animals need a place. He was told we depend on donations only and had no money to build more. That was the first time we got money from him. Michael made sure we got money to build and rent more space for the animals. He thought it was wrong that such things would be all dependent on donations from people. He thought the state, or how you say, would give money too. In some countries there are so many stray dogs, and he felt as bad for them as for the children.

One year after he had made that donation he wanted to come and visit. To get him there unnoticed seemed to be a mission for the White House people, but it wasn´t really. When he came, the first person he met was me with two puppies on my knee. I was on the floor feeding them. He didn´t say hello or anything, he just went down on the floor and started to talk with them in that silly voice you use with animals. It took him a few minutes before he looked up and said he was sorry and he offered me his hand. I still had one puppy in my hand and a bottle in the other. He giggled when I put it down and we said hello. He got up and wanted to take a look around. He was terrified over how many dogs we had there, not so many cats, sometimes it was full with cats, but more or less always more dogs. And he became very emotional and said he wanted to take all of them with him home – like most people wanted when they came there. Me too, it was very hard working there and after so many years I was drained since it became more and more and people do horrible things to their animals. After a round there and being explained how things work, he invited us for dinner later that night. At that dinner he talked about how he could make a donation every year, and how it would take place without the fact that he was making donations getting out. It fell on me to take care of it.

Next time he was in London he wanted to meet and we did. That is when he asked if I would like to come to Neverland and spend some time there. I could bring a friend which I did.

Piccolina, the dog under Michael's car

Zack made Michael laugh so hard

Those two weeks were the best thing ever in my life. Not because of Michael, but because of the place. I was never a Michael Jackson fan. I had seen him in concert, but I didn´t have any of his records. I liked his music though, but not in that fan way, you know. Still, it was very exciting to be at his home. It is an amazing place, really. He was so proud of his zoo and he showed us around. We were allowed to take out the horses for rides whenever we wanted, we were given free space on the ranch. That is how I got more close to him than just making sure his donations went through. I´m not claiming to be a friend of his, but I think I got close enough to make him feel he could trust me, if only a little. I still have a few text messages from him. When I first met him I had no cell phone, it was just in later years he texted. It was hilarious to see him trying to compose a text message. He kept asking someone, "What do I do now? How do I do a question mark? How do I do this?". It was funny.

The second time he visited us we were outside in our rest area for the dogs. It´s a huge fenced place behind our house, with trees and such things. A very good place for the dogs to play around. We had one dog who got crazy at times and started to run around like a mental thing. And they look so funny doing it and you start laughing. And so did Michael, he couldn´t stop really, and as soon as he looked at someone he started to laugh even more. He didn´t stand still and at one point he bent forward and knocked his forehead on the back of a bench standing there. First it came an "ouch" from him but then he broke down completely and so did we. I still had pain in my stomach the day after because of laughing so hard. He got a little bump on his forehead and he kept talking about it the next time we met. He said, "It´s dangerous to laugh at times". Many people did not know how funny Michael was, when he got very silly, he often couldn´t stop laughing. Watching him hitting his head

40

at our shelter or being chased by a flamingo - those memories still make me smile.

The last donation he did was huge and the shelter is still doing good on that one, and will do for long hopefully if nothing unexpected happens.

Very sad to me, however, is how misunderstood Michael was. So many people never cared and never actually knew all the good he did for the world. Partly it was his own decision, too. He chose to make donations privately and he often said he supported many causes and organisations that don´t know the money is coming from him.

What he said that got stuck in my mind is, "There are so many people in this world, especially Americans who make so much money and yes, they do donate, but what I think is horrible is all the boats and private jets they buy. I do travel by private jet at times, too, but I don´t own one. What on earth would I need a plane for? They should really help more". He seemed to like Angelina Jolie a lot and admired her work for the children and animals. As I said, I never cared much about Michael as an artist, but his desire and efforts to help children, the world and the animals left a huge impression on me. I always used to prefer animals over humans, but Michael, for me, was the kindest human being ever. If everyone was like Michael I would get along with people much better.

Spending a lot of time at Neverland, his private home, and taking part in his more private life influenced my life. I think I was humble before, but spending time with him made me appreciate humans more. I know now there are a few out there that are good. Michael's message was to heal the world and to help. We, who can, should help. Even if we can´t give money, we can give our time and support.

I would like the world to know that Michael was as normal as any of us. Some of us are a little different and we think differently. Michael was very European in his thinking. He had one habit that shows his character and way of thinking: He used to flip over beetles who had ended up on their backs. We were out walking with him when he was in Ireland and he turned around every beetle he saw. My friend has a phobia and couldn´t understand why on earth he would do that. Michael just said, "Everyone has the right to live, everyone has the right to a second chance".

Michael, thank you for giving me hope in humanity!

I find in animals the same thing I find so wonderful in children. That purity, that honesty, where they don't judge you, they just want to be your friend. I think that is so sweet.

Invited by the King

by Cécile Duteil, France

Michael Jackson's admirers all know pretty well that there is a place where he loved to stay when he was traveling in Europe: Disneyland Paris. The first job I had after my studies was in this theme park, in 1996–1997. And that's how I had the wonderful chance to see Michael (on two occasions) and to witness his generosity.

One afternoon I was working near the Disneyland Hotel. A group of fans - who knew he was there on that day - was calling for him for hours. Eventually a window would open very quickly. I saw a black hat, black glasses, black curls, a mask and a white glove waving at us. It was so quick I'm not sure it was Michael or a marionette. Anyway, Michael has been seen several times there for sure. I often was in the same hotel, too, but did not have the chance to meet him there. We were never told when there were celebrities at Disneyland, so that the news would not be spread and the VIPs would not be disturbed.

Another day, as my colleagues and I met our team leader at the office, she informed us that Michael Jackson had offered some free concert tickets for Disney cast members (employees). She asked who would like to have one. I would not miss such a great artist! So I took tickets, one for myself and one for my

44

brother. At that time we were both living in the same flat. He was a student. Some of Michael's songs and short films were among my favorite. I was not a fan then but to me, he was one of the best, if not the best entertainer in the world.

On June 29th 1997 my brother and I went to Paris and attended Michael's "HIStory" Concert at the Parc des Princes. It was a great concert. We were impressed by the "lean" effect. My best memory is "Earth Song", when he climbed on the "Cherry Picker" and was hanging on it, like flying over the crowd. This is the closest I have seen him.

I did not know then that I would become a fan, I am very thankful to him that I was able to see him live and this is a souvenir I cherish a lot. I have read that he often offered concert tickets. This beautiful experience shows that he did so indeed, and not only for disadvantaged children. My brother and I lacked nothing but with our little incomes then, we could not afford concert tickets. So if we had not received invitations we would not have had the chance to attend Michael's concert. This was probably Michael's way to thank the cast members, those who contributed to the magic of Disneyland. We were asked by our team leader not to tell about the free tickets. Was that Michael's discretion ?

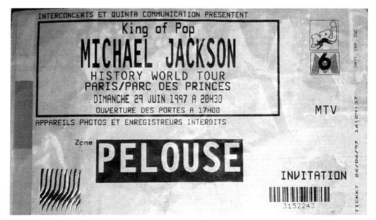

by Cécile Duteil

HE DID IT FROM HIS HEART

by Alex Gernandt, Germany

Michael Jackson is still the King of Pop, the greatest artist that has ever set foot on earth. Michael Jackson changed the world – not only as a god-gifted entertainer who thrilled millions around the globe with his breathtaking performances and larger-than-life stage shows, but also as a true humanitarian who cared for people and tried to help them in many different ways. I had the honor of working with Michael as a reporter for BRAVO magazine, meeting him 13 times during the "Dangerous" and "HIStory" World Tours as well as being guest on the video sets of "Scream", "They don't care about us" and "Stranger in Moscow", which was the greatest experience of my life. I am extremely grateful for having had the opportunity to talk to him, get to know him, laugh with him and just watch him do his thing. He was the coolest, nicest, sometimes funniest person you can imagine. I wish more people could have experienced that...

During my time with him, I was able to experience his humanitarian efforts firsthand. I remember, for example, that, before starting his shoot for the "HIStory"-Trailer in Budapest, Michael and his wife at that time, Lisa Marie Presley, visited two hospitals. Michael brought a whole truck load of toys with him, which he gave to the sick children: Barbie dolls, Batman- and Mickey Mouse

46

figures, comic books and gameboys. Lisa Marie and Michael were visibly moved while going from one bed to another, greeting the kids with pecks and seeing their thankful faces. Their special empathy was directed towards the four-year-old Bela Farkas, who had a liver disease and only a few more months to live. Michael spontaneously decided to pay for his flight to the USA as well as the liver transplant there, which was indispensable for life. A girl with a stomach disease, who had not spoken since three months, suddenly talked again after Michael had tenderly caressed her hair. Michael, the miracle healer, also donated a considerable sum of money to the director of the clinic, Tamas Dizseri, to purchase new breathing apparatuses. In the following days, Michael visited kids in the "Bethesda" children hospital - this time without the press being there. Each time he stayed three hours.

When Michael visited the orphanage "St. Ecatarina" before his "HIStory" concert in Bucharest, we were the only reporters who were allowed to follow him! Michael was distressed. He told me: "There are thousands of children in orphanages in Romania. Most of them have lost their parents, but some were just rejected from their families." Michael sat on the floor with dozens of kids around him. He was very relaxed and smiled a lot. The children between two and four years curiously observed him at first, but when Michael started to put together some Lego bricks, they quickly joined in the game. Michael did not have any fear of contact although some of the children had AIDS. He gently picked up a baby who had been abandoned on the doorsteps of the institute only days earlier. A little girl called Maria started to put candy into his mouth, which was a very moving moment. These children had never known the warmth of a home, nobody wanted them. Their eyes were sad and fearful. For one day Michael brought a bit of sunshine into their lives. During his visit the whole

47

Alex presented Michael with a Golden Otto Award for "best singer" and the first edition of BRAVO Magazine from 1956 on the set of "Stranger in Moscow".

One of the many articles on Michael that were published in BRAVO. Here: Michael's visit to an orphanage in Bucharest

orphanage was filled with a cheerful atmosphere, contrary to the usual sadness. He distributed gifts, flowers, toys and played with the children for hours. A staff member said to me: "I have never seen the children that happy. For them it was like Christmas!" Michael also donated a considerable sum to the director of the institute in the name of the "Heal the World Foundation", which he had founded to help children. It was obvious that Michael did not do this for PR-purposes but from his heart, as there were no journalists allowed; he only made an exception for BRAVO. In the evening, Michael went sightseeing in Bucharest and did a tour of the majestic palace, where he also attended a traditional show in the great hall and gave a speech about his concern for children around the world: "Children are our future! They are the most important thing we have. My greatest wish is that politicians thought more before sending their children to war!"

Other superstars lie in their whirlpools, drink champagne and enjoy their life while Michael spent his time and energy on helping children. And whenever he did you could tell that he did it from his heart!

by Alex Gernandt

I saw this little kid, his name was Farkas. He was very sick. I asked his nurse, "What's wrong with this kid?" She said that he needs a liver. I said, I'm not gonna let him die. No matter what it takes, I'm gonna find a liver for him. So I sent my organization around the world. We went all over the place and it took a long time. I was so happy when I got a phone call. They told me, "We've found a liver!" And he has his life. I'm so proud that I could help him.

Michael's Dream Foundation

by Christine Serene, USA and her team from around the world

Michael Jackson was a caring and loving man with a heart as big as the sky. He never feared to be judged for saying what he felt had to be said. He wanted people to care, and open their eyes and heart to what was going on on our planet.

He was always concerned about the world, and felt so deeply the pain of the sick and deprived, especially when it came to children. He was always very vocal about his desire to help children, and yet remained very quiet about all the gestures and actions he took to help those in need.

He didn't do it to become well known for doing it. He did it because that's what his heart wanted him to do. ~ Tom Mesereau

He mentioned many times his desire to build homes and hospitals for children, but unfortunately, the world never allowed him to fulfill his deepest desire.

Michael's humanitarian efforts were recognized through trophies and certificates, but he always had that dream that he never managed to fulfill, and this dream didn't die with him. It was passed along to us, his fans, his "Army of Love" as he once called us.

51

by Christine Serene

1- The HIStory of Michael's Dream Foundation

On 27 September 2011, Michael Jackson fans around the world braced themselves as the Conrad Murray trial began. While each and every fan was keen to seek justice for the untimely death of their hero, they also knew that the trial would bring many unpleasant revelations about the events leading up to Michael's death.

One such revelation was the recording of a heavily drugged Michael Jackson, slurring his words, but talking about his desire to build a children's hospital, with the proceeds of the "This Is It" tour. "I'm taking that money, a million children, children's hospital the biggest in the world, Michael Jackson's Children's Hospital…", Michael had said.

There can be no doubt that the heart of every fan around the world broke all over again upon hearing that disturbing recording. For many, it opened up the still raw wounds of grief, the grief that was still there and had been there ever since that tragic day – 25 June 2009.

And yet among those millions of grieving, heartbroken fans, there was also a sense of injustice. It had become clear from that recording that building Michael Jackson's Children's Hospital was Michael's biggest dream, and would more than likely be the greatest act of humanitarianism Michael could do. How tragic that he would not be alive to fulfill that dream. Fans within the MJ community felt it incredibly unfair that he didn't get the chance to do it, to build that hospital for the children he loved so much.

And then one fan asked the all important question that would change that sense of great injustice: "What if we could do this

52

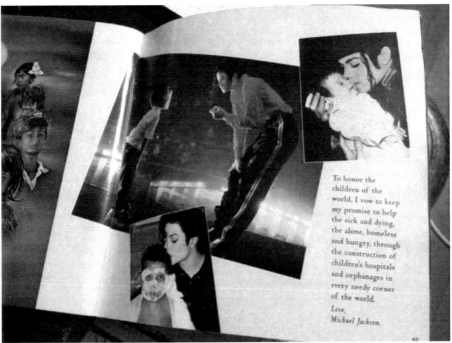

To honor the children of the world, I vow to keep my promise to help the sick and dying, the alone, homeless and hungry, through the construction of children's hospitals and orphanages in every needy corner of the world.
Love,
Michael Jackson.

Michael's message in the HIStory booklet

One of the numerous pillow cases Michael signed for his fans, mentioning the children

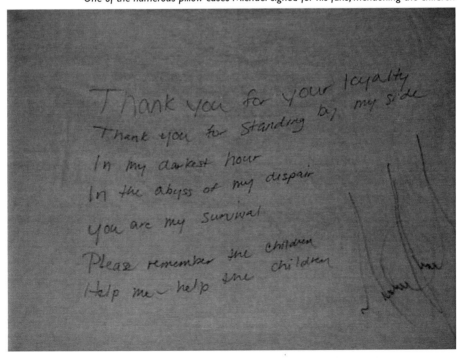

for Michael?" When faced with such a question, perhaps some people would mull it over and decide that with Michael no longer with us it wasn't possible. It would remain an unfulfilled wish, a strong desire Michael sadly took to his grave. But one group of fans pondered the question deeply; "Yes. What if we could do this for Michael? What if we could do it for him?"

Very quickly, that small group of fans sprang into action, setting up a Facebook group to find out if there were others within the MJ fan community who were also pondering that question. Within the space of a week, not only did it become apparent that yes, many were asking themselves if it really could be done, but they wanted to put words into action! The group had grown to over 1000 members and the answer became clear - "Yes, we CAN do this for Michael!"

But there was much work to be done. If the children's hospital Michael had spoken about was going to be built, then it had to be done properly, the way Michael would have done it himself. After all, this was to be the ultimate tribute to a man who had dreamed it for decades, but sadly never got the chance to do it. This was our gift to him, to our hero, our friend, our inspiration, our Michael. And like Michael, we knew that such a hospital would change the lives of sick children around the world. Michael's humanitarian efforts were well documented throughout his life-time. And now we, his fans, are about to continue that legacy through love.

Preliminary meetings with lawyers and accountants were scheduled in an attempt to seek as much advice as possible into the setting up of a genuine and strong non-profit organization, intent on undertaking such a monumental task. A small team was set up to administrate the initiative until finally Michael's Dream Foundation Inc. (MDF) and the Michael Jackson's Children's

54

Hospital Project (MJCH) were born.

Building a children's hospital of this magnitude, from the ground up, takes more than bricks and mortar. We needed, and still need, support, lots of support. This was to be a worldwide initiative, needing worldwide support. A network of worldwide representatives was set up in order to gain that support. They set to work spreading the word in their countries and regions that we were determined to make Michael's last dream come true, and that everyone's support was necessary. Pledges of support started to be gathered, flying in at an unprecedented rate. More and more people from within the fan community came forward, eager to lend their support and help in any way they possibly could and each one fired up by the two things Michael had taught us all – L.O.V.E. and humanity.

That was almost a year ago. Today the MJCH project goes from strength to strength, gaining pledges of support at a rate of about 400 per month. We currently have representatives in over 40 countries and states, and supporters in over 100 countries worldwide.

This incredible out-pouring of love and support for Michael's unachieved dream, learned from a disturbing and upsetting recording in a criminal trial, became so strong that we are determined to go the distance, and do all that needs to be done to achieve what Michael would have done if he was still with us.

2- What we hope to achieve

Michael's Dream Foundation's ultimate purpose, as stated in the name, is to build Michael's dream, his children's hospital with his name on it. This would remain forever a testimony of what he inspired in the world, especially for his fans; those who didn't just listen to his voice, but also to his heart.

I admire the fans who are working towards building the hospital. They understand his heart. ~Karen Faye

This will also be the ultimate tribute, and proof to the world, that Michael was nothing less than one of the greatest humanitarians that the world has ever known. Too many were blinded by the media's lies, and they didn't see who Michael really was. This will change, and hopefully the realization of his dream will help.

Michael had a vision, and that vision is the one Michael's Dream Foundation adopted. He didn't just want to build a children's hospital, where it was a necessity, he wanted to make that hospital as perfect as possible so that the children had everything they needed to feel better not only physically, but mentally too. He spent his whole life going from children's hospital to children's hospital, passing through orphanages and schools, and he saw what all those places had and what they were missing. This allowed him to create in his mind the hospital he wanted to build, the one he mentioned in the recording played in court in September 2011:
"...Michael Jackson's Children's Hospital gonna have a movie theater, game room. Children are depressed in those hospitals, no game room, no movie theater, they're sick because they're depressed, their mind is depressing them...I want to give them that, I care about them, them angels, God wants me to do it,

56

God wants me to do it, I'm gonna do it..." (Excerpt from recording)

Michael's Dream Foundation lives by those words, no matter how sad they, and the circumstances in which we heard them, are; because no matter what people might say, what comes out of that recording, is that, even heavily sedated, Michael had one thing in his mind: Help the sick children whose pain he felt so deep in his soul. That speaks volumes of the heart and soul of this beautiful man, who lived for the children of the world, whom he considered his own children.

Since the building of Michael's hospital is such a huge undertaking, it was decided that our first mission would be something else that Michael mentioned, and felt strongly about: build game rooms in existing hospitals, to uplift the children's spirit, and increase their healing chances. The MDF committee feels that this would not only be something that Michael would have approved of, if not done himself, but also something that will show the community how serious we are. And when the foundation is large enough, Michael's Children's Hospital will see the light of day. When and where remain unanswered questions. We have a team in place that only does research on the different possible locations, looking at the legal feasibility, as well as the costs and needs so that Michael's dream is not only financially feasible, but is also built where it is extremely needed. Just like Michael would have done…

Michael's Children's Hospital is most likely decades away, but with the right dedication and hard work, anything is possible. Michael taught us that, and he is our inspiration through it all.

3- How has Michael inspired us?

When you think about Michael Jackson, what do you see? The entertainer? The singer? The amazing dancer? Or do you look beyond the Hollywood glitter and see a man who, despite his superstar status, always remained humble?

"Even though you become powerful or have power with people, with your talent…underneath all that be as humble as a child, as a baby, and be as kind and as giving and loving." ~ Michael Jackson

Even as a little boy in Gary, Indiana, Michael was always aware that there were people in this world who were less fortunate than him, and he always did the best he could for them. He always believed in giving something back.

When the Jackson 5 first started out, Michael would take his earnings from the shows, and use it to buy candy and in the yard of 2300 Jackson Street he would give that candy to the poor children who lived nearby. His father, Joseph, would regularly criticize little Michael for giving the candy away instead of selling it but undeterred Michael would continue to donate his candy to children who were less fortunate than him.

"Michael, he would give his last to anybody, if they needed it. That's just the way he is." ~ Joe Jackson

Such simple acts of kindness were perhaps the basis for Michael becoming one of the greatest humanitarians of our time. Whenever he became aware of a child suffering, he sprang into action; doing everything he could to help that child. A new liver for a dying boy in Budapest, aid parcels for war-torn countries in Eastern Europe and even instructing his driver to stop so he could chat with the children playing in the slums of Bombay, India. While on tour, he was never too tired or too busy to visit local children's hospitals and orphanages offering love, comfort and gifts to all those children. He regularly referred to the children of the world as his children, because in his heart he felt responsible for each and every one of them. Michael was a person who cared. No matter how big his fame, he never forgot his roots and how lucky he was to have what he had. Just as being the greatest entertainer in the world was his destiny, so was his mission to spread his message of love and help whoever he could, even if it just meant putting a smile on a face.

"You know, sometimes I feel so guilty when I have dinner or breakfast because I realize how so many people don't have those simple things that we so much take for granted. And people, they sit at the table and they pray and all that, which is beautiful, but to do something is the thing, you know, you have to act. I think it's important to help out as much as you can. If one person would just help one child they've done so much and if you can do that, it would be beautiful, just to help one person would be a lot - it's a big step forward because it's a lot to be done, and children all over the world are in such need." ~ Michael Jackson

Some may think that the albums he sold, the many concerts he sold-out, and the records he broke were his greatest achievements. But what he wanted his greatest achievement to be, is what we are trying to do today.

"I'm gonna do that for them, that will be remembered more than my performances, my performances will be up there helping my children and always be my dream, I love them, I love them. Because I didn't have a childhood, I had no childhood, I feel their pain, I feel their hurt, I can deal with it..." ~ Michael Jackson (Excerpt from court recording)

59

In the eyes of every volunteer of Michael's Dream Foundation his greatest achievement was having the most pure, innocent, loving and caring heart, and maintaining it for 50 years, until his tragic and untimely death; and throughout those 50 years, he taught us the lessons of his heart; to love, to care, to always consider those who need help, to be the best that we can be. And most importantly to ALWAYS remember the children.

We, at Michael's Dream Foundation, carry those lessons through our mission every day, in everything we do. In our attempts to gather as much support as possible, Michael's heart is always at the forefront of our minds and our hearts. Each one of us is doing this for love. We are doing this for Michael, with Michael and because of Michael.

Michael once said; "always help the children. Help me to help the children." And through Michael's Dream Foundation and building the Michael Jackson's Children's Hospital, that is exactly what we will do.

There is nothing like a dream to create the future. ~Victor Hugo

Another one of Michael's messages mentioning the children

The official logo of "Michael's Dream Foundation"

Michael's Dream
Foundation

by Christine Serene

4- MDF volunteers and Michael

Michael's Dream Foundation is a 100% volunteer initiative, and because we all have our reasons to be a part of this project, some of us wanted to share them here.

"As far back as I can remember Michael Jackson has always been a part of me. When I was eleven I fell in love with Michael and his music, he was a few month older than me and I imagined Michael being my friend. I was in an unfortunate living situation as a child and subsequently separated from my other siblings, it was a dark time. I was presented with a record album called 'Ben'; I listened to that album over and over again which pulled me out of my dark place and back to smiling and feeling much better about myself.

As the years went by I found great comfort and pride knowing Michael Jackson was experiencing the same teen years with me that came with all the oddities. He became more electrifying and dazzled the music industry. I remember the first time MTV showed his video, he rocked my world. Watching and listening to Michael Jackson whenever I could I soon realized that he was more than entertaining the world, he was teaching the world about love. His humanitarian work and generous giving was spread throughout the world. Michael cared so much for the well-being of the children in this world that he lived his life dedicated to children.

When Michael left this world he made a path for all to follow in his footsteps, his work continues in all of us, he taught this world that love is the answer. His love for children made him dream of a hospital like no other, filled with all the things he envisioned, but mostly with love. Michael envisioned a hospital that felt like a home, a warm and fun place, not a sterile cold

62

institutional building. When we all heard his dreams on that recording it hit everyone like a lightning bolt, straight to the heart and minds of many people. This is where 'Michael's Dream Foundation' was born. What better way to carry on Michael's work than to see his dream fulfilled. I know I owe Michael much more than this, a lifetime of friendship, a lifetime of love. Over the past several years it was a painful transition for me but I feel as though I have calm and peace now. I see Michael's vision and I will follow the path he left us. I truly believe that Michael is still leading the way. Many people have come together because they also feel a sanctuary in what this Foundation is doing. We are healing many broken hearts across the world, bringing unity not just as a fan gathering but doing what Michael would have done. I truly believe that Michael would have built that hospital but now it's in our hands. I love you my dear friend and I miss you so much."

~ *Louise A Greer, Secretary/Board and Committee Member*

"To make Michael's dream come true I will do my best. Michael gave us so much, I want to give him all I can and as soon as I heard about the 'Michael's Children's Hospital' project , I knew it was the way to show him my endless love, my dedication, my faith in a better world for our children if we 'raise our voice as one'. 'Michael's Dream Foundation' is part of my life, volunteers in the whole world are my family and I am proud to say that I am the MJCH representative for France and will be until the 'Michael's Children's Hospital' is built. I love you forever Michael."

~ *Brigitte Laurent, Fundraising Team Coordinator/French Representative/Committee Member*

"Throughout being a fan of Michael Jackson, it struck me that he was a very unique being. Never before have I encountered somebody who was not only enormously talented, but somebody who was so humble and sincere. I have constantly followed Michael's humanitarian efforts, and just by seeing what a loving and giving person he was, it has inspired me to become the same both on a personal and professional level.

When Michael died in 2009, I felt as though a part of me died with him. I went through a whole rollercoaster of emotions in trying to come to terms with his death, and one emotion which stood out for me was a sense of injustice. Michael had given so much throughout his life, and yet the media were seemingly unwilling to tell the world about this. Only content with reporting ridiculous stories highlighting their inaccurate perceptions of him, meant that the true essence of Michael, his heart, went unnoticed by those outside of his fan base.

When I began working with MJCH, not only was I determined that Michael's dream of a children's hospital would become a reality, but that finally, the world would take note and recognize that underneath that amazing talent, Michael really was the kindest, most giving, loving and purest human being the world has ever seen. We will never see his kind again. And that is why I made my promise to Michael, that not only would I see his last recorded wish granted, but that I would work tirelessly to continue his legacy of love.

Not a day goes by where I don't thank Michael for his presence in my life and for the lessons he taught me. Without them, I would not have been given this amazing opportunity to make a difference to millions of children across the world, in his honor. Thank you Michael, from the bottom of my heart."
~ *Kerry Ward, Media & Communications Coordinator/ Committee Member*

64

"When I was around 12 years old, my brother in law told me 'come here, you gotta listen to this!', and he put 'Black or White' on. He thought the beginning of the track rocked, needless to say I agreed. That was my introduction to the man who, years later, would become a huge part of my life.

At the time, I wasn't a fan probably because I had no fan around me, I was young, and I didn't have much access to MJ news. The stronger memory I have was something that happened quite a lot of times during my teen years; I would go to bed, get out of it, grab the 'HIStory' booklet, get back in my bed and read it. I didn't understand much English, but obviously I understood enough. I remember clearly tearing up looking at the pictures of Michael with ill children, and those words 'I vow to keep my promise to help the sick and dying, the alone, homeless and hungry…'. Those words are still stuck in my head today. I just knew it wasn't empty promises. I just knew… I didn't know more about Michael than what was in the 'HIStory' booklet, but it felt like I knew everything I needed to know: he had that sensitivity and love that only a few rare human beings have. His heart and arms were wide open to all those in need.

My admiration for him stopped there. Life went on, and then I read the news of his death…Something in me changed. I didn't understand the pain I was feeling. I had never been a real fan, how could I cry every day because of him? Now, I think it is simply because I always knew Michael's heart, and it felt like a hope for a better world had gone with him. But then, the Murray trial started and I heard those words. Through my tears and uncontrollable sobbing, I heard what needed to be heard: no matter what Michael went through, he still had that promise he wanted to keep! So a couple days later when I read on Facebook 'what if we could do that for him?', I didn't need to think twice. I embarked on this project because I still had that

by Christine Serene

promise that Michael made with 'HIStory', that promise that I read so passionately so many times a decade earlier, going through my mind. Because I felt Michael wasn't done with his promise, and that somehow, the horror of this recording was Michael telling us: 'No matter what, I'm not done'. Now we have a chance to not only make the difference he wanted us to make, but also to show the world who this magnificent man was through the greatest tribute he could dream of: His Dream made into a Reality by His Soldiers Of Love. I think that's the way he would have wanted... It started with Michael, it will end with Us. For Him..."

~ *Isabelle Rieger, Promotions team coordinator/volunteer coordinator/Committee Member*

"When I was a teenager I would watch MJ on MTV, loved hearing 'Heal the World' and 'Man in the Mirror' on the radio. I knew about 'We are the World'. I always liked his music and him but sadly never 'truly' knew who he 'really' was, until after he died. I remember the day he died very well. I was on the computer when it flashed the news story across 'yahoo' and all the media outlets. It was such a shock. His funeral was the beginning of me finding out who MJ 'really' was. After the funeral I began searching to see if anything like the 'Heal the World Foundation' was still in place. I began searching about Michael everywhere. I had always been into being a humanitarian and helping people, but after Michael's death I found that this was reawakened in me, stronger than ever. I remembered how I would sit there and cry like a child, just like MJ did, when watching the children starving in Africa. I remember being floored by 'Earth Song'. It was like everything that I felt right there in one song! It was like everything that was in Michael's heart now became part of mine. I began to grieve for this great humanitarian who had given so much love to the world. I began to feel the pain of all the horrible things he had to endure throughout his life. I knew

66

that my life would be changed forever, from this point on. I met many wonderful fans who have had similar experiences after Michael died. These people also knew his heart and wanted to help heal the world and wanted to keep Michael's love alive in a world that seemed so lost without him. During the Murray trial I heard the horrible tape of Murray recording Michael speaking after being put under sedation. What came out of that was a message strong and clear! The message that he wanted to use his money from the 'This Is It' concerts to build a children's hospital- 'Michael Jackson's Children's Hospital'. This tape also showed where Michael's heart was; with the children and with helping others. Under sedation like that he would not be able to hide his true thoughts and intentions. And what came out of this was the truth, that Michael was a great humanitarian!

As soon as I heard this recording it was an immediate feeling of 'how can we make his last wish come true? We need to find a way to build Michael's hospital.' It seemed that many others felt the same way. I then found MJCH on facebook. It was like a dream come true. We could really make his last wish a reality. What grew from something small has now grown into an initiative in over 100 countries worldwide. After joining MJCH as representatives of the Northeastern, United States my husband and I then additionally began to work as team leaders for the research team; researching countries, hospitals and organizations all over the world that are in need that may become our focus in the future. It has been three years since Michael has been gone; he is still remembered, missed and loved all over the world. His love has made a huge impact on this world. His dream is not gone, it is still with us, waiting for us to make his last wish come true... to build a children's hospital to help the children."

~ *Brenda Pineo, New England representative/Research team coordinator/Committee Member*

67

"I remember the first time I saw Michael Jackson on TV. He must have been about 8 or 10 years old. The Jackson 5 were singing, 'I'll be there'. I asked my father, 'Who is the kid with the big red hat?' My father said his name was Michael Jackson and the others were his brothers. 'You should sit down and watch it, they're pretty good'. So I did, and from then on I followed all of the Jackson 5 shows and cartoons. My favorite song was 'Ben'. When I heard that Michael had died, I was in shock. I could never believe that he would ever die. I just sat down and couldn't move. I could feel tears in my eyes. I felt like my best friend had died. The things that hurt the most after Michael's death were when Paris cried at the funeral, when Barry Gordy gave his speech and when Usher sang 'Gone to Soon'.

I watched the whole Murray trial. When I heard that Michael's last wish was to build the largest children's hospital in the world, I thought that it should be done. Now I think it is the least anyone could do for him.

My wife found 'Michael Jackson's Children's Hospital' on facebook and then we decided to become representatives. We were very excited to be a part of something that would be so much of a reflection of Michael's dreams, personality, and his promise to help all the children.
~ Harold Pineo, New England representative/Research team coordinator/Committee Member

"Michael has meant so much in my life. Since I was a child, I loved his music, and I knew of his humanitarian work.... and he has inspired me to continue his legacy now. Many people are unaware of what Michael has done for children and charity in the world. We, the fans, we should instill in the people his work and imitate. 'Michael Jackson's Children's Hospital' gave me the opportunity to start with this work, thinking of a better future

68

for the world and fulfill his dream."
~ *Nikki Golden Jackson, Argentina Representative*

"Unfortunately, I didn't know Michael well before his passing (I'll never forgive myself enough for this!), but then, I felt like I was being pushed as if it was a magnet guiding me towards him, so I started listening to his interviews, because I wanted to hear his words. When I realized who Michael really was, a new world appeared in front of my eyes...such a Wonderful World: Michael's World!!! From that moment on, I decided that my life would never be the same, because thanks to Michael and his immense unconditional love, I realized that I had the chance to literally follow his great example: helping needy people, especially children!!! That's why, when I found out about this huge project, I enrolled immediately, because this was exactly what I was looking for! My commitment to make Michael's dream come true will never fade away, nor will my love and gratitude to him!"
~ *Federica Cambini, Italian Representative*

"First, Michael is my inspiration 24 hours a day since many years, he never knew but he helped me to be a better person. Michael inspired me through his words, his music, his dance, his presence, his message to make a difference, because we are here to change the world. In my land Guatemala together with other loyal fans we try to help needy children in orphanages and old people in hospitals. But we have one more opportunity to help more children thanks to 'Michael Jackson's Children's Hospital', thanks to the great idea by more loyal MJ-fans around the world, because it is a beautiful way to follow his dreams, his legacy and an opportunity to make a better world how he would have wanted it. And thanks to MJCH this dream will come true."
~ *Sharon Mabel Oliva Zapeta, Guatemala Representa-*

by Christine Serene

tive

"Michael's humanitarian works are like the stars in the sky, shining everywhere and uncountable. Never ever in my life I have seen a man so selfless with a child's heart dedicating his entire life loving and giving his best for mankind and for our planet. Any Michael fan not only looks upon him as a great musician, singer or dancer but even more than that as a human who tried to bring that change and show us the path of unity, love and sacrifice. His innocent heart touches every life, for every single person he helped he is no less than an angel. Whenever I see little kids, whether in my family or in the streets, I feel Michael then and can imagine him playing with them enjoying himself. There are many children in the world whom Michael helped during his entire lifetime and gifted them their life and if he would be here now, he would have continued to do so. Even now there are many new stories revealed about how much he did for us all.

I'm just doing my part for those children suffering in the world, taking that step that whatever I may do must help them somehow to smile back at life again and it gives me a sense of peace and joy that I am doing that for Michael. Whenever I am doing something for MJCH, there is only one voice that I hear, it's Michael's last words about building 'Michael Jackson's Children's Hospital', that is the thing that gives me the strength to move forward and give my best towards making his dream a reality. Working with MJCH has given me a reason and hope to live. Without doubt Michael's music and his words have been a turning point in my life. They have given me a proper direction to move. I am so proud and honored to be following his message of our real existence on this planet that is to love all and heal with love without any kind of discrimination. We are all equal and that is what MJCH is about where all fans from around

by Christine Serene

the world come together as a family for Michael. Staying with MJCH I have learned more about Michael and his effortless work done towards humanity. Just wishing we all get and stand together again for his dream and make it a reality being a family filled with love headed by Michael himself."
~ *Taniya Ghosh, India Representative/ Promotions Team Member*

"MJ is, was and still will be inspiration for me. He showed me love, peace and caring. His love for people on this world, especially for children was so big because he had a big heart.
This all is the reason why I do what I do, I mean working for MJCH. Michael is, was and will be a great man and person, an amazing singer, dancer and father. All people around the world love him so much for what he did for this world. Because he wasn't like all other celebrities in Hollywood.

I've loved him since I was 12 years old and everything I do, my behavior, my mind is like Michael gave me something of him. God bless you Michael. I love you so much forever. With L.O.V.E."
~ *Ivka, Slovakia and Czech Republic Co-Representative*

"I've been a fan for only a few years now, yet Michael has made a change in my life that no one else could ever make. I used to be very different, but Michael changed me into a much more loving and caring person who is concerned about others, especially the children. The longer I've been his fan, the longer I was looking for ways to keep his humanitarian legacy alive, but I've only been a part of some small projects and campaigns before I found out about MJCH. That's when I felt that I found something I'd really love to be a part of. After reading about how tirelessly they are working towards achieving Michael's last dream – building a children's hospital – I felt so touched that I said to

71

by Christine Serene

myself I want to help as much as I can. Sending my pledge of support wasn't enough for me, I wanted to do more. That's why I became a representative for Slovakia and Czech Republic and started doing all I could to spread this idea not just to people in my country, but to people all over the world. The project grows every single day and I'm so glad to see that. The love, strength and inspiration Michael had given us makes it possible for us to keep pushing this project forward all the time no matter what, and we won't stop until we see a hospital built. I truly believe we can achieve it. I feel that nothing would be a more beautiful gift for Michael and the children of the world. They are the ones I love more than anything. It's because of Michael that I understood how important children are for the future of this world and for healing the world, and I dedicate my life to helping them and making him feel proud. Now that Michael is no longer with us, someone needs to help the sick, needy and dying children the way he did. As his fans, we should be the ones to do that. If we can make his dream a reality, we can make a difference in the lives of many children all over the world. It means a lot to me and that's why I'll keep doing whatever I can do to help out. The children need us and this is a wonderful chance for all of us to continue in Michael's footsteps."
~ *Dària, Slovakia and Czech Republic Representative*

"How do you say thank you to the most inspiring, genius, talented, caring and beautiful human being that walked this planet?

Michael was my rock, my best friend, the meaning to my life. I have memories of the first music I ever heard; The Jacksons. The first dance video I learned from beginning to end in my mother's living room; 'Thriller'.

Like Michael, but in different ways, I had a difficult childhood. When times were hard and I felt like I couldn't face another day, I would lock myself away and play Michael through my head phones. This was my escape from my pain, I would let my imagination wander and lose myself in his world of songs. Listening to every word he sang, feeling every beat in my heart. I would read the hate and lies in the magazines about him and listen to him fight back with his head held high through his lyrics. Michael taught me to be strong against the face of evil and that it was ok to be different.

I had dreams of helping people just like Michael did to share the love that I had to give. I have a passion for animals and a thirst to help people in need. I ran away from home and school at a young age with no prospects or money. I took strength that Michael gave to me to better myself and change my life around. Today I'm older and wiser; I'm now a nurse and get to help and comfort people every day. I took a leaf out of Michael's book and I fill my spare time with animal welfare and humanitarian work.

I sometimes look back on my life and I know how different it could have turned out if I didn't put my faith in Michael and his music. I had to get away from where I was, Michael taught me to dream and believe and that I did.

When Michael died a part of me died, he was my childhood. I miss him so much every day and his absence never gets easier. Deep down I know he will never leave us, he has given us a path to which we must continue and for as long as my heart beats I will continue his good work and spread his message of love just as he taught me all those years ago.

Thank you for saving me Michael, you are always in my heart. I love you."
~ *Lisa-Marie Armitage, UK Representative/Media & Com-*

73

"Hello! My name is Jenn Connor and I am an upcoming 18 year old Pop singer from Toronto, Ontario, Canada. I am also the Canadian representative for the 'Michael Jackson's Children's Hospital' project.

I have been a huge fan of Michael Jackson for so many years and I truly consider him to be one of my biggest inspirations in my life and in my career as a singer. As an entertainer, Michael Jackson has been a fantastic mentor for me. Michael taught me the importance of singing from my heart and from my soul. He taught me to never sing a song unless I truly mean it. Michael has also inspired me to learn how to dance and to write my own music. Without Michael Jackson's music and his brilliant, larger than life performances, I would have never grown as an entertainer as much as I have now. Michael taught me to never, ever give up on my dreams and to always go for what I truly want in life and believe in. He also taught me to never listen to any negativity, to believe in myself and in my dreams, and to be true to myself as a person and as a performer. Just listening to his touching music and watching him perform has taught me so much and that means the whole world to me. Michael himself means the world to me.

Not only has Michael Jackson inspired me musically, but Michael has also inspired me to be the best person that I can be. Michael taught me the importance of love and the importance of caring for our world and its people. He taught me that one person can make a big difference no matter where they are in the world or what situation they might be in in this world. Michael taught me that we are all one and that we should all love each other like family. It doesn't matter what country a person lives in, what race they are, or what gender they may be, Michael taught me to love everyone and treat everyone as I would like to be treated. I think that is such an important lesson to learn and I couldn't ask for a better teacher than Michael.

I really respect, admire, and appreciate Michael and all he has done for charities all around the world. Michael donated millions of dollars to help children that were ill and less fortunate. He also donated millions of dollars to help animals that were in need. Because of all he has done for various charities, he has inspired me to donate as much as I can to help children and animals. I really thank him for teaching me to be the best person that I can be. I love you so much, Michael. Thank you so very much for all you have taught me in my life and in my career. I really appreciate it from the bottom of my heart and I hope you're looking down on all of your Soldiers of Love with a smile. God Bless you."
~ Jenn Connor, Canadian Representative

"What brought me to want to participate in this cause was of course, Michael. It may sound strange but losing Michael Jackson has given me a different outlook and perspective in life. He has made me want to become a better person not only to my family and friends, but also within the MJ community. His very many unselfish acts of kindness and love, and humanitarian efforts made me realize that if someone with such a high profile, that has been through so very much throughout his lifetime, can somehow continue to give of himself as much as he did, then I also wanted to try and do what little I could do to make a difference in the world or the life of a child. Working with other volunteers in the MJCH project has shown me more love, strength, unity and hope. I have never been more happy or felt more pride than working with these people who also give of themselves freely and willingly towards a common goal, a dream, of making Michael's Dream come true, not only for Michael, but for the very many children that so desperately

75

need someone to help them and love them with the genuine care that Michael would have been giving to them if he were here today. That thought fuels me to move forward every day in life and in this project. It inspires me to try harder and not give up the same way Michael never gave up on the children of the world. With as much grace and love, he did as much as he could possibly do despite his personal turmoil and tribulations. This dream is one that I whole-heartedly believe should become a reality for I see no one more deserving than Michael Jackson. With his strength and his love, we will all continue to push forward until we see it materialize. Thank you for this opportunity to express myself. I wish you all lots of love and blessings."
~ Nancy Perez, New York State Representative/Promotions Team Coordinator's Assistant

"For as far back that I can remember, Michael Jackson has always inspired me. Not just for his amazing talent but also for the love and compassion he had for the sick and needy. I have witnessed first-hand the joy he brought to the unfortunate and it truly is an amazing feeling. He gave out toys to kids, helped parents pay for medical bills, donated large sums of money to hospitals and youth programs in order to bring about change, but most of all, he wanted to spend time with them just so they could smile even if it was just for a day.

Michael cared about anyone who was in some sort of pain, but he was especially sensitive when it came to children. He would spend all day in hospital playing and meeting children and seeing them smile, but when he left he would often cry. He knew what it was like not to be able to run around and play and live a normal childhood and it truly hurt him to see young children confined to beds too sick to move. 'No child should ever be sick' and he truly believed it. He donated millions and millions of dollars to research for AIDS and Cancer in the hope that

76

one day a cure would be developed so both children and adults could live normal happy lives.

Michael did all this out of his own heart. He would invite hundreds of children to his Neverland Ranch and let them roam the grounds playing and having fun on the rides, in the pool, having water balloon fights, playing with animals from his small zoo but most importantly smiling. Together, Neverland and Michael created some sort of 'magic'. I cannot explain it. Many children went to Neverland extremely sick and months later were completely cured and to know that he had this effect on people really warmed his heart.

Having spent a lot of time with Michael, I believe it is now our duty to continue on with his legacy and make this world a much happier place for both adults and children. He literally has done so much for me and I desperately believe and want his final dream to become reality- the 'Michael Jackson's Children's Hospital'."
~ Kam Costigan, Australia Co-Representative

"Michael has inspired me throughout my life to do good for others. He had the most beautiful soul! I have a life-long goal to pay it forward in Michael's memory. Working for 'Michael's Dream Foundation' (MJCH) has been a dream for me! Over the years, Michael has visited hospital after hospital, helping sick children feel better about themselves and showering them with gifts. Michael wanted to take the money from the 'This Is It' tour and build a Children's Hospital. I can't explain the wonderful feeling I get, to be able to be a part of this. It is up to the fans to keep his legacy alive and MJCH is doing just that. Michael will always be in my heart and many around the world. I can say from the bottom of my heart that MJCH is everything Michael would want. We love from the heart and never judge. I know Michael would be proud to see that we are all coming together

77

to make this happen for him and all the children of the world. Michael is gone but never forgotten, he will always be with us, through us!"
~ **Christina O'Donnell, Pennsylvania State Co-Representative/Promotions Team Member**

"Michael, Michael, Michael. I just couldn't imagine the world when he's not around. He became a part of me when I was 10 years old. Before that, I didn't know myself that much. I didn't know how the world revolves. The only thing I remember before Michael was the Olympics, 'Schindler's List', 1992 Presidential Elections, and Macaulay Culkin. If I think about it, after listing all that, Michael was already a part of me. That thought just slept, and after June 15, 1995, I woke up. What struck me personally about Michael, aside from his music, his dance, his business affairs, was his personality. If it hadn't been for Michael, I bet I would've jumped off a building already. Sorry for that, but that's how I feel. But because I saw how he overcame the hurdles of his life, I knew, if he can make it, so can I. It is when you do something good, something extraordinary, that people will start bashing you, putting you down by making up stories. That's the reality of life, and our way of acceptance is to continue doing something good, something extraordinary.

When I saw a post searching for country representatives for 'Michael's Children's Hospital', I didn't think twice. I went straight to one of my email accounts and right away I presented myself for the Philippines. After that email and being accepted as the Philippines's country representative, I was so happy to finally represent for something other than being a President of 'Michael Jackson Filipino Fans Club Worldwide', for a project that is close to my heart. There were, of course, many opposers to me being a representative, but in the end, I allowed myself to immerse in 'michaeling', and focus on being Michael-like in char-

78

acter so that we can go on to do our work as administrators, along with the MJCH co-administrators here in the Philippines. Having detractors is a way of life, but it is not something that should hinder our planning and implementation on what we can do regarding the hospital.

I am almost done with my Masters' Degree in Nursing at St. Paul University-Manila. What connects this degree to MCH? Well, for one, building a hospital is a task that is not being taken lightly. It has to be handled by the people who know a lot about administering the hospital, and one of its requirements is to have a master's or doctorate degree. It is a great opportunity for children, especially those who cannot provide adequate funds for their treatment, to be in a place that is supported by Michael's fans, by the local government, and hopefully by 'The Michael Jackson Estate'. With this, the children will have a better place for them to be treated. It is also an amazing opportunity, not just for myself, but also for the numerous healthcare professionals who do not work as doctors or nurses, just to get experience in their jobs. They finally are going to be given a chance to grow in their own fields and at the same time they can help the children in a lot of ways. Lastly, we do this for Michael. He had dreamed of having this hospital, and wow, he even thought of that at the verge of being on medication. The dream that he is dreaming is being continued by his loving fans, despite of differences all fans are united to build this wonderful hospital. The detractors' view on Michael will be changed for the better, erasing what the kids were told about him in his later years.

'Michael's Children's Hospital' has definitely influenced a lot of people in a lot of ways. There are fans who hold up their pledges as a 'wall of love', fans who make videos expressing their pledge, and those fans who are willing to give donations

79

for this wonderful cause. What a wonderful experience it is and will be, and I'm very thankful that I am one of those who represent this hospital in the country that I grew up and learned to love truthfully."

~ Diann Margott Santiago, Philippines Representative

"When I think of the word inspire… one person comes to my mind. The one who's inspired me to do so much and in a way helped shape who I am today. That one person is Michael Jackson. I fell in love with Michael because of his humanitarian efforts. Sure, his talent is remarkable but his heart is what I love most. When he passed… it was shocking to say the least. It didn't seem real, it still doesn't today. I'm not sure it ever will honestly. However, I am honored to be able to be a part of a wonderful project like MJCH. I love everyone I work with daily, they're all wonderful people.

When the trial first came about and I heard that heartbreaking recording, I was completely shocked. No matter the circumstance Michael was always thinking of others. It blew me away and I wished more than anything he could get his dream. When a friend of mine called me late at night to tell me the fans were actually trying to make this happen, I instantly wanted to be a part of it. I wanted to be able to be a part of Michael's dream. I wanted to be able to give him something back after all the countless things he gave us. It seemed like a wonderful idea.

Michael inspired me to make a difference through MJCH in many ways. Condensed down, it is who he was and what he was all about. Helping sick children in any way possible, even if it's just by giving them some fun, which helped their recovery. The smile on their face, the laughter they break into is enough to make my heart feel warm. Having fun can mean so much for a child, much more than people think. It gives them a sense of

hope. I wanted to help making that possible, just like Michael did. His spirit, his messages, his heart, all of this, what made Michael Michael, inspires me to make a difference through MJCH, as well as through my life in general."
~ *Sam Shirk, Pennsylvania State Representative/Promotions Team Member*

"Michael Jackson is my greatest teacher; he was the man who inspired me to make a change in my life and become a better person - to make the world a better place. By his teachings of love and peace, I have looked at the world through brand new eyes; I feel things I never did before. I am better, I am stronger. Joining the MJCH/MDF was my way of giving back what Michael gave to me. I have this incredible opportunity to work with a group of dedicated, talented, beautiful individuals from all over the globe; carrying out this dream by our bare hands. The MJCH project will affect everyone - not just sick children but also the people who have lost faith in humanity. Let this project serve as a provider of hope to the people, let it be known that we, the people, can accomplish anything if we join together. The people, if united and dedicated, can make this world a better place. I believe that the MJCH will be a reminder of that, and will inspire others to make that change. I am very proud of being part of the MJCH because I get to be a witness of the power of love, I get to see with my own two eyes HIStory in the making, I get to be a part of something larger than myself. And isn't that what all people want? To belong to something? We are like a family here at the MDF. Sometimes I imagine what the Children's Hospital will be like, and I visualize all the little patients laughing, playing, and smiling - being medically taken care of while still living a happy childhood. Michael taught me to never give up and to do things to the best of your ability, and so I will. I will always look to Michael for advice and inspiration for healing the world, and I will always be a proud member of the MJCH. If only Michael

81

could see that this grand dream is coming true. Now, we all carry the torch of L.O.V.E. that Michael passed onto us. It's our job - we'll make him proud."
~ *Addie James, Washington State Representative*

"I can't remember a time when Michael wasn't in my life. I watched J5 on the Ed Sullivan show, Dick Clark and also the J5 cartoon! My first 45 record of MJ's was 'Ben'. I played it until it wore out. From buying my daughter the 'Thriller' album to my little grandson's favorite video, 'They Don't Care About Us', Michael is multi generational in my family. I think I took for granted that he would always be here, because he always had been. When he died I felt like I had lost a family member. The world was a colder darker place without his beacon of light and his love. I knew I needed to do something but didn't know what. When I heard the tape played during the trial I knew what I needed to do. I believe Michael helped me find MJCH. Our community of love has allowed me to meet the best people this planet has to offer! Everyone involved here are the most loving and giving people there are, and I feel blessed to be a part of such a loving tribute to the love Michael had for all the world's children! I personally believe Michael was sent here to remind us how to love and help people, and I got the message. My MJCH family selflessly gives of their time, creativity, encourage-ment and love. I am honored to be a part of the legacy we will leave for future generations to come."
~ *Julie Dodge, Illinois State Representative*

"I fell in love with Michael during the 'Thriller' era, as I lay across my bed swooning over the photo on the 'Thriller' cover. Although my life did not revolve around him, and I didn't follow him around the world, and I never even saw him in concert, he apparently stayed in my heart all these years, his love seemingly lying dormant until just the right time when it would have the

82

greatest impact on me. I believe fully in all that Michael Jackson stands for: love, unity, healing, compassion and magic. His philosophies guide me in my everyday life and are the reason for me being so committed to the MJCH project. I believe in him, and this project, with all of my heart and soul and I promise to do everything in my power to see it through! I love you Michael, with everything that I am, and I promise to never let you down again."

~ Christine Serene, President of Michael's Dream Foundation/Primary Project Admin

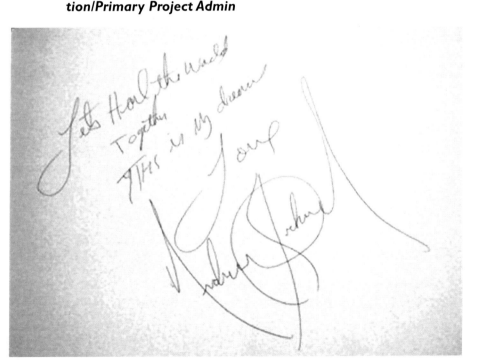

We Will Michael, We Will…

http://www.michaelsdreamfoundation.net
http://www.michaelschildrenshospital.com

by Christine Serene

Precious Human Moments

by Darlene Donloe, USA

Everyone knew Michael Jackson, the King of Pop, as a great singer and an incredible humanitarian. However, very few people have been a witness to both.

As a publicist for a portion of the HIStory Tour in 1996-97, I travelled around the world with MJ and had the privilege of accompanying him on his numerous visits to local hospitals. MJ had empathy and a soft spot for children in hospitals.

Whenever MJ visited a country, province, etc., he would make sure to carve out time in his hectic schedule to visit hospitals and sit and talk to children whose eyes would light up when he entered the room. As soon as word would get out that MJ was coming to a hospital, he would be met with a swarm of adoring fans outside the hospital - all eager to catch a glimpse of the King of Pop. Sometimes his visits would be a total surprise. He would simply walk into a hospital and visit as many of the patients as he could.

It was always touching to watch the King of Pop and his littlest fans, especially when he sat by their bedside. They would smile. He would smile. Soon, the entire room would be filled with smiles. That simple act was infectious.

84

Many of those moments were caught on camera or videotaped by a local news crew. But sometimes it wasn't about publicity. Sometimes those moments weren't meant to be shared with others. MJ simply wanted to spend some precious one-on-one time with his fans who had health issues. He wanted them to feel special. He wanted to bring them joy. He wanted them to get well. On occasion he would dismiss all cameras and even his handlers. Those moments were bigger than publicity. It was about humanity!

Precious human moments are what I'll remember most about my time with MJ. Those were the moments that revealed the real King of Pop! That's when MJ was at his best!!!

From the wings of the stage, I had the privilege of watching MJ perform night after night. There was nothing like it. He was amazing on stage. But, watching him bring smiles to children who were fighting to get healthy – was priceless!

Darlene and Michael on the HIStory Tour

Love,
Michael

by R.M., USA

Everyone was always asking about the red bracelet Michael Jackson wore around his wrist. It was a friendship bracelet that was given to him, and he was told he had to wear it until it fell off. He wanted to have a bracelet like it made to give to the crew of the THIS IS IT tour to solidify the unity in the project and to remind us to heal the world.

Mid-June that year (2009), Michael's make-up/hair artist and dear friend of mine, Karen Faye, came to me and asked if I would be interested in doing it. I jumped on the chance and quickly designed a piece made of silver and nylon, to look like the friendship bracelet he had requested. It said "Heal The World" on one side and "Love, Michael" on the other. Karen showed it to MJ and he loved it.

Unfortunately, soon after, the world suffered the enormous loss of this talented man.

Karen participated in the preparing of his body for burial. After he was lovingly dressed, she tied the bracelet he had chosen around his ankle.

86

by R. M.

In a world filled with hate, we must still dare to hope. In a world filled with anger, we must still dare to comfort. In a world filled with despair, we must still dare to dream. And in a world filled with distrust, we must still dare to believe.

A GIFT TO KEEP ME STRONG

by Mallory Cyr, USA

I am so glad this book became a reality. It was powerful for me to truly relive and reflect on this amazing experience in my life, and a fond reminder of how a community can come together to help one of their own. I hope this story continues to inspire people to reach out, lend a hand, and take a chance. You can't get to yes if you never ask!
Best wishes to all of the Michael fans, and those who believe in good.

-Mallory Cyr, 2012

Because of the media today, we are constantly reminded of the horrible things that happen in our world. With all the negative things that we see, hear, and read, it can be easy to forget that there are still good, selfless people in the world. However, on that hot day in 2009, as I sat in my apartment in Maine, watching the memorial service for Michael Jackson like so many other people all over the country, I was able to remember that I was indeed one of the fortunate ones to know the good of such an incredible icon.

I was eight years old when Michael lent a hand to my family residing in a small town in Maine. My whole life I have dealt with a complex medical condition that prohibits me from digesting

88

food properly. Because of this condition, I must receive nutrition intravenously every day of my life. During the early stages of my treatment I went without key nutrients for several years. This caused many health complications, many of which could be corrected, fortunately. However, it also caused my growth plates in my bones to dissolve, which was irreversible. By the time we had figured out what was happening, when I was only four years old, my legs had begun growing incorrectly, which resulted in me having severe difficulty walking, and extreme pain.

We tried everything to remedy this situation. I remember using my hot pink wheelchair in first grade, and wearing bright blue braces on my legs. They didn't help, but only succeeded in pinching my legs and giving me large bruises in addition to the pain I already had.

By the time I was in second grade we had sought the help of orthopaedic experts out of Boston Children's Hospital. Living in Maine at the time, it was a distance, but we had no other idea where to turn. We were told that the only option was a very intense surgery that would consist of cutting the bones in my legs, straightening them, and inserting large metal fixators to hold them in place. There would be two in each leg that would stick out, and it meant I would not be able to walk for several months while the bones healed. It was a grossly invasive, painful process, but it could mean that I could have my mobility back, and the option to participate as an active kid again.

All of this could not have happened at a worse time for my family. We had no income, were struggling with maintaining health insurance and were looking into a procedure in another state, to improve my quality of life.

It was also at this time that my mother found out she was preg-

89

nant with my sister. Although I had begged for a baby sister all of my life, having another child was a difficult decision for my parents to make, and many people had discouraged them from taking such a step. As a family, we were aware that whatever child we brought into the world had a great risk of having the same condition and medical issues that I had. My parents debated for a long time, and although to this day I am sure there are people who would not agree with the decision, they knew our family was meant to grow.

After the surgery, which we had decided to go through with, I would be using a wheelchair during the three months that I had the "pins" in my legs. This would mean transporting me in it every time we left the house, which meant we would need a special vehicle. With everything that was occurring during this point in time, it certainly was not something we could afford. There were other expenses as well; gas for going back and forth to Boston for the procedures and follow up visits, miscellaneous medical bills, and of course the expenses of every day living that didn't cease when there was a crisis.

During all of this, I witnessed one of the most incredible surges of community support I have ever seen to date. My entire elementary school, members from the high school and our hometown gathered together and began a fundraising campaign called "Mal's Pals." Dozens of people wearing bright purple t-shirts and buttons emblazoned with the slogan, "I'm one of Mal's Pals!" planned events to raise money to support my family. There was a spaghetti supper, dances, a carnival, and so many other events that were simply a blur for me. I just sat there smiling in my wheelchair, realizing that all these people were there to help my family.

Amidst all of these events and fundraising efforts, a young girl

90

who was in the sixth grade was courageous enough to share her idea. "What about Michael Jackson?" she said. "Everyone could write him letters about Mallory!" Her idea was received with head pats and typical comments of "well, isn't that cute", but somehow she persevered and was convinced that this little girl in Maine was worth more attention.

Finally, people agreed, and although the fundraising director had written letters to other celebrities for this effort, the campaign for Michael was different. All of the children in my class, and many from other classes wrote letters. There were dozens of them, scrawled on lined 2nd grade stationary with drawings. The kids all wrote about how I was their "best friend," or just "really cool."

I don't think anyone really expected a response to this effort, especially one as generous as what we got. I remember the day that the letter came in the mail. My mother opened it immediately, as she was walking into the house. Michael had not only written me a letter, but he had contributed a significant amount of money into the bank account that was used specifically for the fundraising events.

In the letter, he had said, "I am sending you all my loving and caring, Mallory, along with the enclosed gift, which I hope will help nourish you and keep you strong," He had also promised that he would call me. That didn't end up happening, I was ok with that. At that age, I didn't know much about him, or what I would say. I just knew that what he had done had made my mother cry tears of relief and joy. Because of his support, and that of our incredible community, our family was able to get back on our feet and have the strength to get through my recovery, and enjoy the miracle of welcoming my sister into the world.

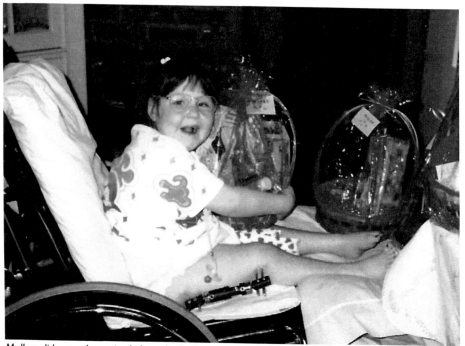

Mallory did not only receive help and gifts from her community but also from Michael Jackson

Mallory and her family

There is a scrapbook that I have from all the fundraising events, with news articles, pictures and letters from the lead coordinator that went out to everyone involved with the endeavours. One of the letters reads, "Mallory is probably way too young to yet realize the impact that those 92 letters have had, but to think that out of all the letters [Michael Jackson] must receive from around the world each day, he chose our letters concerning Mallory, is just amazing beyond belief. But so are all of you, so is Mallory, and Mr. Jackson."

It's true I didn't understand at the time, but as I look back now as an adult, I still revel in the fact that Michael chose our letters, and to help me, in rural Maine, when clearly he has impacted people all over the world. No matter what I have seen, heard, read, or what other people may believe about Michael Jackson, I will stand by my belief that he was indeed a good man. I think he had a big heart, good intentions and perhaps the world was not ready for the messages he brought.

I may not have known what to say to Michael in 1993, but if he were to call me today, I sure would have plenty to say. I would tell him I share in his beliefs that it doesn't matter if you're black or white; we all need to come together to heal the world. I would tell him about the work I do now, advocating for other young people with severe health needs to have better lives, and that I strive to continue his legacy. But most of all I would thank him. I would thank him for choosing my family, for wanting to keep me strong, and for all of the selfless, inspiring things he did for other people all over the world. Thank you Michael. You will never be forgotten.

The Charitable Efforts of MJ

by Vincent Amen, USA

My name is Vincent Amen and I worked for Michael in 2003 - together with Frank Cascio, his personal assistant back then. I got to know Michael as a very cordial and friendly person who never missed a chance to let us know how much he appreciated our hard work.

Me and Frank were childhood friends and since Frank was also good friends with Michael, I first met him back in the 90's when he would visit Frank's house where Frank and I would be hanging out together. When I first met Michael, I said "Nice to meet you Mr. Jackson", and he quickly said "Call me Michael, no need to address me by my last name." Michael wanted us to be casual around him, he was very nice and open to meet Frank's friends, like me, even though he was a superstar and I had to be a teenager of 16 years at the time.

Working for Michael taught me many lessons, but two have engraved themselves deep inside my mind. First, I learned that when you are successful with what you do, such as Michael, it is important to always give something back to the people, not once but every day. Often it is not material things but more importantly love, kindness and appreciation.

94

Secondly, through working for him, I also experienced how it feels to be falsely accused by people in front of a global audience, people you trusted and helped, such as Janet Arvizo. I will never forget that terrible experience and therefore can relate to what Michael had to endure almost all his life.

As you know he helped Gavin Arvizo to get over his cancer disease. He helped the whole Arvizo family personally and financially and took immediate responsibility for them after the Bashir documentation was aired, and relocated the family once harassment by the public and press in the aftermath of the TV airing began, which made them lose their home and schooling for the children. He realized it was a mistake to put them in the spotlight and did everything he could to bring the family back to normal.

As we now know, all this led to very hard and cruel times for Michael. I would like the world to know that the whole situation was a set up, an entrapment which led to the "Michael Jackson Trial". Janet Arvizo pushed her children to call Michael Daddy for an apparent gain of money, fortune and fame. However, all this pain and torture did not stop his charitable efforts in the years following the trial.

Michael once said to me: "I want to help all the children of the world". This seemed like an over reaching statement to me at first, however I must admit that through his charitable ways he did contribute to help many and it seems that he did accomplish his statement in a lot of aspects.

There are numerous examples that show the good nature of Michael. For example in the summer of 2003, Michael opened the "Neverland Valley Ranch" for a charity event based off of the "Neverland Romero Britto Event". I was impressed that Michael would not only open his private home and fund

95

the event but also give his time to make a special appearance onstage. He also personally called several of his friends, like the Carters, Mike Tyson and others and asked them to make an appearance at this benefit charity to help collect money. The opportunity to meet those celebrities, and him of course, helped a lot to motivate the guests to give money and so that day celebrities and the invited guests mingled together for one common goal that was charity. The event turned out great and in the end over $100.000 were raised.

Another time, when Michael was exiting the gates of Neverland, he stopped his car to talk to a waiting fan. When he heard that this fan's younger brother had cancer, he opened up his car door and invited the fan into his limousine to specifically tell him about it. As the empathetic person that he was, Michael wanted to reach out to this sick child and make him feel better. Knowing he was sick with cancer at such a young age, he wanted to do something special for him and for his family. That's the way he was. He took the time to reach out to people in need despite his very busy schedule and at least tried to make them feel better and give them something to look forward to, something like a telephone call from Michael Jackson or a visit to his ranch.

While staying at Neverland, I often witnessed Michael allowing groups of underprivileged children to come and tour the ranch, enjoy the rides of his amusement park, watch a movie in his theater and have food and candies as they wished. Eventually Michael would then choose a moment to meet these groups of children and sometimes join them to tour his ranch with them. Michael told me the joy of these children made him happy, and he believed that this special day full of fun gave them, sometimes for the first time in their life, a feeling of being welcome and being special. And he hoped that they would remember this day and it would help them to be in-

96

spired and not loose hope in difficult situations of their life. I realized Michael's true inspiration were children. He always included children in his work, his shows and he would keep enlarged photos and posters of children over his working areas.

Michael said the innocence of children and being child-like inspired him and his music and how he lived at the ranch, which was all geared and centered around that fun time of being a child.

Michael donated to so many charities and helped so many people from behind the scenes, without the public or press knowing about it. If we take something from his example, it should be that giving is important and to help one another should be a part of our daily lives.

Michael, I saw first hand your work and your wish to make this world a better place - and you truly excelled. I saw your charitable efforts and they made and make a difference for so many people. I also saw first hand what Janet Arvizo tried to accomplish and she truly failed in front of the world.

MJ AND THE BLANK CHECK

Gwen J. Cariño, Philippines
  PR practitioner

When I was a public relations officer of Manila Hotel, I headed the annual Orphan's Christmas Party of which 300 children from different orphanages around Metro Manila were to be treated to a day of fun and surprises. It was one of the biggest projects on my plate, and was such a challenge to focus on work the day before the big event knowing that Michael Jackson was billeted in the hotel. Two nights before, I had been fortunate to be part of his welcome line at the hotel lobby together with the rest of the PR and sales staff but was content enough to see him walk by amid a huge crowd of fans and well-wishers.

The hotel atmosphere was filled with excitement. Much as I hate to divulge the info, I sensed that nobody really seriously worked from the time Michael Jackson arrived. Everyone was waiting for him to either cross the lobby, walk along the hotel hallways, be in the elevator, pass by the backdoor to avoid the crowd or even the employees walkway and entrance. I saw a colleague with a highly esteemed position literally press the down button to make sure the elevator door opened on the same floor she was in so she'd get a glimpse of MJ when she knew he was to pass that way.

98

Callers heard songs from MJ's "HIStory" CD while put on hold, mainstay lobby pianist Joselito Pascual played MJ ballads and our corporate print ad, which was published in 3 major dailies, read "Another King sets foot at The Manila Hotel and makes History." The hotel entrance signage read "Welcome to the King of Pop and the King of Beers" as Budweiser had a big event at that time, too.

The day before our orphan's affair, a guy who claimed to be Michael Jackson's aide from Mamarao Productions came to our office. I couldn't recall his name but he looked for the 'person in charge' and said that his boss had read the announcement about the event in the "Dear Guest" flyers we had circulated to all the rooms a week before, and Michael wanted to know how he could help. So his aide found himself going up the Penthouse Suite and coming down again to our office several times, as both of us suggested how he could participate.

Michael offered to fill up 300 loot bags with goodies and toys, candies and chocolates but having been able to solicit close to 50 sponsors, it was already a problem for us to dispose of everything.

So I thought hard…how can the King of Pop meaningfully join the affair? I couldn't possibly have him be with the kids during the games as he might end up getting mobbed! And since the annual event was really all about giving, I mustered all my courage and told the Mamarao guy that the best thing I could think of was for him to literally be present to help distribute the loot bags, be available to sign autographs and pose with the children for photos. Say it was far fetched but really, it was the only way I could think of for him to bring genuine smiles and joy to those kids. "Wow, that may not be easy. You're talking about handing goodie bags to 300 children and I can just imagine the chaos.

We'll see, Ms. Jacinto, and I'll get back to you," he said.

Lunch break came and it was the most hurried one I ever took in my entire life. The afternoon hours passed and no aide was knocking at our office. It wasn't until after 5pm that he came back and said, "Michael is more than happy to do whatever you suggest! How do we go about it tomorrow?"

I wanted to scream! This is the living legend – the only meteoric person on the planet who could have that kind of a marriage with one's emotions just through his amazing music! And here you're talking of a girl who collected MJ albums, magazines, and painstakingly got the lyrics of his "Off the Wall" and "Thriller" album songs by playing and pausing the cassette tape over and over from her boombox in her elementary days! But I had to calm myself and get composure as the Lizzie Maguire in me said "Get real, get back into focus!"

We agreed that Michael would join after the games, musical program and snacks – at last part to give out the loot bags. My colleague Annette Africano and boss Dulce Agnir requested for additional security around the event venue and its stage area where we decided to distribute the gifts so that we could get him as far away as we could from a possible crowd. We also made sure we had a line for the children to come up orderly.

Then it came. The moment arrived. It was at the Champagne Gardens on December 7, 1996. I was surprised to see The King of Pop walking towards us, guided by his aide he came up to me knowing I had to brief him. "Hi, how are you? Thanks so much for letting me join. I know I'm early coz I didn't want to miss the program!" I said, "Are you kidding? Thanks so much for volunteering! Here's what, Michael, why don't you just sit here and watch the musical numbers before we get into the gift

100

Michael, Santa and Gwen having fun giving out loot bags to the kids

Michael with an orphan at the event

giving. I will have to tweak the order of the program a bit." He replied, "Sure, anything you say….(pausing to look at my name tag) Gwen!" I was stunned at how incredibly sweet and modest he was. And in my mind it was, "Oh my God, this is really happening!!!"

Amazing how he patiently sat through the whole program. One of our child entertainers, Carol Banawa, who was then a popular TV kids program mainstay couldn't believe that THE Michael Jackson was watching her perform! She had her red blouse signed by him right after her number. Then followed Stefano Mori's dance number, another popular child star. Later on, Michael's back up singers and dancers came up on stage followed by select kids from different orphanages who all danced to the beat of "Billie Jean". Oh, the smile in Michael's face was just amazing, seeing those kids perform.

Then we announced that Michael would be distributing gifts onstage. I explained to him that there's a loot bag for the younger kids and another for the older ones and he nodded. It was really the thrill and excitement he gave those children that was incredibly touching. And it was, too, in between the gift bag distribution that I saw a glimpse of not the performer in MJ, but the person that he is.

It was one in the afternoon and Santa Claus (David Endriga, a friend of fellow PR officer Francis Capistrano) joined us on stage. The heat was scourging and I was worried that MJ felt so hot with his black long sleeved signature attire. "Are you alright Michael? We can let you take a break." He said, "I'm cool Gwen, just imagine how Santa feels inside his velvet suit and beard! We'll be fine." I never heard him complain or say a word about how hot it was or how long the line is. He had the most beautiful manners. He didn't even ask for a drink or a towel to wipe

103

his sweat but one of our banquet staff made sure he got a glass of fresh orange juice.

At one point, when I mistakenly handed him the wrong gift bag for an older kid, he kindly reminded me that the 10-year old won't enjoy the goodies inside the bag intended for the younger ones. I thought it was responsible of him. An hour had passed and we were halfway through gift-giving when we noticed that the garden was getting filled up. There suddenly were people from the media, politicians, officials, hotel guests including guests of a wedding at the nearby Champagne Room who all deserted the bride and groom to get a glimpse of Michael.

"Uh oh, this isn't supposed to be, I'm so sorry," I said. "It's alright, we'll get through it," he said smiling. And as we finished giving out the last loot bag to an 11-year old orphan, a new line of more kids and even adults formed. Michael's bodyguard, Wayne, said, "We can leave now!" And calmly MJ replied, "We can't leave when there are still people in line. It's Christmas, dude." Wow, I felt my heart beat faster and the hair on my arms and the back of my neck stood up. He wasn't just the most electrifying performer, but the most generous person!

One of the most memorable moments was when a lady came up to him for an autograph. Laughing and holding his tummy, he said, "Hey Gwen, you've gotta check this out," he whispered, "It's a blank check. The lady is making me sign on a blank check!" We laughed hard and little did we know that it wasn't even half of the comedy. He later showed me and Wayne other stuff people would use or pick up on the ground when they couldn't find paper for him to sign on. One lady made him sign at the back of her elegant, designer, Filipiniana gown. One teenager came up to him holding a dead leaf and another one a popped balloon to sign on! Imagine how much our laughter ballooned

104

Gwen getting her photo signed by The King of Pop

A signed picture and an autograph on the cover of the HIStory album

as well. It was an unbelievably amazing and genuine experience. At one point he asked if I was going to catch his "HIStory" concert and I said, "Tomorrow night." "Oh, you'll have a blast!" was his immediate remark.

At this point he became concerned about the stage as adults literally outnumbered the kids and became too crowded. His face had nervousness written all over but he still didn't complain. He tapped the wooden floor with his left foot several times making sure it was sturdy enough not to fall apart. "I've experienced the stage collapse and I just want to make sure we're all safe here."

Half of me wanted the line to finish because we were literally melting and worried about our safety, but half of me didn't, knowing that once the line ended, he was also going to leave.

And at some point it did end. I managed to get an autograph for me and my sisters before our general manager, Clem Pablo, requested him to sing "Give Love on Christmas Day." Cesar Sarino, one of the hotel's officials, addressed his thank you note to The King of Pop, then I saw his guards and aides whisking Michael off the stage. I said in my mind, "Oh man, I didn't even have the chance to say goodbye."

Suddenly, I saw Michael return on stage and say, "Thanks so much to you and your team, Gwen. This really means a lot." Then he held me beside him and said, "I'll see you at the concert."

Michael stayed in Manila Hotel for four more days after that. When he had to leave the hotel, aside from his two-night concert, these were all visits to cancer wards, hospitals, to the sick, the poor, and the needy. Not a single guesting in any of the

106

noontime variety shows or television specials.

When he left on December 11, Annette and I immediately ran to the Penthouse Suite where he stayed. We were very curious. There we found an empty Paperoo popcorn bucket, about 3 or 4 flavors of Haagen Daaz ice cream inside the fridge, and Snickers chocolates wrappers on the table. No wonder Paul McCartney called him a "boy man" and it's not surprising that he saw himself as Peter Pan. He was such a child inside.

And while Michael Jackson is laid to rest and returned to pristine condition in the afterlife, two incredible acts of the King of Pop – volunteering for charity, and unselfishly spending time with the less fortunate - will forever be the way I will mirror this man.

PNCC Grounds

THE KING OF POP

MICHAEL JACKSON

The HIStory World Tour

MANILA PHILIPPINES

Sun Dec 8, 1996 8:00pm

SECTION	NO	ADULT
RED	1610	P1751

Gwen's ticket for the HIStory Tour concert on Manila's Asia World City Concert Grounds

Travelling the world has been a great education for me. And if there is one insight I've had, it is this: wherever you go, in every country, on every continent, people yearn and hunger for only one thing: to love and be loved. Love transcends international boundaries and it heals the wounds of hatred, racial prejudice, bigotry and ignorance. It is the ultimate truth at the heart of all creation.

MYSTORY: PAST-PRESENT-FUTURE

by Steven Hodges, UK

PAST

My "Michael Connection" started many years ago. I think I was about 8 years old and I think my father had the Motown 25 "Billie Jean" performance on VHS. I distinctively remember us pulling back the carpet and trying to learn to Moonwalk, that is where it all started for me. From then I ended up becoming a silent fan as there weren't many others around me.

My sister used to take disco dancing lessons at a local dance centre and I guess I was inspired enough by MJ that I also ended up taking part and was the only boy there. I remember one of the dance teachers said she could get hold of "Bad"-Tour tickets and I was so excited, you have no idea. This was an opportunity to see MJ LIVE. Unfortunately this was not to be and we missed out on tickets in the end. I was devastated. It didn't stop me from getting various certificates and medals for dancing though and this was a very fun part of my childhood. It is always nice to take a look back at the medals and certificates now, even if I was only about 8 or 9 at the time!

Later on I ended up coming across a Michael Jackson fan magazine called "Michael Jackson News International" (MJNI). I

109

subscribed and became a member and eventually had a letter printed in the magazine describing my experience of being an "Isolated Fan" in the world. This was a result of having a previous pen friend request in an earlier issue of the magazine and being inundated with pen friend requests. I later volunteered with MJNI and helped them out at some of their MJ Day events and it was so much fun, Michael even turned up one day! I got to see MJ in concert at Wembley for his "HIStory"-Tour and it was awesome. Through the club I managed to also get to see the MJ & Friends concert in Munich with some other fans I met through the magazine. I am still good friends with some of the fans I met back then to this day. It was such a great experience, one which I will never forget.

PRESENT

After time, the "MJ drought" turned into total amazement when the "This Is It"-Tour was announced. I was so excited. The only thing is that I remember thinking "is this real, is he actually going to tour again?" There was just something not quite right with it all. I snapped up as many tickets as I could afford as I knew various friends wanted to go and had been trying to get hold of tickets but couldn't. I ended up with approx. 30 tickets on various dates, but it wasn't to be.

I remember getting a text from a friend as I had just got home from the cinema, it simply said something like: "Have you heard the news, mate?" I felt my life changing and destiny unfolding as I watched it all happening. After the news I tried to be around the fans I met through it all to make sure they were all OK. It was difficult. I know the pain I was feeling, I couldn't imagine what they were feeling, but I needed to man up, so I made sure I was around to be able to help and took the day after off work

by Steven Hodges

so that I was around. I knew I wouldn't have got ANY work done if I had gone in.

I got to visit London on the weekend after the news broke and it confirmed to me what I already knew: Michael was loved. A LOT. But up until his death I never really paid attention to what Michael had been trying to tell us for years. WE are the ones that can help Heal The World. Michael knew that. I am sure that if he were alive today we would all be able to unite as a fan base and start to really get things changed. It turned out that we were going to have to tackle this without him and tackle it we will.

I reached out to the "Heal The World Foundation" after Michael's death as I felt an immediate urge to give and feel connected to him to somehow reassure him, that his work wasn't in vain and that his fans WILL carry on for him. The "Heal The World Foundation" had issues of their own, so I decided to see if there was something else I could do. I decided to try and tackle it myself, and find out how many other fans would be behind me.

I started "Michael Jackson Fans For Charity" (MJFFC - www. mjffc.org.uk), it was a cause on Causes.com where it encouraged fans to donate directly to a children's charity in memory of Michael. I felt it was important for fans to have the "Michael Connection" when it came to them donating. In time over $1,000 were donated by various fans. This was all fine, but it didn't feel like I was a part of something, it felt like it was just a donation to a charity. I needed something more, something that gave positive feedback, acknowledgment, and ultimately love, and so did the fans.

I cracked on in making MJFFC a larger venture. I spent hours on getting the idea to where it is today, which now includes ways

111

UK donors can text in their donations to various charities. I had a bigger picture in mind. One that covered all of the things I have wanted to cover and plugged all of the holes I wanted plugged. It was a simple idea and it was able to sustainably give thousands of pounds to various charities by means of monthly donations by Michael Jackson fans. The trick? ALL it needed was for just a small percentage of Michael's MILLIONS of fans out there to donate just one unit of their currency per month in memory of Michael, and at the end of the month it would be given out to a beneficiary, that the very same donors have voted for. I started running some numbers and as soon as I realised what was possible, I made sure I could dedicate as much time as I could to it, remembering that for it to work, I needed to make sure 100% of the donations went to the winning beneficiary.

We are almost there with all of the money going to charity less the PayPal fees. It is such an exciting time for myself and the other members of the project and it just grows and grows the longer we do it. To date we have given over $2,000 to charity in total and have continuously maintained our Global Total, which is a comprehensive list of all of the other known Michael Jackson fan made initiatives over the world. This so far has been calculated to be at least $150,000 which has been donated and raised by Michael's fans globally since his death. This, just like the man himself, is simply MAGICAL.

FUTURE

So what does the future hold? To put things in perspective with a 100% donation model, if just 250,000 fans donated $1 monthly, fans could be a part of an organisation that literally gives $250,000 per month to good causes (or even 1 MILLION for that matter!) Just imagine that. Just imagine funding a child's emergency operation. Just imagine being able to give money instantly to a natural disaster that has just occurred. Just imagine being able to completely fund the building of 50 water wells PER MONTH in memory of Michael. Just imagine being able to sustain the running of a Michael Jackson Children's Hospital. Just imagine what Michael would be feeling. It CAN be done. It just needs fans to discover the underlying message in Michael's songs… that he has been trying to tell us since day one AND ACT ON IT. Give. Love. Change the World.

http://www.mjfc.org.uk

Steven in London on June 27th, 2009

by Steven Hodges

Fight Against Indifference

Dr. Patrick Treacy, Ireland
Medical Director of Ailesbury Clinic

I befriended Michael while he stayed in Ireland 2006/ 2007 and was looking for a doctor to take care of his dermatological conditions. Getting to know the man behind the myths, it was quickly apparent that he was not only an exceptional multitalented artist but also an avid reader, a very intellectual person, a fun-loving guy, devoted father and simply the kindest human I have ever met.

By the time he came to Ireland he felt deeply hurt and betrayed by what had been done to him, and very disappointed about the indifference most people had for him and his fate. What an irony that someone who cared so much about the rest of humanity was rejected by his own country, his own people. It was a pain he felt deeply and whenever we touched on the subject he would stop talking and looked into the empty space. The memories related to the Santa Maria trial were too painful for him to emotionally go there again. As a result of all the bad experiences he had made in the past, he was often unsure of people's intention. He needed someone to trust and ask advice of and so soon Michael called me on many occasions to ask about my opinion on certain things.

114

Michael and I shared the same humanitarian ideals and a deep love for the African continent. I was very surprised to learn that he knew a lot about my personal attempts and struggles to help there. He was very troubled by the suffering he saw in our world and even more by the indifference to it. His first words to me were: "Thank you so much for helping the people of Africa". On top of all other problems that the continent faces, the terrible plague HIV, which wipes out whole villages, was one of his main focuses. He often stressed that we must do something together for them. One day, when I was with him, Nelson Mandela called and Michael wanted me to speak to him and handed me the telephone. It was just amazing. And so our plans for a charity concert in Rwanda began to take form. Michael was very enthusiastic and had many ideas and already knew that there was an old airfield that could be rented to hold the concert. Sadly these plans never saw the light of day.

Michael, being a very spiritual person, believed that private acts of charity should stay private. In Matthew 6:1 it is said: "Be careful not to do your acts of righteousness in front of others, to be seen by them. If you do, you will have no reward from your father in heaven." That is the reason why only people very close to him really knew about the considerable time, money and energy he put into giving. The majority of things he did for others were from behind the scenes. To this day most people will not even know that it was him who helped them.

Michael was also the most empathetic, compassionate and gentle person I know. While he lived in Ireland, a terrible petrol bomb attack from gang warfare in the town of Limerick injured two 5-year old siblings very seriously. He heard about the horrific injuries and agonizing pain the children were suffering in the news and from that moment on he wanted to go and visit them in hospital. Michael could relate to physical and psychical

115

pain very much and hoped that he could ease suffering with his presence somehow. So he asked me to go with him - but I declined. I feared that once the press heard about it and his whereabouts, he would not be able to live in peace – not even in Ireland. On top of that the press might again twist and turn the truth, as they usually did with him, and make his visit appear in a sinister light.

To spare him from all that, I insisted that I would go and check on the children and if there was anything we could do for them, alone. Michael was not happy at all with that, to say the least and bombarded me with questions about the children once I got back. "How badly are they injured?", "Were they in pain?" "Were they scarred?" "Are they getting morphine for the pain?" But the question that tormented him most was: "Why can't I go and see them?"

Again I tried to explain him my fears about what the media could make up about him, especially then, in the aftermath of the trial, but it seemed that he did not want to hear about that.
He asked me: "Patrick, do you think I would ever harm a child?"
I said: "No!"
He asked: "You mean that from the bottom of your heart?"
I answered: "Michael, I think you are like a modern day Jesus Christ!"
He said: "So, if Jesus was here now, would you stop him, too?"
I thought for a moment and honestly had to say: "No!"
Then he said: "You never met Jesus and you do not know him as a person, yet you would stand behind him. You say you know me and you won't? That is being a hypocrite!"

As you surely can imagine, I won't forget that conversation for as long as I live. He was right and I had to admit it, yet I feared for him and his well-being in that moment and declined his wish. I must say I regret it to this day that I did not walk beside him when he needed me most.

The children and their mother have contacted me since and said that one of the greatest moments in their lives was the fact that Michael thought about them in their darkest hours and cheered them up with his "get-well" wishes.

To me Michael was (like) a spiritual leader, someone who shelved his own happiness to help others and to heal the planet. His artistic work is filled with the message of love and the call for a change to make this world a better one for our children. He was the voice of the voiceless and a spark of hope for the hopeless and despaired.

In the end his goodness was his vulnerability. I am annoyed that the world never got a chance to get to know him as a person. The sad fact is that people only needed to be in his company for less than five minutes to feel and experience his total radiation of goodness. People will realize the real treasure they had one day.

I believe Michael would want us to continue his legacy by standing up for the things he stood up for, to wipe out injustice, combat disease and try to save the planet we live on. And to fight against this terrible "dysfunction" called "indifference" that is spreading amongst people all over the world like a disease.
He once said: "To be indifferent to the suffering of the world is what makes human being inhuman".

So what would Michael do?
Maybe he would say: "Let's start with the man in the mirror."

117

Flowers from Michael

by Denise Fergus, UK

The first time I heard Michael Jackson's music it was coming from my older brother's bedroom. I'm not sure how old I was, but I can say I was very young. The song my brother was playing was "Don't Stop Til You Get Enough". As soon as I heard the music I was hooked. I needed to find out who the singer was.

After learning it was Michael Jackson, I had to go and buy his album, which, of course, was "Off the Wall". I learned every song on that album very quickly as I played it constantly. My number of albums started growing as did my obsession with Michael Jackson. I started putting pictures all over my bedroom walls. I got Michael Jackson dolls that I placed on my dressing table. I had to buy every magazine, newspaper, in fact, everything that contained anything about Michael Jackson - even if it was the tiniest picture, I would still have to have it. I made my own scrapbook and stuck all the cut-out pictures from the magazines and newspapers in it and did my own write-ups to go with them. Unfortunately, I no longer have that scrap book.

Time went by, but my love for MJ hadn't changed. I bought every song and album that he released. I'd stay up till late to watch his new videos, which I always knew were going to be very entertaining.

118

I had a son. A little boy called James. From an early age in his life James began to recognise Michael's voice as I always had either an album or a video playing. As soon as James could talk and walk he would tell me to put on one of Michael's videos, so he could sing and dance to it. One of James' favourite videos was "Remember the Time". I used to love watching and listening to James sing and dance to Michael's songs. He even tried to dance like my idol. It was very funny to watch. Everyone I knew would tell me I had brainwashed James into liking him. I didn't see it like that. I just saw it as a mum and son enjoying listening to music from a legend.

I never had James for long as he was cruelly taken away from me in February 1993. It was two weeks before his third birthday when he was abducted at a Shopping Centre by two teenage boys who were both 10 years old at the time.

I still have my memories of my darling son James, singing and dancing to Michael's music. These are memories that will stay with me forever. I had a song played at James' funeral. At first I couldn't decide if it should be "Gone Too Soon" or "Heal the World". Because of the way James was taken I felt like the world did need healing, so that is why I chose "Heal the World".

I'm not sure who it was but someone got in touch with Michael Jackson's people and explained what had happened to James and how much he loved to sing and dance to his music. Shortly afterwards a huge basket of flowers arrived with a short poem attached. It was labelled "A Child of Innocence". To this day I still can't believe that Michael Jackson took time out to send me flowers and a note from his heart. I was really touched. I only wish they had been sent in different circumstances and James could have seen them.

119

by Denise Fergus

The last present given to me from my son James was a Christmas present. It was "Thriller" and the "Making of Thriller". James had been helped to hide it down the side of our sofa, but he couldn´t wait to give it to me, so I got it late on Christmas Eve in 1992.

In December 1993 I gave birth to another little boy. I called him Michael James. I named him Michael after a priest who helped me through a tragic part of my life when I lost my son James. I also gave Michael his elder brother's name. To this day Michael is proud to have his brother's name included in his full name. When I was younger I always jokingly said I would call my boy 'Michael Jack' and say he is my son, so I nearly got there with that one! Still at least I had MJ as his initials.

In 1997 I heard a rumour that Michael was going to start a new tour. Unknown to me my boyfriend at the time (Stuart) had got tickets to see him at Sheffield on his "History" tour. I couldn´t believe it when Stuart rang and told me. I was so excited I was finally going to go and see Michael perform live in person. I couldn't wait - I counted down the days.

The concert was on July 9th at Sheffield's Don Valley Stadium. Michael James was only three-and-a-half years old. The concert was unbelievable. The tickets we had were right at the back and I actually felt sick as I knew I most probably wouldn´t be able to see him. Stuart saw the look on my face - he took me by the hand and picked-up Michael. "Follow me!" he said. I could hardly stop him as he began walking through a maze of people. Without realising it, Stuart had taken me and my son Michael right to the front. I couldn´t believe it! Now I was only 10 feet away from him.

The concert was magical from the count-down of video links

by Denise Fergus

of MJ crashing to earth to the explosion of the stage being torn apart and a spacecraft protruding from the stage. Smoke, screaming (good of course), chanting and then...there he was sliding out of the spaceship. It was my idol of all those years - Michael Jackson!

A few days later Stuart was acting a little odd and then after a while he explained to me. A close friend had managed to get some more tickets for the London concert. Our friend had bent over backwards to help. I wasn't going to complain, I was getting to see Michael Jackson again.

I remember thinking as we travelled to London how much James would have loved to have been there and getting to see Michael Jackson live in concert. To be honest I wished he was.

The Wembley concert seemed so much better. Whether it was a bigger show or just the hysteria from the crowd, I don't know, but I loved it. After the concert we managed to stay at the Park Lane Hilton Hotel.

The following evening Stuart had arranged a lovely meal in one of the restaurants located in the hotel. To be honest I couldn't remember much of the meal we had as I was too busy talking about the concert the night before. I never noticed a waiter wheeling a trolley to the side of our table. He removed the cover, smiled and walked away. I turned to say something to Stuart and there he was on one knee about to propose. What an ending to a fantastic week and of course I did say "Yes". Together we have two more sons today, Thomas and Leon.

In 2009 Michael Jackson announced that he was going to do a final tour "This Is It". Stuart spent hours on the computer trying to get tickets. He filled in the forms for the official website. The first lot of emails with the codes were sent out - none sent to ours. So Stuart tried again. Eventually he got a code and typed like crazy. He shouted to me "I got four tickets, hun!". I couldn't believe it. The millions of fans who wanted tickets and my Stuart had got the maximum four tickets. Tears welled-up in my eyes. I was going to see my Michael Jackson again - AGAIN!

I sat and watched every news clip when Michael came to promote his final tour. He kept on repeating, "this is it... This Is It". I told everyone I knew I was going to watch Michael again. I didn't need to have bothered as they all knew that somehow I would have gone.

One Thursday evening whilst relaxing with Stuart in the kitchen, my niece Natalie came in and kept telling me to put the news on as it was important. So I switched on Sky News. God, I wished I hadn't! That yellow scrolling bar telling me that there was a possibility Michael Jackson was fighting for his life... I couldn't believe what I was seeing and hearing. I prayed that Michael would make it. Once again my prayers were never answered. Michael Jackson passed away on June 25th, 2009.

I was devastated. It felt like I had lost a close family member. Then again I feel every MJ fan must have felt like I did. I had friends and family ringing me to see if I was ok and they came round to see me because they knew just how much I had loved and adored him.

A few days later, Stuart sat me down and explained to me that because he could only get four tickets and there was five of us, he had spoken to my press agent and very close friend Chris Johnson. Chris had spoken to Michael's people and managed to arrange to get five tickets all together for one of the concert dates. I felt happy and sad that I would have got to have seen

122

him another time. But it was not meant to be. Then Stuart added another bit, Chris had also managed to arrange it for me to get to meet my idol Michael Jackson. I couldn´t believe the man I had listened to and watched for all those years had agreed to meet with me and my family. So sad that he was stolen away from us.

I kept my ticket as I couldn´t bear to part with it. When I feel the time is right I shall pass it on to my son Michael with the programme from the concert that never was. Michael Jackson may no longer be here in person but his music will live on forever. He was a very talented artist who brought a lot of entertainment into the lives of so many people all over the world. Even more, he will remain in the hearts of millions of people whom he helped to make their lives better and brighten up their darker days – like he did by sending me flowers and words of comfort in my darkest hour ...he will always be very deeply and sadly missed.

Since my son's murder I have been involved in many charities as I felt I wanted to try and help as many people as possible. I have met so many lovely people with the work that I have done.

It was in spring 2009 when a close friend of mine, Stephen Linder, got in touch to tell me a lady he knew, called Terri Ann Devine, wanted to meet up with me as she and her brother and a few local artists had got together and sang a song which they wanted to use to help raise funds for the charity I was involved with.

We met Terri Ann and her family who were really lovely people. After a good long chat Terri Ann and her brother Lewis showed us to their music studio in which we were asked to listen to the song they had recorded. We stood there waiting for Lewis

123

to play the song – I couldn´t believe what I was listening to. The song they had chosen was the same one I played at James funeral. I turned around and explained it to Terri Ann who didn´t know that. I still couldn´t believe it, out of all the songs this one had been chosen. There and then I knew it was meant to be.

Afterwards Terri Ann got in touch with a company called Matchbox recordings which then got in touch with Michael Jackson and his people. When in June 2009 MJ agreed to let us use the song, it was all systems go. The artists worked really hard putting it all together, Terri Ann co-ordinated it whilst her brother Lewis produced the song. We got a lot of friends and family together and over two days we had shot the video for the single.

The single was released in October 2009 and we had backing from Tescos and HMV who stocked the CD in local stores. The single made the Top 10 in the downloadable charts and also at one point was in the Top 40. It turned out we were the last group of people to be given permission from Michael (shortly before his death) to use one of his songs. I still feel strange about this even to this day, but maybe it was a sign, Michael Jackson telling me to continue with my efforts to heal the world in my son's name. The song helped a lot in raising money and the profile for the charity I was involved with at the time.

With time, I wanted to broaden out that work to help bullied children and their families, and young victims of crime. In 2011, the year that James would have turned 21, I set up The James Bulger Memorial Trust (JBMT), which will operate under the name "For James". The charity will support young people who have become the victims of crime, hatred or bullying, but we also want to be able to reward children for good behaviour - those who have made positive contributions to society in all

124

The holiday and respite facility "James Bulger House" near Blackpool in the UK.

Denise and her son Michael at the opening of "James Bulger House"

A picture of James

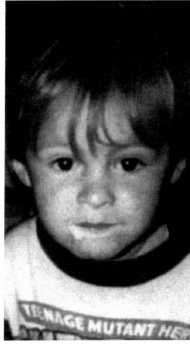

kinds of ways. Too often the victims and simply the good kids are forgotten and we want to help change that.

Several "For James" events raised more than £20,000 for the charity. Then an anonymous well-wisher donated a £28,000 six-berth static caravan. Stuart, my three sons Michael, Thomas and Leon (all teenagers by now) and myself have worked hard to get the caravan to the highest standards possible. In August 2011, the JBMT was finally able to establish a holiday and re-spite facility, the "James Bulger House", for the use of deserving children and their families, at a gorgeous luxury 5star resort at Ribby Hall Village, near Blackpool/UK.

I promised James after he was killed that I would always fight for justice and do my best to keep his memory alive. "James Bulger House" is there to help heal lives that have been dam-aged and to reward youngsters who have done good things for the community or other people. Seeing it become a reality is my dream come true.

If it can help put a smile on the faces of a few children then all the effort will be worthwhile. This is the only real, tangible me-morial to James and we aim to carry on from here to do more good works in his name.

If anyone would like more information on my son's charity or would like help raise funds or to nominate a child from the northwest area (UK) please go to www.forjames.org.

by Denise Fergus

Do I really believe that we can heal this world, that is riddled with war and genocide even today? And do I really think that we can heal our children, the same children who can enter their schools with guns and hatred and shoot down their classmates, like they did at Columbine? Or children who can beat a defenceless toddler to death, like the tragic story of Jamie Bulger? Of course I do, or I wouldn't be here tonight.

THE REAL
MICHAEL

by David Nordahl, USA

I first met Michael in March, 1988. Previously, I had done some paintings for Steven Spielberg. One of those paintings was hanging in his office. Steven called in January to tell me to expect a call from Jon Voight because he had displayed a genuine interest in my work.

Shortly after, a secretary from Los Angeles called me and requested photos of my work for her unnamed boss. I just assumed it was Jon Voight's secretary. I sent a group of photos of my work and I included a brochure of my upcoming show in Scottsdale, Arizona on the second weekend of February.

A few days after returning from my show I was working late at night. Sometime between midnight and 1a.m the phone rang. Usually, if the phone rings at that time it's either a family emergency or a late night drunk calling the wrong number. I was surprised to hear the voice on the other end of the line say, "This is Michael Jackson". I was sure this was a prank call. After all, why in the world would Michael Jackson be calling me? The voice said, "Thank you for sending the photos of your work". Being of average intelligence, I quickly put two and two together and suddenly realized I had sent photos not to Jon Voight but to Michael Jackson. After I got past the shock, we settled down

128

to a long, pleasant conversation.

During the hour long conversation, Michael asked whether I gave painting lessons. I replied that I didn't. He then asked if I would give him painting lessons. I explained that I was painting for an upcoming show and I would have limited time. I asked him to give me a few days to try and work it out.

A couple of days later, the TV said Michael would be opening his "BAD Tour" in Kansas City, Missouri. I then assumed that he would be way too busy for art lessons. To my surprise, his assistant Jolie phoned and told me Michael was excited about meeting me and she gave me a list of cities he would be appearing in. She said, "Pick one". I picked Denver, Colorado, because it's close to my state of New Mexico. Michael called soon after and asked if I could pack up all my equipment - easel, drawing board, lights, paints, etc. and ship it to the hotel where we would be staying. I complied.

Michael had arranged for a limousine to take me to the Albuquerque airport (about 67 miles from my home in Santa Fe). When I got to the Denver airport there was a limousine waiting to take me to the hotel. I would have a personal driver for the next five days that I would be in Denver. When we got to the hotel, the staff was lined up by the curb to welcome me to the hotel. Holy mackerel, I'd never been treated that well at any hotel I ever stayed at.

My crate of equipment had arrived and had been placed in my suite. I began to unpack when the phone rang. Jolie told me Michael was eager to meet me and could he come down right away? I said, "Sure".

Shortly after, Michael and Chuck, his bodyguard, showed up at my door. Michael is normally very shy, so Chuck hung around for a few minutes. When he realized that Michael was comfortable, he excused himself and left us alone. I arrived in Denver on a Tuesday, so that gave us three days before his concert. We visited art galleries, bookstores, even had a private showing of Egyptian artifacts at the Denver Museum of Natural History. We also drew, painted and generally had a great time together. I found him to be intelligent, thoughtful, compassionate and above all, funny. The man had a great sense of humor.

Finally, the first night of the concert arrived. We had to leave very early - about an hour and a half before the concert started. We had a hair-raising ride to the stadium in 3 vans - 70+ mph sprint aided by police cars with sirens wailing and complicated by a car with two Japanese ladies who were determined to arrive at the same time we did.

Upon entering the stadium, Michael headed straight for an area marked "absolutely no admittance". It was a curtain wall where I could see children in wheelchairs - some with nurses, some with families and some were even on respirators. Later I found out a little boy had actually passed away while he was with Michael. These were critically ill children whose last wish was to meet Michael Jackson. It broke my heart.

After the concert, I asked Michael how he could spend time with these children and then go directly onstage to deliver a mind - blowing performance. His response was, "How could I not?" I found out that Michael always made himself available to sick or dying children. Often, at a moment's notice, Michael would fly to visit the bedside of an ailing child. Just as often, he would leave a personal item, a glove or a hat, and tell the child that he would be back in a specified time to see them again. Michael said, "I know I'm just an ordinary man, but Michael Jackson

130

David with one of his drawings of Michael

the superstar may be able to inspire this child to live another day or another week or longer". I admired his compassion.

I've been to many concerts and they all seem to attract a specific age group. I was surprised by the wide range of ages present at Michael's concert. There were kids, teenagers, young parents, middle - aged people and yes, even the elderly were present.

That summer, Michael invited me to spend some time with him at the ranch. He had closed the deal on the 2800 acre estate north of Santa Barbara. It was an exciting time. The estate had fallen into disrepair and needed a face - lift as well as all the attractions Michael was planning. By the time I got there, the ponds had been dredged, the grounds replanted, new gates, a theatre and they were in the process of installing a magnificent merry - go - round and a train that would carry children around to the attractions. Michael said, "I want children to feel special when they come here. I want to give them a time out from all they're having to endure".

The ranch was not only a sanctuary where Michael could roam free from security, but his gift to children who desperately needed an uplifting experience. All the rides and attractions at the ranch were wheelchair accessible and all of the rides were modified so arms or legs or hair could not be caught in the equipment. Further, the people in charge of the rides went to Kansas City every six months to practice extricating special needs children from all the rides.

Michael and I also worked on plans for a water park and condo units at Neverland where very sick children and their families and health care workers would be able to spend overnights at the ranch. He knew that critically ill children heal better in an environment of hope, positive thoughts, laughter and magic. The

132

darkened and quiet sick room fosters depression, not joy and joy heals according to Michael.

His condos should have large bay windows in the front and they were supposed to look like tree houses in the forest. He wanted the large windows because he knew that very ill children often can´t sleep and wake up at night afraid. His idea was to build an outdoor theater with a huge Sony screen (similar to the one on Times Square in New York) facing the glass walls of the condos. Cartoons would be played there continually all night, in case the children woke up, they would be able to have some entertainment.

Later, in November 1994, Michael summoned me to New York City. He wanted me to help plan and illustrate a project he was interested in. I stayed with him and Lisa Marie at Trump Towers.

I often traveled to where Michael was to work on projects. During this time Michael had provided aid to a lot of people and children in Eastern Europe (esp. the Balkans - Sarajevo). He had built an orphanage and also supplied a 747 Airliner filled with doctors and medical supplies for that region.

Michael and Lisa Marie had agreed to bring a little boy to the United States and to pay for his much - needed heart surgery. The surgery was to cost $125,000, but when they found out that Lisa Marie and Michael were going to pay, the price suddenly became $250,000. For a man who continued to do so much good, these acts were hard for him to understand.

Soon after I met Michael, he told me, "We're all put on earth for a purpose. Mine is to help children. I am so grateful to be chosen for this god - given talent. It allows me to do what I was

133

Michael's "Heal the World Foundation" was responsible for an AmeriCares airlift delivering $2.1 million worth of humanitarian aid to Sarajevo and also helped provide 47 tons of winter relief supplies including medical items, blankets, winter clothing and shoes.   Pictures © AmeriCares

purposed to do".

In the two decades Michael was my friend he never changed. His driving force was always to help the sick, the abused, the neglected, the poor, the under - privileged and the environment. No matter what people tried to accuse him of, Michael loved children; he lived for children. They were the most important thing in his life; in fact, they were his reason for living. All of Michael's work was dedicated to children - to the children of the world or to the child in all of us.

It has been reported that Michael contributed more than $300 million to charities during his short lifetime. I personally know of many surgeries Michael paid for to help sick or injured children. I feel the loss of Michael's passing, but the world has lost one of its greatest gifts and philanthropists.

I wish the world could know the real Michael. Michael always said that if you talked about the good you did in the world, you cancelled the beneficence of the gift, so he was very private about his humanitarian work.

Nobody will ever know how much he did for this planet and for the children. The world will never know what it lost because they took Michael from his work and that cheated not just him of his future, but it cheated all of us.

Just right the way he was

by Mark Lester, UK

I got to know Michael in the early 80s. He was on tour with his brothers and came to London. At that time I was more into heavy mental, but of course I knew the Jacksons and their music. Michael's favorite musical was "Oliver" and as I had played the title role in the film version in 1967, when I was eight years old, Michael had asked his manager to arrange a meeting with me. Of course I said yes when I got the call. When my sister and I arrived at the hotel, I realized that Michael had booked a whole floor. I had never seen something like that and felt a little intimidated. But then Michael opened the door in jeans, a sweatshirt and trainers. I would have expected something fancy, but he just appeared like a normal guy. That impression increased while we got to know each other. He was basically my age, just one and a half months younger, and so we got on very well immediately and talked about films and music and whatever else was on our mind for four full hours.

From that day on we got together whenever Michael was in London or I would visit him in LA, Neverland or elsewhere. Our relationship got even closer when our children came. We not only shared our experiences of fatherhood, but also our children became friends. My girls are a bit older, my son a year younger than Prince. They loved to play together and of course

136

my kids were crazy about being at Neverland. For Michael's kids it was also an advantage to be around children that did not grow up in show business. Although I was an actor for many years, I'm now working as an osteopath in a clinic for acupuncture, that I opened in 1993.

One thing that was so wonderful about Michael was his childlike nature. I remember once when we were together in Los Angeles, Michael had rented the penthouse in the Beverly Wilshire Hotel, the one made famous by the "Pretty Woman" movie. Michael, in his playful mood, had filled up water balloons and threw them from the balcony. Then he hid and carefully peeked to see if anyone got wet. One poor guy who was at the wrong place at the wrong time literally got soaked. Michael was laughing so hard. But that guy got quite angry and went into the hotel to tell the manager what happened. Security was sent out to find out who had thrown the balloon. Fortunately for Michael they did not figure out it had been coming from his room.

He would also often call me imitating accents like Cockney, pretending to be someone else. He actually was quite good at it and could often fool me for several minutes before I realized who it really was.

I think this childlike character of his as well as the fact that he himself had an unusual childhood made him sensible for the suffering of children and dedicate his time and money to underprivileged youngsters. He was always very quiet about his efforts to help, he would not brag about them, sometimes not even mention them at all. He often turned up at hospitals and orphanages anonymously so that nobody knew he was coming. The fact that he gave these kids a little escapism, something to hold on to in their suffering was enough for him, he did not do it for the publicity. Once I was at Neverland and Michael

by Mark Lester

returned from Los Angeles and he told me he had just visited a burn unit there. To put a smile on the children's faces was all he needed to make his effort worth it.

While I was at Neverland there were often busloads of kids. Michael regularly invited children from the ghettos, nearby schools or just sick youngsters to have a day of enjoyment on his ranch. He gave them entertainment for the whole day, played with them and showed movies in his especially designed theater, which had places equipped even for very ill visitors. It's sad to see what happened to Neverland now. I think Michael would have liked it to become some kind of children's home because to be a place where you feel happy and at home away from home was already its purpose when Michael lived there, and especially so for underprivileged children.

Michael always expressed his concern for the destruction of the world. He was very upset about what happened and tried to do his part, give his contribution to make this world a better place. I guess due to the fact that he was so ardent about it and that we spent a lot of time together, traveled together and were longtime friends, this kind of rubbed off on me as well. I just hope that the world is aware that we have not only lost an incredible musician and performer, but that someone was taken away from us that had so much more life in him! Someone that you cannot even describe in words! Someone that was unique and that had an aura and presence around him like nobody else! And someone who had a genuine love for our planet and our children. It might be argued that he maybe should have been a little more sensible with kids he allowed in because he made it so easy for people to take advantage of him, but after all that was also part of Michael's innocence! If I had the chance to tell Michael one thing today it would be that he shouldn't have changed anything! He was just right the way he was!

138

My source of faith

by Stefania Capasso, Italy

God gives each one of us the strength and dignity to face our fate and places people in our life who have the power to motivate and help us through difficult times.

Since my childhood, Michael was not only my favourite artist, but felt like that true friend everyone wishes for, who is always there, in good as well as in bad times. Through his music, he accompanied me and one can say that his music is like the soundtrack of my life. As it were, I even met my husband Giuseppe through Michael, during his "BAD" concert in Rome. Guiseppe was also a big fan and only two years later we married. In 1991 our first child Tania and in 1993 our baby-boy Vincenzo were born. Needless to say that both of my children knew Michael and his music since they were in their mothers lap.

Getting married and having children never reduced my love for Michael, on the contrary, it increased! Perhaps that was because I identified with him a lot, not only for the fact that I too had three sisters and five brothers in my family but more so because of problems I had to manage in my life, that occurred almost simultaneously as Michael's biggest problems. In 1993, Michael went through hell because of false accusations by a

139

greedy family that wanted to extort money from him, which they succeeded in. That same year was also a very dramatic one for me, because shortly after my second child, Vincenzo, was born, I was told that my first child, Tania, had been diagnosed with autism. I was only 22 years old at that time and could not handle the bad news at first. I believe nobody would have, no matter what age. So my daily life had become very difficult and energy-sapping in many ways but Michael's songs and messages kept me going.

A few years later, in spring 1996, I heard the announcement for Michael's next world tour, which would start in Prague, Czech only a few months later. I was so excited and happy about those news but soon my feelings changed because I realized that with two little children and especially one child who needs extra care, I would not be able to travel with my fan friends to see his concert.

Our neighbours at that time knew about my love for Michael and how sad I was that I would not be able to see him at his concert. They knew how difficult the situation for my husband and me had been since Tania's diagnosis and how it had changed our life. They were the kindest people and tried to cheer me up but they knew it would not really work.

One evening they came over to our house and wanted to speak with my husband. I had no idea what it was about and was stunned, to say the least, as they began to speak. They told him that they believe a change from everyday-life would do me good and give me strength to keep on, after all. They offered him help with taking care of our children for the time I would be away and told him that they still owned a house in Prague, the city they originally came from, with a vacant flat, where my friends and I could stay. They were so convincing and had thought about everything, that my husband simply could not decline. The moment I heard him say "Yes" was the moment I swore myself that I would use my chance to let Michael know I exist and to tell him what he means to me.

During the following weeks I felt like recharged already, because I had something to look forward to. Even though I was tired in the evening from all the work, I wanted to create a present for Michael and came up with an idea for a big painting (2x3metres), showing Michael under a tree with Walt Disney characters all around him in a landscape with a river, a lawn and many children and a character popular in Italy called "Topo Gigio", holding up the Italian flag. I also wrote a very personal letter to Michael, telling him about everything and what he means to me.

When finally the day of my departure to Prague drew nearer, I became more and more excited. Luckily all my preparations were finished in time and I could not wait to begin my journey. However my heart was with my children and husband also and while packing, I decided to take pictures of them with me.

I met my fan friends in Prague and felt so incredible happy that I had gotten this chance. We immediately walked to Michael's hotel and I could not believe my luck when I saw him departing for his rehearsals the very moment we arrived there. I was so excited that I almost could not sleep that night.

The next morning we arrived early at his hotel and I took the chance to place my painting for Michael right opposite the main entrance, so that he would see it when coming out of the building. Soon more and more fans arrived from every part of the world and many came over to admire my painting. I was very happy that they liked it but when Michael's photographer and a little later his cameraman came over, too and started tak-

141

ing pictures of my painting, I got really excited. Finally, around midday, Michael came out of the hotel. Seeing him that close for the first time, I couldn't believe my eyes. He was just a few metres away, when he suddenly looked over and his eyes met my painting.

He immediately seemed to like it and gave me "thumps-up" for it, before continuing his walk along the crowd barriers to greet fans. Then he entered his van and obviously told his bodyguard Wayne to tell something to Teddy, Michael's tour assistant, who would then walk over to us and said: "Michael likes this painting very much and would like to have it". By then I had lost my ability to speak but my friends luckily answered for me: "Oh yes! She drew it just for him! But she would love to give it to Michael personally, if possible?". So Teddy went back to Michael to report about it and when he came back to us, he said: "OK, Mr. Jackson is going to visit the President now, but when he gets back, you are invited to visit him in his room.". Then they drove off. I could not believe this and started to laugh, cry and tremble simultaneously.

The moment I entered Michael's room, I saw him talking to some kids and their mother. As transfixed as I was in that moment, I was glad that his bodyguard, who had brought me up to the room, motioned for me to open the wrapping around my painting. But it was quite big and heavy, and so accidentally I clashed the wrapping against the chandelier with a terrible clatter. Luckily it didn't crack but I was so embarrassed and all I could say in the audibility of a whisper was: "Oh, sorry!" It was that moment when Michael's eyes caught mine and he smiled at me with the sweetest expression and came over to me, looking at my painting. He was happy to see it again and said: "Oooohhh!" I was so nervous but he tried to make me feel at ease by smiling at me and commenting on my painting:

142

"Oh my God, it's wonderful!" Then he came closer and discovered something that made his eyes light up like those of a child: "Ohhh! Topo Gigiiio!" He accentuated the final "i" of the name with his voice. Everyone in the room started laughing. Michael asked me if I was Italian and I confirmed that. The woman who was there with her children immediately came over to me and began to speak Italian with me. She asked me which part I am from and when I said: "Naples", Michael seemed to have understood that and said: "Oh, I love Naples!"

Then he went on to analyse my painting and repeated: "Oh boy! It's wonderful, wonderful!" Luckily that woman now helped me with talking English when Michael asked why I had chosen to portray him underneath a tree. I answered that it was an inspiration I had, like a picture in my mind before I started painting. He was excited and said: "Oh, you had a vision! You know that tree means a lot to me", and continued talking, which the woman translated to me and said that he wants to take my painting home with him and put it in his room. I couldn't believe it and almost speechless said: "Thank you!". But Michael replied: "No, I thank YOU! You gave me such a beautiful present! It is full of love! Thank you, I love you!"

Then his bodyguard was told to take a picture of us with the painting. Michael gave me his hand and drew me closer to him, his fingers touching my skin. I will never forget how he smelt of some sort of vanilla perfume. That was the most beautiful moment in my life and I trembled from top to toe. He felt my state and asked concerned: "Are you ok?". But instead of an answer, I threw my arms around him and all the tension inside of me, my hopes, my sorrows, simply everything, broke out of me in that moment and I sighed: "Oh Michael!". He held me tight and as much as I tried, I could not stop my tears from falling. I felt him comforting me by caressing my head and back and I swear if I

143

have had the opportunity to stop time, I would have and stayed in his arms forever.

As soon as I had calmed down a bit I began to feel very embarrassed and said: "I'm so sorry". But Michael replied with his indescribable kindness: "Oh, oh, it's alright." Then he curiously asked me, what I brought in my bag. I had completely forgotten that my bag hung on my shoulder all the time with my letter for him and the pictures of my children. "These are my children.", I said giving him the pictures. Astonished he said: "Oh, congratulations! You already are a mother! They're such beautiful kids!"

I told him that Vichi was imitating him since the age of one, which made Michael smile and say that Vichi was really a beautiful baby boy. Then I showed him Tania's photos and told him that she's autistic. Michael's expression changed and with pain in his voice he said: "Oh no. I'm sorry! I do know about autism, they live in a world all on their own". I told him this was true

144

but also that he and his music were part of her world since she was a newborn girl and that whenever we needed to calm her down, the only thing that helped was playing his songs or watching his videos.

Michael closely looked at Tania's pictures and visibly touched he said: "She is beautiful! Her glance and smile are wonderful! Can I keep her pictures?" Stunned I replied: "Certainly, you can". Then he wanted to know Tania's age and if she was speaking. I had to tell him that I had never heard the sound of her voice. He said: "Oh no! Oh my God. But she is so beautiful, is there something I could do for her? Do you need help? How can I help you?" I was so overwhelmed of his kindness that I could not ask him of anything in that moment. Michael suddenly took my hands and while intensely looking me in the eyes, he said: "Please don't ever loose your faith, your hope and don't stop fighting for her! Never! Don't give up!" Then he embraced me again, and again I could not hold back my tears. It seemed like all the years of having to be strong broke out and while crying I murmured: "Thank you Michael! I love you!" And he replied: "I love you, too, I love you more!". It was such an intense moment, so special and I felt as if a heavy stone fell from my heart and I was recharged. Now so many years later, I regret my shyness, because I know Tania would have been so happy to meet Michael, the hero of her life.

Then my time to say goodbye came. His bodyguard already waited for me at the door when I remembered to give him my letter and told him that it would be important for me that he reads it. He replied: "I'll read it tonight, I promise." But then one more important thing I felt that I needed to let him know about came to my mind. Although I had written about it in my letter, I wanted to let him know how sorry I feel for him, for everything he had to go through regarding the fake charges and all the pain and suffering because of it. But I was too overwhelmed and all I brought out in that moment was: "Michael, how are you?" For another moment we looked into each other's eyes and although my English was not good, he understood what I asked him about and told me that all the love he receives from his fans gives him strength to keep on and that he is fine. "Please don't forget to take care of yourself, you will always have our support and we will always be there for you", I told him and he thanked me, saying "I love you so much! God bless you!"

While I walked to the door, I reminded him once more about my letter and he indicated me with kissing his fingers and placing them above his heart: "I swear it!" In the last moment, before walking through the door, the presents my friends had given me for him, came back to my mind and so I turned around once more and said: "Oh, I forgot to give Michael these presents!". So I went back up to him, gave him the big bag and instead of telling him that those were gifts from my friends, I said: "These are my friends!" Everyone in the room started laughing and Michael pretended to look inside the bag with an surprised expression on his face. Although embarrassed again, I had to laugh, too and it made my goodbye-moment easier.

After this meeting, my life was changed forever. He had given me, an ordinary fan, a lot of his time and made me feel special and loved. He really was a gift from God, a unique human being and I will never forget the pain and love written on his face while looking at my daughter's pictures, he hardly held back tears. Michael's hugs were full of LOVE, positive energy and regenerative vibes. In them, you could genuinely feel at home.

I know Michael really wanted to change the world and he did in many ways. Even though he was so famous, Michael has always been humble and helped so many people without wanting at-

146

tention or publicity. Through the most shameful abuses of human evilness, he preserved his dignity and never seemed bitter, on the contrary full of forgiveness and love. He truly is a role model to strive for. Like many other fans all over the world, my friends and I have created a non-profit foundation called "MJJ's IYouWe Foundation" (https://www.facebook.com/MJJIY-OUWE) after Michael's death. Our goal is to continue his message in our small way by helping children and people in need. Although we know this is only a drop of water in the ocean, we remember that Michael taught us to start with the man in the mirror, or else nothing will be done.

147

THANK YOU, MICHAEL, I'll never be able to thank you enough, you are an angel indeed. You taught me unconditional love, strengthened me in my difficult times and taught me to never give up, to believe and to fight for my dreams. You will always live in my and my children's heart because you are a part of me and I LOVE YOU!

Children show me in their playful smiles the divine in everyone. This simple goodness shines straight from their hearts. Being with them connects us to the deeper wisdom of life. These children are a reminder of the preciousness of all life, especially young lives untouched by hatred, prejudice and greed. Now, when the world is so confused and its problems so complicated, we need our children more than ever. Their natural wisdom points the way to solutions that lie waiting to be recognized within our own hearts.

Dreams Become Reality

by Julie Windsor, Australia

Thursday, November 28th 1996 will remain to be a day that is forever etched in my memory, as this is the day that a long wished for, long awaited dream of mine actually came true! I got to meet my absolute hero, the moonwalking, singing, dancing, thrilling legend himself, the one and only
Mr. Michael Jackson.

I've always told people that I became a fan of Michael's the night I was sitting at home looking for something to watch on TV and saw that there was a special playing of Oprah interviewing Michael. I'd heard a lot of people over the years saying how weird and strange Michael supposedly was, but I didn't really have any opinion of him (or any other singer at that stage) for myself. I knew a few of his songs, but nothing at all about the

150

man himself. I knew he had a sister, Janet, but I didn't even know that he had any brothers or was a singer from such a young age. This night back in the early 90's was about to change my life in a huge way and forever change and shape my taste in music. Now, I've always said this is when I first became a fan of Michael's, but I think a superfan, is more like it because when I think back now, I loved the songs from "Thriller" when they first came out. I can vaguely recall singing and dancing along to "Billie Jean", "Thriller" and "The Girl Is Mine" when they were first released, I would have only been three or four years old. I remember walking to school around the time "Bad" came out and singing "Thriller" songs, songs from "Bad" with my school friends, trying to outdo each other to see who could moon-walk or side step the best. So I would definitely say I have been a fan the majority of my life now.

However, that Oprah interview was just mind-blowing for me! I couldn't see at all why anyone would think he was strange or odd in any way at all, he was a normal, kind, caring, loving indi-vidual who gave everything he possibly could to everyone he could possibly reach. Not only through his music and dancing, but by his fundraising, giving so generously to so many founda-tions, creating his own foundations, donating the profits from concerts and singles. The thing that really reached me, however, along with how amazingly talented he was - just being aston-ished by hearing and seeing him sing, such a tiny boy, only ten years old with his brothers as the "Jackson 5", for the first time in my life - was to see how he had such a huge heart for sick kids. The way he not only invited them into his private home to give them a day they would never forget, but to see he actually built sections of his home, to accommodate these kids and their medical and physical needs. Building hospital beds into the walls of his theatre so that kids who were bed-ridden could still en-joy these amazing shows he would have put on for them. Their

151

happiness and seeing them being able to smile through the pain and enjoy a day away from hospital, is what brought the real joy into Michael's life. I don't think I can name one other celebrity that exists today who has opened their home and their heart so much to fans, sick kids and just random strangers, people they don't know in the least, so that their lives can be improved so much, even if only for a single day or a few hours!

I think one of the reasons this hit me so much was because I was also incredibly ill at the time, spending months at a time in hospital, tied to numerous drips at once, even going weeks or months without being able to eat a single thing.

I was 12 years old and had woken one morning with the most severe stomach pain I had ever felt in my life. I was taken to hospital that day and the doctors could not work out what the problem was, other than finding out that I was diabetic. After several months in hospital and thanks to my sister staying at a friend's house for the night, the father of who just happened to be a doctor in the field I was needing another one in, gastroen-terology (dealing with all sorts of issues to do with the stom-ach), at the Children's Hospital, Princess Margaret Hospital (or P.M.H. to us locals), I was finally diagnosed as having something called Pancreatitis, which is an incredibly painful condition to suffer from. It's very rare for children to be diagnosed with, as it is generally known as an alcoholics condition. People will drink so much that it destroys the pancreas beyond repair, causing hideous pain. In the rare occasions it has been diagnosed in children, it is normally from an injury to the stomach. There was only one other case the nurses looking after me could recall at the time I was first admitted, and that was from a young boy falling off his bike, flipping over the handle bars and having them somehow stab into his stomach, which damaged his pancreas. He was lucky however, and recovered after a few

152

weeks. Pancreatitis is basically a disorder where the pancreas will deteriorate, basically eating itself away from the inside on out, causing what doctors say is the worst pain known to man, while it does this. Needless to say these years of my life were not the least bit pleasant!

By the time the Oprah Winfrey interview aired on TV I had already been sick for two long years, spending months in hospital, home anywhere from a few hours to a few days or if I was really lucky, a couple of weeks before being admitted again to try and come up with new ways to control the pain I was suffering from each day. I'd had a lot of tests and scans run on me, along with surgery by this point also. The first one was to have half of my pancreas removed in the hope they could remove all damaged parts of it and I would be fine again once I recovered, and also removing my appendix "just in case"! Sadly, it only seemed to work for a few days before I was in agony again. I used to think it would be more pleasant to cut my arm or leg off with a butter knife than go through this pain each day.

A while later they were considering whether or not to remove the rest of my pancreas, but it was a pretty radical surgery that had never been done anywhere in the world before, at least not on a child my age, and they weren't even sure if I could survive or not without the pancreas! We eventually went ahead with the surgery, again hoping this would stop all the attacks of pain, but no such luck. The doctors had decided that whatever caused this in the first place, had continued to spread to all the nerve endings in my stomach and would leave me needing further surgery in the years to come, in more attempts to ease some of the pain out of my life.

Throughout these times of such severe pain, music became my best friend. Having seen this Oprah interview, where they de-

153

buted Michael's single "Give in to Me" from the album "Danger-ous", along with showing the amazing and so cute "Jackson 5" clips, I was gone! The only music I cared about was Michael's! The only books I wanted to read were by Michael or about Michael! When I was having a well day, I'd be allowed out of the hospital for a few hours at a time, so I would get my Mum to take me to a music store or a second hand book store to find anything I could possibly find about Michael. I wanted to collect every single CD I could possibly find by Michael or the "Jackson 5", even if it only had one song on it that I didn't already own, it was worth it to me. Any video tape I could find that had foot-age of Michael and his brothers on it also became mine. Shows such as "Motown 25", "The Wiz" and "Moonwalker", anything that showed an interview with Michael became much sought after for my new collection! I am still sure, to this very day, that I must have driven the hospital staff crazy with the non-stop playing of Michael's music and videos, as loudly as I could pos-sibly play them, over and over again. I wanted to make sure I had every lyric, every spoken word memorized!

It wasn't long before my bedside drawers in the hospital room were filled with Michael Jackson memorabilia. I would constant-ly have the CDs out, trying to re-organize them from year of release, or J5 in order of release date, then MJ in a separate pile in order of release date, unsure which was best. Whether Young MJ albums such as "Got To Be There" and "Ben" should be with Adult MJ's solo works, or should they stay with the J5 albums, since his brothers did sing backup for him on them and they were recorded in the J5 era... not an issue for most people, but the order mattered a lot to me, so that I had the correct rotation of songs played and they would all fit in the drawers correctly. I was completely and utterly obsessed! These days of utter obsession are where my luck really changed for me.

154

It must have been late 1991 or early 1992. I had seen the Oprah interview, "The Jacksons: An American Dream" and almost everything else ever recorded! I was so in love with Michael Jackson and all I wanted, all I ever dreamt about was trying to find some way of being able to meet Michael myself, but how does a 14-year-old girl, stuck in hospital and tied to numerous IV poles at a time, make such a huge dream happen, when so many other people in similar situations throughout the world want the exact same thing? Every night I would wish on the first star I saw, I would pray that somehow I would get to meet him. Then one day I recalled reading in a book a few years earlier something about a group of people who would grant a wish, of any kind, as long as it was humanly possible, to kids who were seriously sick in hospital. I remembered reading in books about Michael how he would quite often grant wishes for sick kids to go to his "Neverland Ranch" or he would visit them in hospital when he was on tour in the area and so forth… so that was my plan! I tried to lay hints with some of my doctors without being too obvious about the "Make A Wish" or "Starlight Foundations". I guess maybe I was a bit too subtle though, because no-one ever picked up on it!

Then one day a lady had started coming to visit me ever so often, her name just happened to be MJ, so I thought that was pretty cool. We'd get talking for a few minutes until she had to head off elsewhere. I never really had any idea who she was; where she came from. I only knew she worked in the hospital and was something other than a nurse or doctor as she didn't have a uniform of any sort. My Mum then told me one day when she was visiting that she was actually the head of the hospital's promotions or fundraising department. Something similar to that anyhow, she was kind of a big deal in the place and involved with a lot of things on all the wards and was always shown a lot of respect. Well, one day I was sorting through all my CDs

155

and getting frustrated that they wouldn't all fit into the drawers anymore when this lady, MJ, walked into my room, reached for one of the discs and said, "Oh, this is my all time favourite album of Michael's, I see you're a big fan also, I absolutely love him! Did you know that he is planning to come to Perth, when he starts the "Dangerous" tour?" Well, of course I knew he was coming to Australia, and I knew he'd been to Perth several times before, so I could only hope that he would be including Perth with those tour dates since he would already have his show in the country and said he liked it here so much! Then MJ continued, "Well, as you probably already know, when Michael visits different cities around the world, he also likes to visit the hospitals there to visit some of the kids, like yourself, who are so sick! Quite often he will also give those kids tickets to his shows… and for those kids who are too sick to go along in a regular manner, we are able to take them in the ambulance transport so they have the medical help they need nearby and a way back to the hospital if there's any emergency. I'll make you a promise now, if Michael does make it to Perth for the 'Dangerous' concert, I'll make it my business to make sure you are one of the first people to get tickets and that you personally get to meet him!"

Wow! I was about ready to float out of that hospital bed! It was the most exciting thing I had heard for a long time!! When Mum returned back to my room and any other visitor that came to see me, I couldn't keep my mouth shut about it! I was absolutely thrilled. I didn't even realize that this lady, MJ, was a fan. I thought those just happened to be her initials. I had no idea she had so much power at the hospital, she was just a nice lady who came to see me ever so often. I asked Mum what she thought her name was one day, obviously something that began with an M, and she said no, nobody actually knows what her real name is! She is such a huge Michael Jackson fan that she started call-

156

ing herself MJ and it stuck, so now nobody actually knows her real name, she just goes by MJ!

Sadly, the rest of us fans know what happened next in Michael's life though. A greedy, fame starved, money hungry father got his son to become good friends with Michael, got him to use and abuse that friendship so that they could take further revenge on Michael, and for what?! Even more money and fame and because he, like so many other people, didn't want to see such a lovely, caring, beautiful, African-American man become even more rich and famous than he already was, through his latest album and a new world tour about to start. Sadly, he didn't only succeed in trying to ruin Michael's good name in the eyes of certain people and the media (who weren't interested in looking to find the truth for themselves, the lies sold more copies of magazines and got more people watching their TV shows to worry about that!) but he also stole from a lot of really poor children the world over.

Michael had planned to give all the proceeds from certain individual concerts to his newly created "Heal The World Foundation". Funds raised from the single, from selling memorabilia at his concerts were all going towards this new Foundation. Millions of dollars were raised from kind people donating, from the shows Michael did get to perform, from the singles that were sold. However, because of this one greedy individual, nowhere near the millions of dollars got delivered, because so many shows were cancelled. The loss of those millions of dollars to help aid so many people was the only crime committed, and Michael was not to blame for that happening! Something that was finally admitted by the child involved, but sadly not until after Michael passed away, and then the boy's father also committed suicide from living so long with the knowledge of how he destroyed the life of an innocent man.

157

Like all of Michael's other fans, millions of people worldwide, I was absolutely devastated that anyone could think Michael would do such dreadful things and I was positive it was going to be over really quickly. My friend MJ came to see me in hospital, also upset by it all. As she was leaving the room she said to me, "And don't worry, my promise still stands. I heard an interview with Michael where he said he was going to be releasing a new album as a thank you to all the fans that stood by him over this time and as an apology for those who missed out on seeing the 'Dangerous' tour, who had bought tickets but were never able to attend, he is already planning to do another world tour to make up for the one that was cancelled, going to all the countries who missed out on the 'Dangerous' tour! So my promise still stands, when Michael comes to Australia next, even if he doesn't make it to Perth for some reason, I will get you there somehow!" That really brought a big smile back to my face again, as I had thought that maybe every chance I ever had of meeting Michael had been erased.

It was now mid-late 1995, I was still in and out of hospital a lot, aware that I was starting to get too old to be in the "Children's Hospital" as a patient, and would have to move over to new doctors at the adult's hospital soon. I really didn't want to do that as I had made great friends where I was, the hospital was decked out with it's own radio station that you could call up and make requests on, had its own big activity centre for teenagers so you could cook, play pool, video games, had a punching bag, drum kit, anything you could imagine to entertain yourself on those long stays. It was a fantastic place to escape to. I was also a bit worried that since my friend MJ's words to me those couple years earlier were finally starting to happen, I might miss out on meeting my idol! Michael had released the "thank you album" to his fans, "Blood On The Dance Floor", and he had also released a new two-disc album entitled "History", or as Michael wrote it, and us fans read it, "HIStory"...His Story! A fantastic album that included one disc of some of his best known, most popular hits over his solo career and the other disc consisted of entirely new material. Some of these songs just blew me away, just like the tracks from "Dangerous", "Thriller" and "Bad", music from his entire life had done so.

As mentioned earlier, my days would be full of such extreme pain that I honestly couldn't see an end to it at all. I could not see what the point was in continuing to live that way, I was rarely able to get to school to see friends, because I'd now started high school. Or my friends had at least! Naturally their lives continued and they would become too busy with so much homework and other friends to really keep in touch too often and the news of Julie being sick in hospital again was no big deal and something that was said on most calls. Not exactly many interesting things happening there! The friends that did continue to visit me became fewer, which was understandable especially with everyone going to new schools and so forth. I also switched to a new high school, really close to the hospital and had made just a few really good friends there, the sort you know will be in your life for the rest of your life. So they would come over and visit me after school or at lunch break or if they wanted to miss a few classes of school! Life could be pretty hard though and I soon found one of the few things getting me through each day, other than family, friends and prayer, were the amazingly insightful words that Michael had placed in his music.

When I first bought "Dangerous" and was reading along to all the lyrics and trying to memorize them all, "Keep The Faith" soon became one of my very favourite songs: "And you can say the words, like you understand, but the power's in believing, so give yourself a chance, 'cause you can climb the highest

by Julie Windsor

mountain, swim the deepest sea..." Lyrics like these just really helped me so much and taught me that I just needed to keep on fighting through everything and, like the song says, "All you need is the will to want it and a little self esteem, don't let nobody turn you round, you gotta know when it's good to go and get your dreams up off the ground, so keep the faith! Believe in yourself no matter what it's gonna take! Don't let nobody take you down brother, just keep your eyes on the prize!" There are so many terrific lines in that one song alone, I would listen to it 10, 20 times a day. It just helped me so much. If I ever wanted to lead any part of a normal life, make my dreams come true, I just had to keep my eyes on that prize!

"Will you be there" was another really great song that helped me. With such emotional lyrics in the song, it showed me that I wasn't the only one who felt so alone and hard done by at times, that other people go through similar things and we just need to be there to support each other.

Those are just two short songs out of hundreds of songs Michael sung that I owned and listened to daily, that helped me so much. He wasn't just another singer out there amongst the masses to me. He was someone who shaped my life, gave me the moral support I needed and when I needed it. When I was at my lowest points and just wanted to curl up and die, Michael was there when no-one else in the world seemed to be. He meant absolutely everything to me and it would really crush me to think I may not ever get to meet him if I left this hospital as a patient to be at the adults hospital. I couldn't stand the thought, I just had to meet him, and thank him, somehow.

I soon heard that Michael would be coming to Perth for the "HIStory World Tour" and I was so excited. I was secretly wondering if my friend MJ had remembered that promise she'd

160

made me a couple years earlier. I had now left the "Children's Hospital", PMH and was seeing different doctors at one of the adult hospitals now. Unbeknownst to me, however, when I left PMH for the final time, one of those doctors, nurses or other members of staff had actually gone and written to the "Make A Wish" and "Starlight Foundation" about me and what I had been through.

One day my Mother checked the mail and said, "Julie, there's a letter here for you!" I didn't have a clue why I would have a letter from anyone, I looked at the envelope and saw the "Starlight Foundation" logo on it. Inside was a letter saying they had heard my story from some important people and wanted to know, if I could make a wish, for anything at all, what would it be? There were boxes to make three separate wishes in case the first one or two just weren't possible to be made. Well, it didn't take me long to fill this form in! Number 1 was to "Meet Michael Jackson at his Neverland Ranch and see him perform live in concert!!" I wanted to make sure I didn't miss a single thing, so I made sure I put all the Michael things into the first box together, so they would hopefully make all three wishes come true within the first wish! I wasn't sure if I would quite get away with that though, so for number two, knowing Michael was on his way to Perth at the end of the year anyway, I wrote the next answer. 2: "See Michael Jackson perform live in concert and meet him!!!" Number 3 I didn't really want to fill in because I had to see him perform and I had to meet him somehow and I hadn't heard from my friend MJ for ages, I didn't think she'd even know how to contact me now. So I figured I could always buy tickets to go to a Michael Jackson concert, but I may never get the chance to meet him again, so wish number 3 was simply just "To meet Michael Jackson". We were then asked why each of those dreams were so important to me, so I somehow had to work out how to write that in such a short space, did so and

161

had the bit of paper sealed in an envelope and copied in case it got lost and I needed to send it a second time! I didn't want to leave anything to chance!!!

Time seemed to be passing quickly and I was rather upset that I hadn't heard back from "Starlight" about my wish yet, the concert tickets were going on sale any day now. Michael was only doing one show in Perth at this stage, but he had been adding extra shows to other cities and his timetable allowed him enough time to do more in Perth if he needed to. All his shows in Australia were selling out immediately, and with possibly only one show the question running through my head was, "Do I risk that my dream will be fulfilled or do I go ahead and book a ticket when they are released?" Well, when release day came around and I still hadn't heard back, I was panicking. They had just announced that Michael would perform first of all a second show and then they announced a third show in Perth, all were selling quickly. I didn't want to risk anything though, so for what would be an early Christmas present, my Mum got two tickets to the second of those shows, because "who knows if he will ever come here again and we will get the chance to see him again, I don't want to risk not seeing it at all!" So I was pretty happy with that plan.

A few weeks went by and the tickets arrived in the mail, I was thrilled to have those in my hands at last, I put them away in the safest place I could find and still remember where they actually were, as the show was still months away. Then later that same week I peered in the mail to find another little package from the "Starlight Foundation". In the package was a letter, a small little stuffed toy; the star which is the foundations logo. I looked at the toy thinking it was pretty cute but I was rather hesitant to open the letter and see if a wish had been granted. I was thinking maybe the toy was instead of the wish! How could that

162

ever make up for missing out on meeting Michael or seeing his concert? I finally opened the letter to find two opening night concert tickets to the "HIStory Tour" in Perth!

I was pretty excited but still kept looking for the part saying where I'd get to meet Michael, but it just wasn't there and I was pretty devastated about that. I was back to square one and trying to think up new ways to meet Michael while he was in my city. "How can I make it happen? Maybe I could book a night at the already pretty expensive hotel and hope somehow I'd run into him waiting by the elevator...?"

The days, weeks and months kept rolling by, during this time, since the tickets were fairly expensive, I decided to sell the tickets I had bought for the second show to a good friend of mine, another huge fan who just hadn't been able to get any tickets, and she was really excited to be able to get some seats as she thought she was going to miss out all together. It was now about three or four days before Michael was due to arrive in Perth. I'd been watching every news clip of him on the news to see what was going on, so excited for him when the news came out that he was expecting his first child, to Debbie Rowe.

163

I could not have been happier for him, as I knew how much he loved kids and had always hoped to have his own some day. Then to see the news that he had married Debbie while in Sydney, that just seemed to top things off! He looked to be so absolutely thrilled with life and could not have been happier with how things were going again. Good on him! My Mum had gone out for the morning and I was home alone, talking to friends on an internet chat line I used to chat on a lot. The phone rang and it was someone asking to speak to me.

Me: "Yes, hello, this is Julie speaking!"
Caller: "Hi Julie, how are you doing? I haven't seen you for what seems like such a long time! Have you been keeping well?"
Me: (a bit annoyed that someone who wouldn't even tell me who was speaking to me, was interrupting my internet chat!) "Oh yeah, I'm ok, I guess…have been better of course, but I'm ok."
Caller: "Oh, do you realize who this is, by the way? It's MJ from PMH!"
Me: "Oh, wow! Really? Hi! How are you doing?"
Caller/MJ: "Yeah, I'm doing great, but I was wondering if you would be able to come up to the hospital in a few days? To PMH?"
Me: "Oh, well, Mums not here to say yes or no. I don't think we have anything else on. I guess I could…why?"
Caller/MJ: "Well… do you think I might get a yes if I were to say it's because Michael Jackson is going to be here and I want you to meet him, like I promised a few years ago!!!"
Me: "Oh my gosh!!!!! Are you serious???? I will be there if I have to crawl the whole way there and back!!!! When? What time? How? What do I need to do?"
Caller/MJ: "Well, I haven't got all the exact details now until we get Michael's flight schedule, but at the moment he is planning to fly straight in to Perth, come straight to the hospital where

yourself and a few other kids will get to go into a room and talk to him for awhile, get autographs and everything! So make sure you bring something you really want him to sign for you!"
Me: "Oh, wow, this is so amazing. Thanks heaps!!! I'll wait to hear back from you for more details then!!"

I was so absolutely ecstatic and was standing there in shock for a few minutes after hanging up the phone! I couldn't believe she had kept to her promise after all this time and was still going to help me out like this! The smile could not be wiped off my face! My Mum finally arrived home and as soon as I heard the car engine, I ran out the front door to greet her. "You will never guess who just rang and what I am going to be doing in a few days time!!!!"

As the days slowly passed by, we got news from my friend MJ who told me that since Michael had been putting on extra shows in Sydney and gotten married, the plans had changed slightly. Michael was now on a later flight into Perth, so instead of going straight up to PMH from the airport, he would be going directly to the hotel at Scarborough Beach, "The Rendezvous" at Observation City. So I was to go straight there mid afternoon by about 4pm, Thursday November 28th. One day that is constantly lived over and over in my memory.

Since the area had been newly renovated, I was no longer so familiar with the layout there, and I had never been into the hotel itself, so Mum and I thought we'd better check it out ahead of time to see where to park and where to meet the people that I was meant to meet ahead of Michael's arrival.

So Mum and I drove down there, only a five minute drive from home, on the evening of the 27th. We found a perfect place to park so we wouldn't get blocked in by other fans hoping for a

by Julie Windsor

glimpse, found our way into the Hotel to see where we would meet my friend MJ along with a woman called Di Rolle who worked for "Dainty Entertainment", the company that has promoted all of the tours Michael had ever done in Australia, going right back to the "Jackson 5" days. This was seeming more real every second that passed by. My excitement levels were off the charts, I felt just like I used to on Christmas Eve, waiting to fall asleep and for the next day to arrive, just even more so! There's just no way to correctly describe the way I was feeling, other than a pile of nerves, major excitement with what seemed to be a lifetime of wishes right within my grasp finally about to come true!

I went back home and started looking around everyhwere for a couple of really good, near new pens, black markers that I could have in my pocket for Michael to sign something for me. But what out of my huge collection do I choose for him to sign? So my next big job was to search through my "MJ wardrobe", a closet in my brothers old room which was by then devoted to storing all my "Jackson 5" and Michael Jackson memorabilia, so it took a fair while to sort through it all and find things that were small and light enough to take with me for Michael to sign. I eventually decided on one of my favourite t-shirts, Michael's book "Dancing The Dream", an old autograph book I had with other autographs in it and my favourite Michael t-shirt I had bought on a trip to the USA a year earlier.

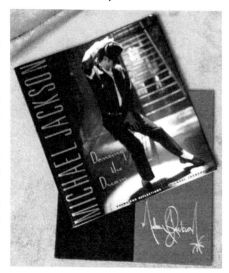

by Julie Windsor

The only thing I had left to do was find something to wear! I thought about wearing something rather fancy, or something really casual as I'd normally wear anywhere else, but just couldn't decide, so in the end I went for comfort. I grabbed my new and favourite pair of jeans, bright red with an almost fuzzy feel to them. And I decided I had to wear one of my Michael shirts if I was meeting the man himself, so decided to wear that same shirt I was wanting Michael to sign, as it was such a gorgeous photo of him and I had two of that shirt, one I could keep wearing and one that I could wear on the day, have Michael sign and then put away so that the signature would never wear off it. Everything was finally planned and organized for my big day ahead of me, all I had left to do was work out how on earth I could possibly sleep that night!

Finally Thursday had arrived!! I was awake by about 6am, showered, dressed, eaten breakfast by about 7am and doing anything I could think of to try and pass the next few hours until I would head up to "Rendezvous Observation City" hotel to see Michael! I totally felt like a child on Christmas, so excited to get all those great gifts but not being allowed to open them until my siblings and parents were awake! I just could not contain my excitement. I went and made sure I had the marking pens and they were working, so I could get Michael to sign my shirt with it, found the items I wanted to ask Michael to sign for me, made sure my Mum had a camera with extra film in it so she could get photos of Michael and I, and got it all packed in a bag, put in the car and ready to go!

After what seemed like a lifetime, but probably only another hour or two, it was time to go. I couldn't understand my body at this point, I was excited beyond belief, yet my stomach was tying itself in knots, my palms were sweating like mad…and we had only just pulled out of the driveway!!

We made sure we got there quite early, around 3:30pm as there wouldn't have been many parking spots left if we left it too late, as it was, being right on the beach and with so many other fans just as excited, all hoping to catch a glimpse of Michael. It was going to be rather hard to find a parking spot. We eventually found our way into the hotel to meet with Di Rolle and everyone involved with making this dream come true for me. Di and I spoke for awhile. She was a lovely lady, told me that she worked for "Dainty Entertainment", who had been the company that Michael had worked with for every tour he had ever done in Australia, going back to 1974 or so, when the "Jackson 5" came over for their first tour here. Di had met Michael on a few previous visits and could see how excited, yet nervous I was, and told me not to worry or let the nerves get to me, he is the nicest, most caring person you could ever hope to meet!

He was expected to arrive at 6pm, so we still had a bit of time to fill in! After I had been sitting around there for a bit longer, two other girls – Casey and Alicia - came along, who were also there to meet Michael. I was a bit too nervous and excited to say anything much to anyone, though, unfortunately, but I clearly remembered thinking how gorgeous they both looked. Casey was wearing a navy blue dress with pale blue flowers scattered over it, while Alicia was wearing a white t-shirt beneath a denim and flowery blue dress, topped off with a black hat. I do recall thinking she looked as though she had been through a lot, having lost her hair and black circles around her eyes. I was just really thrilled for her sake, that she was well enough on this day to be able to come along and also meet Michael, as another friend of theirs from hospital, Stephanie, was too sick to make it along that day. That may have been to her advantage, though, as she was lucky enough to meet Michael backstage before each of his shows and go onstage during "Heal The World" instead, along with Casey, so she really scored from that one in the

Three hours before Michael was due to arrive, there were already numerous fans waiting outside the hotel, while Julie nervously waited inside, preparing herself for the event of her life

Julie (right) meets Di Rolle while waiting for Michael to arrive

end!! I was amazed to get in touch with Stephanie recently, not having ever actually met her before, but was saddened to hear from Stephanie that Casey had very sadly succumbed to the cancer just two years after the November/December concerts of 1996. She seemed so healthy on this day and with her long gorgeous hair I never would have guessed there was anything at all wrong with her. She was one absolutely gorgeous young lady who I'll never forget. What was about to happen has remained to mean so very much to myself, and without wanting to put words in other people's mouths, I am sure it would have meant even more to Casey, to help keep that beautiful girl fighting right to the very end, and to help Alicia and Stephanie continue fighting throughout their battles also. I am unsure how Alicia is doing, or if she went into remission at all. I am very hopeful that this happened and she is still with us today. I am thrilled to be able to say that Stephanie, who was only six years old when Michael visited, did continue to fight the cancer for many years, but has now been in remission for three years and doing wonderfully well. Casey was one of her best friends at the time and I have a lot to thank her for in helping me write this story, as there were several bits of information I'd completely forgotten and she was able to remind me of these. So Stephanie, thank you so much. Alicia, I hope and pray you are out there somewhere alive and well. Casey, you beautiful young girl, may God bless you and rest in peace! I'm so glad your dreams were fulfilled in this way, which would also have given your family many great memories to look back on during the tough times ahead and to comfort them in the years to follow.

***

After waiting at the hotel for about another 15 minutes, we were told Michael's plane had been delayed about half an hour, but it shouldn't be too much longer than that. Shortly after that, around 6pm, another man, Mr. Linney, came over and said he had a small gift for Michael, he turned to Casey and Alicia to ask them if they would like to present it to Michael. I was so devastated that he didn't ask me, because I was just the biggest fan and I couldn't even imagine at the time that it could possibly mean even half as much to these two girls as it would ever mean to me! So I was hoping and praying that they would be too shy and say no. Then my prayers were answered, Casey first said no, then Alicia also said no and my face just lit up as Mr. Linney asked if I would like to present it to Michael! To which I said: "Absolutely!!!"

This "little" gift was a piece of jewellery, worth more money than I was ever likely to hold in my hands again! Mr. Linney, you see, is the owner of a wonderful chain of jewellery stores called "Linneys", located all around Australia; he was holding a beautiful brooch made with diamonds, which I was told were Argyle Diamonds, which come from the Argyle Diamond Mine in the East Kimberly region of Western Australia! He opened the box to show the three of us what was inside and it was the most gorgeous brooch of Snoopy sitting in his aeroplane. Snoopy was made from a gorgeous white pearl, his scarf tied around his neck and flowing gracefully behind him featured an Argyle diamond. Snoopy's eyes and nose were created by the natural shape of the pearl. The plane itself was 18ct yellow gold and included a spinning propeller. It was a one of a kind item, made especially for Michael, as they knew how much he enjoyed cartoon characters, worth...I can't begin to image how much..., and placed inside a large gorgeous wooden box. I was so transfixed on the brooch and how much money I was holding in my hands that I'd almost forgotten what I was doing there and getting even more nervous; if at all possible! I closed the box to keep it safe and see how spectacular that alone looked. I came to realize again that this box, this brooch, this gift for Michael, was my

171

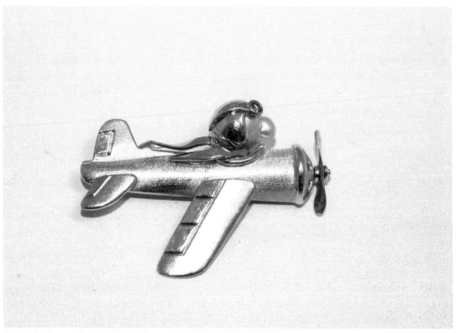

Beautiful Snoopy brooch especially made for Michael by Linneys

Top from left to right: Mr. Linney and Stephanie's Mum. Bottom row from left to right: Casey and Alicia. Centre: Julie taking another glance at the brooch to be presented to Michael.

gateway to spend a bit more time with and actually talk to him as well! I was so grateful to Mr. Linney first of all, along with the other girls who had said no to presenting Michael with this gift; even though they were probably a bit annoyed with themselves by now, but it meant the absolute world to me!

Just a few minutes later we got word that Michael's plane had finally landed! Now I felt as though I had elephants stomping around in my stomach rather than butterflies! I didn't know what to do with myself! We were all led out the front of the hotel to stand at the top of the stairs where the hotel doors are. Down the bottom of the stairs was a driveway that comes in from the busy road to the front of the hotel to let people and luggage out, then it leads either to the right and back onto the road, or around to the left for undercover parking. On the far side of the driveway is a low brick wall, and just in front of that some gates had been put up to try and stop people from breaking through. There were already numerous people out the front there, screaming their lungs out just watching the three of us, Di Rolle, and some of the security guys walk out of the hotel to stand at the top of the stairs to wait for Michael. To the left of me was a DJ to play Michael's music. Down the bottom of the stairs, each in their own little corner, were the camera crews from all the local TV networks. There were green and gold balloons, hundreds of them, tied into a large archway over the stairs where you enter in and along the wall and gates out front, it's hard to explain exactly how amazing it looked, but it was just spectacular!! I had already known this was true and happening…but now…seeing all this stuff here and so many fans out the front…I knew it was really going to happen.

Di Rolle was standing on my left hand side with us both near the tops of the stairs, Casey and Alicia were standing to my right, one step or two lower down. Casey suddenly realized she didn't have anything for Michael to actually sign for her, so I tore a page from the back of my autograph book as neatly as I could and gave her one of my pens I'd brought with me so she could make sure she had her autograph. Alicia was all organized and we stood there pretty much in silence from then on, watching the fans, the reporters, the security. There was such a buzz around the area and so much to take in and try to remember.

My mind was running a million miles an hour! Michael would be there any second now, standing in front of me, hopefully maybe having a quick casual conversation as I handed him the brooch. My mind came up with numerous different situations: "Maybe I could pretend to fall over in the excitement and Michael would help me up to my feet and make sure I was ok... no, that won't work, what happens if I accidentally dropped and smashed that gorgeous diamond badge/brooch I'd been entrusted with!"

As I came out of that daydream, I heard someone talking over the speakers. Michael would be delayed about another 20 minutes as he was taking his time at the airport to be fair and say hello to all the fans who were waiting at the airport for him to arrive. There was so much electricity in the air at the "Rendez-vous", that it was just unbelievable. Fans were screaming their heads off, the DJ was playing a mixture of songs from Michael's catalogue. We soon got word that Michael was leaving the airport. I could hear the radios buzzing through on the security guards two-way radios/communication devices continuing to talk about where they were on the trip to the hotel. "ETA 20 minutes". I was shaking with excitement with the hugest grin on my face. This, somehow, was actually happening! "ETA 10 minutes, traffic a bit busy at this end". I was busy looking in each direction trying to work out which end he'd come from. I was so nervous, yet excited. Michael Jackson, The King of Pop, the legend, would be right in front of me within minutes now; how

174

on earth did this even happen? Funnily enough, just thinking this through, everything that happened, I'm feeling the exact same emotions right now as I re-live the moment.

I was shaking with excitement and in disbelief, but it clearly really was about to happen! The security guard's two-way crackled again. "ETA in less than 5 minutes, we are just around the corner, but taking it slow. As expected there is a lot of traffic and even more fans surrounding us!" I looked up at Di Rolle just grinning my face off, trying hard not to just drop that precious brooch Mr. Linney had given me, making sure my pen was in my pocket and I had my autograph book with me. I started looking around for my Mum to see where she'd gone and suddenly thought: "Oh no, what if security shut her in or out of the building or she runs out of film, that would be a nightmare!" I couldn't even see her then, where had she gone? Michael would be there any minute! She had been standing next to me, now the doors to the hotel were locked and no-one else was going in or out, no matter what!! I eventually caught a glimpse of her watching me, camera at the ready. That was a relief. "Good job Mum! Just don't waste any photos yet!"

I was wiping my hands as they got sweaty and started aching from the excitement and nervousness. All of a sudden to my right, down the very bottom of the driveway, a black car pulled in and stopped. Some security got out of the car, three kids also got out. There were two boys and one girl who I'd say were about 9-13 years old and the girl possibly 14-16 years. They looked really familiar and I just knew I had seen them somewhere before. The girl, wearing a black jacket and fairly long black curly hair was absolutely stunning. It suddenly clicked that they were two of Michael's nephews and one of his nieces, who were on tour with him. Thinking about it and looking at photos, I thought that the girl was quite likely Brandi Jackson,

Jackie's daughter. She certainly looked very similar to her anyway from the photos and videos I had and have since seen of her around that time, such as her appearance in Michael's "LA Gear" commercial from the "Dangerous" era. About the boys I'm really unsure as there are so many Jackson nephews! I tend to think the older one was Jermaine's son Jeremy Jackson and the younger one may have been Jourdynn, who was born in 1989, that would have only made him seven years old, though, and I don't think he was quite that young, so it may have been Marlon's son, Marlon Jackson Jr, as he fits the age range that I am recalling, being born in 1985 – making him 11 years old. The only other nephew that fits the age range is Rebbie's youngest son, Austin "Auggie" Brown, having been born in 1985, so he was also 11 years old at that stage.

Anyway, all the (massive) family tree information aside, I felt like my heart and every vein inside me was about to explode and just burst right open! Right there, about 100metres in front of me wass Michael's car! Just stepping out of the car and walking right in front of me were two of his nephews and one of his nieces. They kept walking forwards to patiently wait at the bottom of the stairs, and looking back at the car and preparing for the screams they knew were about to drown their ear drums. Then all of a sudden one black boot, a second black boot and then one awesome black fedora and a red shirt appear as Michael steps out of that car and the screaming is beyond belief! I don't think the audience at his concert were even screaming that loud and there were a lot more people at each of his shows!!!

Michael slowly started walking up the driveway, about 200 metres long, from my right hand side all the way down to my left. There were people sitting and standing on the low walls, people pushing over and on top of people, pressing them against the

176

Michael walks towards the throngs of fans, followed by his niece and two nephews while Alicia, Casey and Julie watch from the top of the stairs. He gives the victory sign as fans push forward items, hoping to get an autograph from him.

gates to catch a clearer view of Michael, the screaming never ending. I was somehow just standing still at the top of those stairs, watching every step and movement Michael made. I don't know how I kept myself planted there and didn't just run up to him and grab him, except for the fact I knew how much of that treatment he'd received his life over and feared it to a certain degree, so I didn't want to appear to be absolutely crazy and risk doing anything stupid that would stop me from meeting him.

Michael very slowly kept walking his way along the hundreds of fans that were there, shaking as many hands as he possibly could and signing so many autographs to those fans holding out paper and pens to him. I remember watching him as he was halfway up the driveway, giving his trademark Victory sign to some of the fans and one guy in particular. This guy would have been about 16 or so, and gave the "rock on" symbol back to Michael. Instead of just holding up pointer and middle fingers in a V shape, this guy held his hand up with thumb, pointer and little finger up, and waving it around a bit and yelling something, Michael looked straight at him and gave the victory sign again, at which point this 16-year-old reached forward, pushed Michael's middle finger down and pulled up his pinky and thumbs to return the rock on symbol. One of Michael's security guards tried to stop this guy from touching him but Michael kind of pushed them back with his other hand, saying it was ok, before giving his hand a bit of a shake back at the boy as if telling him to rock on! Michael had his mask on, so I couldn't tell for sure if he was laughing or not, but from his posture and the way he walked off, it appeared as though he thought it was pretty funny! I sure had a bit of a giggle at that one.

I was now starting to get a bit annoyed that it was taking so long for Michael to reach me, but understood Michael and how

178

important it was to him to try and meet all his fans, how incredibly important we all were to him, just as much, if not more so, than he was to us. So I kept on waiting.

Michael eventually made his way to the end of the driveway and line of fans. There were two young boys, possibly twins, who were dressed in an MJ style with little fedora hats on, who started dancing along to the music right in front of Michael. They would have only been seven years old or so. Michael alerted someone to allow them to come inside the fencing so they could continue dancing for him, and for everyone to see. They were amazing, doing classic MJ moves and moonwalking around the little area between Michael and the fence there, dancing their little hearts out. I watched Michael as he was watching these boys, enjoying their dancing, bopping his head along, he was definitely impressed with their moves. They jumped back behind the fence and Michael signed one last autograph and turned around, looking straight at ME. OH MY GOSH!!! My knee's were wobbling, my feet and hands aching with nerves, excitement, with all this adrenaline running straight through my body.

Michael started his walk towards and then up those stairs, as if in slow motion. He'd just spent what seemed like hours meeting all his fans there. I'm sure it wasn't quite that long, but it sure would have been close to an hour. I remember thinking, as painful as it was for me to stand there waiting to meet him, it was so wonderful of him to take so much time to try and meet as many of those fans that were there as he possibly could, I don't know how many celebrities as famous as himself would take that much time out of their schedule to greet their fans. This was just one of the many things that made Michael so special. He never forgot where he came from or who we were; that he was still only in this business because of us fans, who

179

loved him so much and continued to buy each and every album he released. He knew that we were the reason he was able to continue doing what he enjoyed and loved so very much.

After what seemed like such a long time to walk a very short distance, finally he reached the bottom of the stairs where he turned to wave at all the fans again and get a good glimpse of them all. Making sure his personal videographer was getting footage of the front of the hotel, decorated in hundreds of green and yellow balloons, of those of us still waiting to meet him and of the rest of the fans out the front, who were still screaming so loudly! I almost wished I had taken ear plugs with me!

The moment was finally here. I was looking down…right at Michael, thinking how much taller he was than I had ever thought he'd be. I know all the websites claimed he stood at 5 foot 11 inches tall, but in those shoes he was wearing and with that huge hat, he seemed well over 6 feet tall! Alicia and Casey were standing directly to my right, they were two steps below me, Alicia on about the 4th step from the top, Casey on the second and myself near the top. The three of us were staring at all those other fans below us, screaming Michael's name, who no doubt would've been wishing they could have been any one of us at that particular moment in time – to be watching Michael himself as he signed an autograph book for Alicia, and he then stepped up to meet Casey and sign the piece of paper I'd handed to her. My heart was now beating so fast, I couldn't believe it. There was more adrenalin running through my body than I think could be possible, I felt like I was about to collapse. My hero, Michael Jackson, was only two steps away from me. I could not take my eyes off him, I was just entranced, everything around me went silent as he took one step up. I was just one step above him as he reached out to hug me. I felt so lucky as I

Michael signing autographs for Alicia, Casey and Julie

Michael gives the thumbs up to all his fans who are still screaming wildly for him

*Julie is clearly thrilled as Michael reaches out
to give her the hug of her life*

Julie:"This hug is something I'll never forget as long as I live.
You couldn't wipe that grin off my face if you tried!"

was the only one who was given a hug from him, and it seemed to last so long. Half way through he took a step up to be on the same level that I was on, right at the top of the stairs. I tried to take in and remember everything, any scent, the feel of the hug, his strength and most of all just how kind, caring and loving it felt. There was such true warmth and care in that hug, as though he already knew me and everything I had been through. It felt like meeting an old friend you'd known for years but who hadn't seen you since becoming so ill and wanted to hug you as hard as they could in the hope that they could share their health with you, in the hope everything would be ok for you from now on. There was pure concern and love for everyone felt through him, as odd as it may sound to some.

I can't really recall if it was before or after the hug that I gave Michael my autograph book to sign, as I went to look for the t-shirt and my copy of "Dancing the Dream" and felt devastated when I realized I had given it to my Mum to look after for me when I was given that brooch earlier on in the lobby of the hotel. Although slightly upset at that, I was too busy watching Michael's hand as he signed that book right in front of my eyes.

I then pulled that wooden box out from behind my back. I'm not sure if Michael had been alerted in the car on his drive up to the hotel that I had an important gift for him and his people had then given Michael a description of me and what I was wearing or if that's why Di Rolle had walked up behind him to tell him about it. However, he almost instinctually stayed there next to me a bit longer before leaning down to hear me as I tried talking to him. My only regret to this day is that I did not ask for the microphone from the DJ standing to the far left of Michael and a police officer now, who had earlier been announcing how long it would be until Michael was due to arrive and playing his music, so that Michael would have had more of a chance to hear exactly what I was saying along with the rest of the fans there. However, I just continued to slightly yell towards Michael, telling him what I had been asked to say: "Michael, this is a gift for you, from all of us here today from Perth." At this time I opened that beautifully hand-crafted box to reveal the brooch pinned onto a white satin pillow inside the box with white felt lining to the inside of the box to keep the brooch safe. "This Snoopy brooch was made especially for you by 'Linneys Jewelers' and the 'Argyle Diamond Company' as a gift and memento of your trip to Perth. We love you, I love you!"

Michael reached his hand out with those long fingers and received the gift from me, nodding his head forward to gesture and say thank you. I could see his eyes smiling with appreciation and thanks underneath the brim of his hat. At that point Michael turned to face all of the rest of his fans once again as he signed an autograph for Alicia. Michael then gave everyone the thumbs up sign, and signaled for the three of us to follow him as he started to walk inside the hotel. His guards were close behind him, Di Rolle grabbed my arm and rushed the three of us inside quickly, Alicia and Casey both holding his hands and getting inside just as the doors were shut and locked behind us again.

We could still hear all the fans screaming for Michael while inside for him to come back out again. I stood there looking around for my Mum, but I couldn't see her anywhere, so I didn't worry. I made sure I kept standing really close to Michael. Thankfully having been standing at the top of the stairs, I was first in right after Alicia, Michael and then Casey, which left me standing next to him once inside, just to the left hand side of Casey, and I made sure to stay as close to him as possible!

185

We walked a short distance inside where there was a choir of about 20 children. We all stood circled around the choir as the opening notes to "Heal the World" started playing, and these children were introduced to us all as being the choir from a deaf school, all of them ranging from partially to fully deaf, being legally deaf at any rate. They then started singing and really amazed not only me, but everyone in that room that evening was deeply touched. If we had not been told they were deaf, I don't think anyone would have ever realized, other than the fact some of them were using sign language to sing along to the song or along with singing to the song. I have no idea how they were able to know when to sing what part, when each verse or the chorus started, but they were absolutely incredible.

I deliberately took a slight step behind Michael so I could watch him a bit closer without seeming like I wasn't paying attention to the choir. I had read that when Michael hears music he enjoys and it has a good feel to it, he just can't keep still. If he isn't dancing to the song, then his feet are at least tapping along to it, head bopping along or hands moving. He shows some form of expression in dance or movement. So I really wanted to see this up close for myself. I watched his head first; there it goes, just slightly bopping along, trying not to move it too much to take anyone's attention away from the choir. I watched his mask, and if he wasn't chewing some gum all of a sudden when he hadn't been previously, then he was singing along or at least mouthing the words to the song. I then glanced at his hands; nope, his right hand was now holding that of his younger nephew. Alicia was standing next to him, his left hand was holding Casey's right hand. I looked next to me to notice his niece was standing directly to my right and grinning slightly amused at me trying to pay such close attention to someone who was merely her uncle, so I grinned back to her, still feeling quite important. Then I looked down at Michael's feet and there they go. I don't know if he even realized he was doing it, but those toes were sure tapping away in time to the music, one foot for awhile, then the other.

I thought "Well, this is the closest thing I'll ever get to having Michael dance just for me, right in front of me!" I looked back to the choir again as they reached the end of the song, singing the last chorus of the song. I looked back up at Michael just in time to see, like mine were, his eyes welling up and a tear running down his face in amazement at these kids. The hours of work they must have put in over the previous weeks and months to get that song sounding so beautiful and just perfect. Everyone was clapping very loudly in appreciation, Michael doing the loudest of all.

As the applause settled down I noticed Michael giving the thumbs up sign to some people with cameras. His younger nephew had taken a step or two backwards and to the right to stand closer to Michael's other nephew. Michael now had one arm around Alicia's shoulder. She was looking a bit wobbly on her feet, the poor girl. She didn't look too well at all, but was taking it all in her stride. Michael's other hand was still gripping onto Casey's. Michael then looked a bit further to his right, past Alicia, to notice a woman holding a very young Joey Kangaroo which was wrapped in a blue babies blankey. He found it hard to take his eyes away from that and I could see him wanting to make his way over to have a hold of it, but in what I can imagine was typical for an event like this with Michael, he was drawn back into the crowd once the performance was over. So he continued yet again to sign more and more autographs: for those kids, their parents, people who must have been staying in the hotel and had come downstairs, along with people who must have been working there also. He must have spent at least another 45 minutes just signing his autograph and saying hi to

Michael with one arm around Alicia's shoulder, the other holding Casey's hand, looks over to see a lady in an orange shirt, holding a very young Joey Kangaroo, snuggled in a blue baby blanket

Michael claps in appreciation and gives the thumbs up for the choir or deaf children, who had just sung "Heal The World." He was greatly moved. Left to right is: Alicia, Michael, Casey and Julie

everyone that he possibly could as he slowly tried to make his way to the elevator so he could escape up to his bedroom and get some rest. I was still doing my best to follow Michael, tailing right behind him, with Di Rolle right next to me again now. I told her that I couldn't see Mum anywhere and that she had some other things I really wanted to get signed. What could I do to get that done? It looked as though Michael was going to leave up to his room any second now. Di asked one of Michael's security men if it was possible for us to go up in the elevator with Michael to his room and have a quick chat or at least just get an autograph. The security man went to ask Michael and returned saying: "Sorry, at this time Michael is exhausted and is wanting to go upstairs and get some sleep, but if you give the items to me with instructions of what you want the autographs to say and where you want each item to be signed, then Michael will do it later on for you and you'll get them returned again." So although I was a bit disappointed at being so close to going up to Michael's suite with him briefly, I was very appreciative that he would take the time to sign these other things for me and for a friend also at a later date.

Michael then entered the elevator and had gone from sight. I quickly found Mum and I went outside and got the book and shirt from her to give to Di Rolle, who also wrote down my name, phone number and address to return them to me, just in case she didn't get the chance to see me again before she had to head back home to Melbourne and needed to post them back to me (I sure hoped she would have time to see me again to get them back to me sooner) and to get the direct instructions from me of what I wanted written on everything and where about I wanted each item signed exactly, as she knew just how important they were to me.

As I said goodbye and thank you to Di, we started walking back

190

to the car and overheard some fans saying "Yes, Michael's room is on the very top level, on the right hand side, overlooking the beach, come around here, if we scream loud enough he might put his head out the window and wave or throw a note down or something!" So quite a few of us stood there screaming his name out for awhile before being asked to move on by his security saying Michael was extremely exhausted and needed to get some rest now. But if we came back tomorrow, we might manage to get another glimpse of him. By this time it was about 8pm or later and most of the fans had left to head off home except for those stubborn few who really wanted to see Michael again or were camping out there overnight "just in case".

As I was walking to the car, grinning away, talking to Mum, half skipping, half walking, I saw two girls talking together with a lot of excitement in their voices, squealing a bit as they spoke. Suddenly something made one of the girls look over at me and she came running at me and said "Oh my gosh, aren't you the girl that just hugged Michael Jackson?? What was he like? Did he say anything? What did he smell like? Oh, do you mind if I hug you, it'll be the closest I ever get to hugging Michael, you probably still have his smell on you, I'll even pay you if you like!!!" Oh, she made me laugh, because I knew I might have been exactly the same if the roles had been reversed, I probably would have asked to take a photo with her! So I answered her questions. "Yes, that was me. Michael was just the nicest, most caring guy. The love this man has inside him just seeps through his pores, he has such incredible energy surrounding him! Michael said thank you for the gift, it was very hard to hear if he said anything else at all with all that screaming though. He didn't really smell like anything though, he wasn't wearing any aftershave or particular lotions. He just smelt like him, and the slightest hint of baby powder, which a lot of adults use. Yes, that's fine if you hug me, if you really want to, but no, you definitely don't need to pay me!" So she gave me almost just as big a hug as what Michael had done! She thanked me as much as she could and went off with her friend, up towards the hotel. I'm not quite sure who seemed more excited: the girl from meeting and hugging me, or me from meeting and hugging Michael!

Once we reached the car I asked Mum where she had been, did she see or get close to Michael at all? Get some good photos? "What happened, I thought you would've tried standing next to me or down in the front of all the other fans or something!" To which she said: "No, I got stuck inside for awhile once Michael was nearly here and they weren't letting anyone out, then as you went inside with him, I was coming out to meet up with you as I didn't realize there was anything else that was going to happen, then they locked the doors behind you so quickly." But I did manage to get some photos and thankfully I met people in the following months who had been there who also managed to get some great shots inside and outside the hotel that day!

Mum continued on by saying, "I told one of the security guards that my daughter is in there, could I be let in also, please?" To which he turned around and looked at her, unsure if she was another fan trying to trick her way in to get close to Michael or if she was telling the truth. He replied he was sorry but that he wasn't permitted to open the doors for anyone for any reason. So Mum told me she went and sat outside and was watching the news crews from Channels 9 and 10 packing their gear away, getting ready to return back to the TV studios to put their footage together for the news the following night, when Mum heard one of the camera men say to another, "Hey, does anyone know who that girl was at the top of the stairs, red pants, who gave Michael something and hugged him? Why was she there? What about the other girls?" The other guys looked at each other and shrugged, suggesting they didn't know. Naturally

192

Mum was also still on a bit of a high, amazed to have seen that after everything I'd been through in my 18 years, her daughter had actually just met and hugged the most famous person in the world. So still being rather excited herself, after seeing him so close-up for herself, and being there amongst the thrill of it all, Mum walked up to these men and said, "I'm sorry, but I couldn't help but hear you asking about the girl who hugged Michael Jackson. Well she's my daughter!" Well, at those few words, apparently the camera crews thought they had hit gold and Mum was now feeling rather important also! They were all handing her their business cards, saying who they worked for, they would love to get an exclusive on who I was and why I got to meet Michael. "Do you think your daughter would agree to an interview with us?" So Mum at that point, I suppose, became my very temporary, one day job only, promoter and manager! I have to admit that I was just a bit excited, on the car ride home, to think I might also be getting interviewed for the news the next day and put on the news on Australia wide TV!!!

We arrived home that afternoon, too excited to do anything much besides call a few friends who I knew were also huge fans, and tell them about what I had just done! Not long after I hung up from my friends I actually got a call back from Di Rolle. She wanted to let me know Michael had been given everything from me, with instructions, ready to sign and would get it done as soon as possible to give to her and return them back to me again. She also had another message for me. She knew that I had tickets to the opening night concert and said to me that she had been talking with the people in charge of "Make A Wish" and "Starlight Foundations" along with "Linneys". They had heard that I was going to be interviewed for the news the next day. Di asked if I could please ensure that I thanked "Linneys" on the news piece for the gift that was created for Michael some-how. Of course I wanted to thank "Linneys", "Make A Wish",

"Starlight", Michael and everyone who'd played even the tinest part in helping me to meet Michael! Then Di continued, "You know how Michael brings people, children onstage with him during the song 'Heal The World'? Well, if you are able to thank those few people during the interview, we just might be able to get you backstage before the shows and you'll be able to go onstage along with the other kids (which as I found out later included Alicia, Casey and their friend Stephanie) while Michael sings the end portion of 'Heal The World'!" That was just extra cool! I quickly wrote down their names and memorized them so I wouldn't have a chance of forgetting for the following day! I was seriously unable to wait until that concert now!

I woke the following morning, had times for my interviews all set up and was expecting the first news crew to arrive around 10am and the second at around 11am. I was feeling hugely important. I really couldn't wait for them to arrive for all the neighbours to see and wonder what was going on! The first news crew arrived fairly quickly. I had decided, as a bit of proof and ongoing good luck, that I would just wear the same clothes I'd worn when I met Michael! They definitely felt like lucky clothes now!!!

Well, we welcomed that first news crew in from channel 9. There was one camera man plus another man to interview me. They set the camera up, got me hooked up with a microphone, asked a few very quick questions and before I knew it the interview was over and they were packing up to head home. It was all done so quickly that I wasn't even quite sure what I'd said other than it was such a spin-out to actually meet Michael! I was amazed at how quick it was done, but rather upset with myself when I realized it was over so quickly and I hadn't had the chance to thank the people from "Linneys" who created the brooch! So I had to make sure I got Mum to remind me to

194

Channel 9 News, Perth arrive at Julie's house and unpack the lights and camera's from the car, before setting up in her room, ready to interview her.

say something with the second interview in case I forgot while they were recording. Once they said they were about to start recording, could she mention to them that I had someone to thank, so they could put it into a question for me, so I'd get a chance, a little reminder to actually mention them.

The channel 10 crew arrived not too long afterwards actually and quickly got me setup with a lapel microphone. They also got the cameras set up, so they'd be showing a small selection of my many Michael Jackson posters, drawings and key-rings that I had stuck all over my walls and set out in very particular positions, planned out with precision over the years. They started off by asking if they could get a shot of me putting one of my Michael Jackson CDs into my CD player, so I chose a CD I had, which was a picture disc, and carefully made sure to hold it the right way, so the picture of Michael wearing the "Jam" outfit from the "Dangerous" tour could be seen. Then I was asked if I would crank it up and dance to the music, really get into it. Well, I'm not the most outgoing of people, so I felt really embarrassed to dance and goof around like that in front of anyone at all, especially if it might go on nationwide TV! So I did the lamer thing of mouthing the words and just bopping up and down a tiny bit, sadly it's all I could make myself do. Thankfully after a couple of seconds they said, "Ok, that's fine then. You can turn that off now!" Either they were embarrassed for me or could see how uncomfortable I was or how dodgy I looked attempting to dance, and stopped it fairly quick!

Then they wanted me to sit on the bed, so I was positioned between the larger cluster of posters. The interviewer, a woman this time, was talking to Mum just outside my bedroom door as I looked over to see what was happening and when this was all going to start. She was apparently finding out more information about my illness, getting a bit of background info and since

196

I hadn't had a chance to talk to her at all yet, I was assuming, maybe hoping more-so, that Mum was asking her to please ask me about the brooch I gave Michael to lead into thanking all these people for making yesterday happen. I was trying to get Mum's attention about it without butting in and saying anything as I'd been asked not to say anything while the camera man got his levels right and got some random footage. The interviewer must've noticed me watching them or gotten all she needed to know, because she then walked over and sat on a chair to the left of the camera, just to my right but also in front of me. I remember thinking how nice she seemed to be, she seemed genuinely interested in me and what happened yesterday, how long I'd been a fan now, what it felt like to finally meet my idol after being a fan for so long, and she wanted to know what his hug was like, what it felt like. I didn't really know what to say as it seemed a rather odd question at the time. So I just giggled through it a bit, saying, "Oh, I don't know...just a long, proper hug!" As far as I was concerned, I thought we were just talking; she was getting to know me a bit first and would then maybe suggest a few things before alerting me they were now filming, like the previous crew had done. Then all of a sudden she said, "Ok, thanks very much for that, I think we've got all we need." I was rather shocked, I didn't even realize they had turned the camera on and started recording yet!

Again the woman went to talk to Mum about something else and I was trying to be polite and not butt in on them, I just wanted to say, "Oh, I'm sorry, that was so quick and felt like a regular conversation so I didn't even realize we were filming yet. There is just one thing I wanted to add if that's ok, it's very important!" I had this whole bit thought up and ready to say, if they'd ever stopped talking, but by the time they did, I realized the man had the camera packed away in its box and he was about to leave my room and the house to pack the car up. Realizing how long it had taken him to set it up and would have to set me up with another microphone now, I didn't want to seem rude by now asking them to unpack all over again for a quick two second piece. So I decided then that well, I had been really lucky and my dream had totally come true yesterday. I had met Michael like I had always wanted to. I was going to his concert like I'd also always wanted to. There are so many other people who would also love to meet Michael, and if I go up onstage with him, then maybe I'm just being greedy by meeting him twice and maybe I'm taking someone elses dream away from them. Maybe there is someone else who has always wanted to meet Michael, and if I go on stage, then I may be taking the last place and that person would never get to meet Michael and experience that amazing feeling that I already got to experience. Should I be greedy and take up someone elses chance, so I can see Michael twice or should I be nice and leave that spot open so that another person can live their dream and get to go backstage, meet Michael and go on stage with him? Would I really enjoy it that much or even be able to get up on stage in front of that many people, even if they wouldn't be looking at me? I decided to leave it. I didn't want to inconvenience these people who probably had more important things to go and film and report on and I had been lucky enough for my dream to come true. I thought, as much as I'd love to see Michael again and thank him for everything, I would leave my spot on stage open, for another child's dream to come true so that they could experience what I had. It was only fair. Michael gave me such a huge gift, now I felt a bit like I was passing it forward to someone else that I didn't even know. So that made the sting of not being able to do it a lot better, and I decided it was something that Michael himself would also be quite proud of.

All these years later, since I got in touch with Stephanie and heard how she got to go backstage at each of Michael's shows,

by Julie Windsor

along with her friend Casey, who'd met Michael along with me on that Thursday, it may seem like blowing up my own ego a bit, but I like to think that it was possibly thanks to me not thanking everyone on the news, and not going backstage myself; that it left enough room for one or both of those girls to experience what they got to experience by going backstage and on stage with Michael those three nights. Something that would have given Casey the most amazing moments to remember during her last days and Stephanie some great moments to remember with her best friend, as the only thing better than going onstage with Michael would have been doing so with your best friend and having someone important to share and recall those wonderful moments with, to talk about them together during the next few years that Casey had left.

I am still incredibly sorry I didn't get the chance to thank "Linneys" at the time however, being so awestruck with this huge camera mere inches away from my face, because without those people's incredible talent in doing what they did to create that amazing brooch for Michael, none of this would ever have happened at all. I would not have had anything to give Michael, I may not have been interviewed for the news, and some other exciting things I'm about to talk about also may not have happened. So "Linneys", Mr. Linney, I am very grateful and I thank you so very much!

Well, it was a rather long wait to see the news that night!! These were the days before DVD recorders, so I had our videotape (VHS) recorders all set up at home. One was programmed onto channel 7 to record the entire hour of news that night, and another in my Mum's room was programmed onto channel 9 to record their full hour of news so that I didn't miss a split second of my interviews! I had never been so excited, or even really wanted to watch the nightly news! Both pieces came on

199

and we managed to record them both, as did some friends of ours and my grandparents, so that I could have a few copies of it, just in case something went wrong with anyone's video player! I now finally had the proof I had wanted of myself meeting Michael; and in video format to top it off! I was still desperate for some photos of us hugging though, so I immediately played back the video footage, set up my new little digital camera (with its huge 1.2 megapixels! haha) on a table, I stopped the video approximately every 1.5 seconds so I could take a photo of the TV screen and get those photos with Michael! During the footage of the hug, I think I tried to pause it every half a second, to take a photo! I was just glad to have those photographs to show friends and family, as grainy as they were!

I was busy talking to some friends online and in the USA about my experience, when the phone rang and Mum yelled out that it was for me. Assuming it was another friend ringing to say they had seen me on the news, I was kind of laughing as I said hello and asked who it was, only to hear through the receiver "Hi, it's Di Rolle here! I am just up here with Michael in his room!" I start thinking all in a split second, 'Oh my gosh!!! I am talking to Di again, that's fine, but she's in the same room as Michael?! I'm possibly on speakerphone? Michael could be hearing everything I'm saying right now? I'm about to die!! What do I say? This is too cool! No-one will ever believe this!!' Then Di continued, "Yes, we were just watching the news and saw your interviews come on, and right as he was signing those things for you actually, and he said 'Oh, she's the girl that I'm signing these for, who gave me the Snoopy brooch, isn't she?' So I told him that was correct. That is when he asked me how these items would be returned to you; did I have Julie's number? I told him yes, it was right here, so Michael himself, just a moment ago, asked me to call you and tell you what a wonderful job you did on the news and that he hoped you were feeling well and would continue

200

to heal and get a bit better each and every day." I was really taken aback, I couldn't believe how sweet that was, wanting to give me of all people a phone call, even if it wasn't directly from Michael himself. It was the thought that counted! I thanked Di for that and said: "Can you please thank Michael for me? He will never understand just how much this has all meant to me." I was stopped for a second when I heard someone talking in the background. I could just make out that it was Michael talking to Di! Di returned to the phone, "Oh, I'm sorry about that, Michael just wanted me to ask you and see if you had been able to get any concert tickets." I told her that yes, I had been given opening night tickets from the "Starlight Foundation", and I could not wait to go. I was just assuming she was planning to meet me there to give me back the signed goods or something. Then she asked me to hold on for a moment as she spoke to Michael again. A bit more mumbling through the phone and Di came back on again. "Are you there still Julie? Michael just said to tell you that going to only the opening show was not good enough for a fan like yourself, everyone knows the closing night show is always the best one of all, as it's like his farewell to the city, so he has told me to ask you if you would be interested in going to the final show also, and how many people were in your family?" Now, although I knew my Dad would not be interested in seeing a Michael Jackson concert, and my brother was in the USA, I cheekily still counted the two of them, saying there was the five of us." I heard Di relaying this information back to Michael before she returned to our call again, "OK, Julie, Michael said to say that he will be sending a limousine around to your house to pick you all up before the show, you will just need to go to the ticket booth on the night and say that Michael has left five tickets there for you in your name! The limousine will then return you home after the concert. This is Michael's gift to you and he hopes you will really enjoy the show!" As you can imagine, I was totally amazed and even more in love with

201

him for just handing out over $700 worth of tickets along with whatever a limousine costs to hire for those three hours or so! Di then ended the conversation by again congratulating me for the news interviews and letting me know where she'd be at the concert on the closing night so that I could get the autographs from her. I thanked her with my life and hung the phone up again to run into Mums room. "You'll never guess who that was and what they wanted!"

Well, this had all happened on the night of November 29th, 1996. The following night, November 30th, would be Michael's opening show, which I was attending thanks to the "Starlight Foundation". Again, I had no idea how I would sleep that night, because the next day the rest of my dream was being fulfilled! I was going to see Michael performing live - for now the 1st of two of his three shows! I kind of wished I hadn't given my friend the other tickets for his 2nd show now, as I could have gone to all three!

I eventually made it to bed that night and got to thinking that I never really got to tell Michael, himself, what I had always wanted to tell him: how much his music had helped me over the years, what an inspiration he was, and just THANK YOU for taking the time out of his life, trips and tours to meet his fans and people such as myself. It had made my life! Not only that, but to basically give up his entire life to create so much fantastic music for the world, to make us all feel better, even though it was to his own detriment at times, and he had missed out on so much from such a very young age, just the basic things in life such as going to a friend's to play or enjoying a game of basketball or going roller skating. I wanted him to know that us fans knew exactly how much he had been through since he was a six-year-old boy, that we really did understand how much he gave up, which was basically his entire childhood. This was

202

by Julie Windsor

clearly such a sore point for Michael and something he always kind of wished he could have somehow gained back again. So I wanted him to know that, although it caused pain for him, the fact that he did so, to create the music and entertain the world, easing the pain of so many hundreds of thousands, millions of other people throughout the world, especially myself, well, we just can't thank him enough for that gift. Eventually I fell asleep and had lost that train of thought by the time I woke up again in the morning. There were other things to be excited about!!!

After a very anxious day, just waiting for the hours to pass, I was finally dressed and ready for the show. Only Mum and I would be attending this concert on the 30th, Michael's opening night in Perth. It was his first trip here since 1985, when he appeared on our "Telethon" show to raise money for the children's hospital that I would be going to regularly five years later, PMH. It was that year he was given the key to the city of Perth and made a secret visit up to PMH, where he had signed a picture of himself that he dedicated to the hospital. It just so happened that this poster would hang out the front entrance to my hospital room for about two years. I used to stare at it, trying to work out if there was any way possible of sneaking it out of the hospital to take home with me each time I was discharged, but figured it would be just a bit obvious, so photos of it would have to do! The real reason Michael was in Perth that year however (since there were no concerts or performances of any kind booked!), was as part of the deal to purchase the "Beatles" catalogue! The last time he had actually performed in Perth, however, was with his brothers as "The Jackson 5" in approximately 1974. It was written in one of the many books about Michael, that they all loved it in Australia (how couldn't you?!) and all the other brother bought really cool souvenirs, but Michael, who really took to the saying "a diamond in the rough", bought himself a rock polishing kit. So while he was here (remember he

203

Michael visits Perth in 1985 and makes one single public appearance, to be given the key to the city

The poster Michael signed while visiting Perth in 1985, which sat outside Julie's hospital room for many years, leaving her to dream of way to get it home as her own autograph, or to think of ways to meet Michael for herself!

was only about 16 years old at the time, it may have been a year sooner or later!) he collected different rocks and, unlike his brothers who would buy gems or nice jewellery, Michael bought the gems still in rock form, so he could buff them himself and watch the beauty come from these dirty looking rocks. Anyone from Perth who may be reading this might also be interested to know, that "The Jackson 5" also actually performed at "Beatty Park Swimming Centre" of all places; not exactly a comfortable concert hall! I can't recall what book I read it in now, but the book clearly described the layout of "Beatty Park". The stands were packed with fans, there was a long Olympic sized pool and they were performing on another pool, a deeper diving pool which had been solidly covered up with staging. They hoped, having an Olympic pool between them and the fans would keep anyone from storming the stage as the fans generally would during most shows, in some cases forcing the brother to have to leave the concert hall early and ending the concert all together, but typically a simple pool didn't keep us Aussies away from Michael and his brothers. Michael said he would never forget that show as long as he were to live. The image of all these fans just jumping straight into the pool, in all their clothes, and trying to get out of the pool to storm the few metres ahead to get up and onto their stage…it sure gives me a laugh picturing it. No wonder Michael had also always recalled it! So those were two of Michael's previous experiences here in Perth. Michael was a much bigger star now, 22 or so years later, but thankfully there are no pools at "Burswood Theatre" for us to have to swim across to reach Michael!

It was finally time to leave for the show. I had been waiting for this moment for months now, and it was so hard to believe it had finally arrived. I had seen all of Michael's, "The Jacksons" and the "Jackson 5" concerts on tape, I had been able to locate and pay a fair bit of money for a lot of video footage over the years! What a shame "YouTube" didn't exist in the early 1990's! So I had a certain idea of what to expect, but all of Michael's shows had all been so different from each other. When the "Dangerous" tour was first aired on Australian TV, I recorded it and would watch it every single day, and probably did so for nearly two entire years straight! I knew every second of that concert. However that show was so different to the "Bad" concert, which was again so different to "Victory". So even assuming "HIStory" would be similar to "Dangerous" in any way at all didn't make much sense to me. The only thing I could really imagine was Michael's favourite J5 Medley, so that I expected that to be in the show and similar to how he usually seemed to do it, as an ode to his brothers and the start of his life long career. The rest of it, including the track lineup, would be a complete and utter surprise.

We got into the arena and headed straight to the souvenir stand. I needed to get a tour program, a t-shirt, key-rings, the little glowing hand on a stick in the shape of the Victory symbol that Michael always shows. I wanted one of everything, but unfortunately couldn't afford that!

Since I met Michael those few days earlier, my Mum had suddenly become a bit of a mini fan herself. It was funny to see someone who used to believe all the media gossip about him, who was always telling me to turn his music down, suddenly coming to his aid, saying what a sweet, genuinely caring person he was. She could see how caring he was towards myself and the other kids when he met us. She was now busy telling people how Michael Jackson called our house to thank Julie for her interview and kind words, that he gave us all free tickets to his show. It was so funny to see. It was also an extra bonus to see her purchase a concert program and glowing fingers for herself to wave around during the show!

206

The front entrance to the "Burswood Arena", announcing the three dates for Michaels show

Well, the concert was finally due to start. The opening act was a wonderful Australian Vocal Group who I was also becoming a fan of, appropriately named "Human Nature", who was the support act for the entire Austral-Asian part of the "HIStory World Tour". They had a number 1 hit in our country at the time, called "Wishes". People were really excited to see them perform and were singing along to them, but let's face it: nobody pays to see the opening act, no matter how good they are! We were all just counting down the minutes for Michael to arrive on stage and those opening notes to be played through the speakers. Everyone was running in and out to the toilets to ensure that we wouldn't have to miss a second of Michael performing to get up and go, and everyone was buying more souvenirs while they had the chance to do so! Then all of a sudden the lights slowly started dimming; and then darkness!

The audience went wild, thundering their feet on the ground, drumming their hands on the banners, rails, their laps and people everywhere just screaming their lungs out!! The moment we had all been waiting for had finally arrived!

207

I could not have imagined the screaming and noise inside the "Burswood Dome" getting any louder than it already was at that moment. As the first bars of music began to play through the speakers, Michael's mini movie started playing showing him on a roller coaster ride through his life, showing snippets of him and his brothers rehearsing back in Gary, Indiana, performing on different shows as "The Jackson 5" and other momentous times from his life, before eventually arriving on stage in a roller-coaster/space capsule. I was proved wrong about the noise not being able to get any louder earlier! I now thought my eardrums would quite literally explode! All of a sudden there was a strange looking pod sitting there on stage, having seemingly exploded through the stage floor and now surrounded in smoke that was filling up the stage. After what seemed to be a very long time, but must have only been a few seconds at the most, the front door of the pod was kicked open to reveal Michael standing there, still as a statue, all clad in a silver and gold space suit, including helmet. After a few more seconds of soaking up the applause and atmosphere, Michael carefully stepped down from his space pod…pauses again…and as the music begins to play behind him, Michael suddenly moves to pull off his chest plate, followed by his helmet, throwing each one forward but off to the side, so they wouldn't remain on stage for anyone to fall over. Michael then started the big performance and had already entranced every person in the building that night from the start of his very first song, the performance of "Scream", "They Don't Care About Us" and "In The Closet". What an incredible start to the show. Part 1 continued with "Wanna Be Startin' Something", "Stranger in Moscow" and then the amazing performance of "Smooth Criminal"! What an incredible start to the night that had been! The entertainment certainly didn't end there. Michael performed approximately 16 songs and medleys during that night, finishing off with "Heal The World" and then, just as everyone thought that was it, the show was over, Mi-

208

chael had packed up to leave, he returned to the stage amongst thunderous applause to perform the album's and tour's title track, "HIStory"; and what an incredible rendition it was, with all his dancers carrying flags from all the countries throughout the world that they had or would be taking the tour to. The two dancers up front, closest to Michael, carried the American flag; for Michael's home country of course. The other dancer was carrying the Australian flag, for the country they were now performing in and having been welcomed into. They weren't just little flags either. These flags were huge and on poles about three times longer than the dancers were tall. They must have been heavy enough just to walk around the stage with, but to march and dance with at the same time…wow! They did an incredible job!

Naturally none of us wanted to see Michael leave the stage and have to go back home again that night, but after screaming the house down for a reasonable amount of time, calling Michael's name over and over, we all came to the realization that he had probably already left for the night and was possibly nearly back at his hotel by now! This had been just the first out of three huge nights, with some very lucky fans holding tickets for the remaining two shows and others, such as myself, having a ticket to at least one more performance before Michael left Perth again. There was one night remaining which I just could not wait for!

After eventually arriving home that night, it took me a long time to finally fall asleep. I kept replaying every moment of the concert and meeting Michael, just how all these dreams I had dreamt of for so long now had finally come true within just one week! I felt like the luckiest person alive, if only I hadn't had to have gone through so much for it all to have come true, though! Soon my thoughts went back to a night or two earlier

209

and how I'd been thinking that I really wanted to thank Michael somehow, but I just had no idea how on earth I could do that and how I would be able to get that close to him again to be able to express what I wanted to. Then it finally came to me. Well, what do most people do when they want to thank someone? They write a card, a letter and send it to the person! Well, Di Rolle still had the material that Michael had autographed for me, which I was to pick up on the night of Michael's final concert. So I finally got my plan into gear! I would get to a local card store tomorrow, write a letter to Michael, then, when I would meet up with Di Rolle before the concert, I could take my autographs from her and ask her to please give the card and letter to Michael before he goes on stage!

So first thing the next morning I went straight to the store and bought a really cute thank you card. Nothing was written inside at all, so there was plenty of room for me to write in it. I got back home again and started writing and writing, planning out a draft first of all thankfully, because I soon realized that all I wanted to say was never going to all fit into this one little card. So I wrote the basics in the card, and wrote on the front and back of two sheets of paper, barely able to find enough space to sign off at the end! I put the card inside a gorgeous envelope I had from an old letter writing set, showing Mickey and Minnie Mouse hand in hand walking along the beach at sunset; the cutest thing I had ever seen and thought Michael would also like it. So I folded the letter up and stapled it inside the card, so it wouldn't get lost or separated from the card, and fitted it inside the envelope, addressing it "Dear Michael". I felt like adding for a joke: "You'll probably never get this letter, Michael. I wrote you a thousand times before..." but I figured it might look a bit odd or creepy on the envelope, rather corny in the very least! With some serious hand cramps, I was finally finished with it. I put the envelope aside ready for the night of Wednesday, De-

210

cember 4th.

Those few extra days passed quite quickly, this time I made sure to pack a camera into a bag, along with a neighbours voice recorder so I could attempt to record the concert onto cassette tape. I wanted to be fully prepared to capture as many memories as possible. Michael would be leaving Australia to head to Manilla the following morning to continue his tour, I would most likely never get the chance to be so close to Michael again. After what seemed like hours of just waiting around, yet again, everyone I had invited to come to the show with me in place of my Dad and brother with the extra tickets that Michael had so kindly given me, started arriving. My sister Jennifer was already at the house, a great family friend, Gay, who I had actually first met at the hospital when I was admitted and who became a great friend, arrived, followed by Fiona, who was another woman not too much older than myself, who was a nurse at PMH but also helped out at the Activity Centre at PMH and had been another amazing friend to me over the years and was also a fan thanks to my constant playing of Michael music and videos in the activity centre. Before the tickets first went on sale, I talked another family friend into buying a ticket and going

Tony, Fiona, Gay, Julie and her Mum in front of the limousine that Michael sent to pick them all up in

along saying he would totally regret it if he didn't go see at least one of Michael's shows. It just so happened that the only ticket he could get was for the final night! So having a spare seat in the limousine, after Michael had given us these tickets to the final show also, we told him to come on over and he could ride along in the limousine that Michael was sending over for us! There was no point in wasting a good seat! So everyone had arrived and we were all really excited about the whole thing! No long after everyone had shown up, the limousine arrived also. We all climbed on in, very glad that we wouldn't need to find a parking space there this time or get caught in the crowd of cars trying to leave all at once afterwards!

I have to say, I felt very important when I got in line at the ticket booth at the concert venue, got to the front of the line and said in a voice quite a bit louder than it really needed to be: "Hi, my name is Julie Windsor. MICHAEL JACKSON has left some tickets here for me!!!!" I wouldn't be surprised if someone told me I'd actually screamed his name out loud to get noticed a bit! I watched as the woman at the counter reached for an envelope of tickets with both my name and Michael's on the front and passed them to me.

The tickets that Michael himself had left for Julie to pick up.

Impressions from the third HIStory Tour show in Perth on December 4th 1996, which Julie attended on Michael's invitation

We were on our way to one final show of amazing entertainment; not just a mere concert but an entire stage production of a musical genius!!! We all stood at the doors for awhile waiting for them to open so we could get to our seats, which I was happy to see were quite close to the stage. While waiting for "Human Nature", the opening act, to come on stage, I spotted where Di Rolle had arranged to meet me and went to see her. She kindly handed over all my lovely autographed material, for which I thanked her very much.

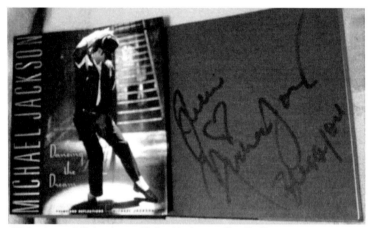

Michael signed: "Julie - Love - Michael Jackson — Bless You"

Next to come was the favour that I really hoped she would be able to do for me! "Di, do you have access to backstage at all or will you be seeing Michael again tonight or at least before he leaves? I just have this thank you card for him that I'd really love to be able to get to him somehow, is there any way at all you could possibly pass it on for me please?"

I was very pleased to hear Di reply that she was actually just about to head back there now to talk to him about something, so she would pass it straight over to him and then find me during the interval if she didn't see me before then. So I thanked her yet again and headed off to my seat with a huge grin on my face. After what seemed like only minutes this time, the room had darkened again and out came the vision, the realization of some of the magic created from Michael's imagination; another incredible performance that I was so ecstatic to be able to witness for the second time within a week. I was even more thankful to catch up with Di Rolle at the interval and listen as she told me that she gave the envelope to Michael a while before he went on stage, and that she stood there next to him as he read my card and letter, witnessing his eyes tearing up as he read my story and how much what seemed like such a simple act on his part, actually meant to me, and how it would have meant the same to all the other thousands of people around the world he had previously met; which clearly included Alicia, Casey and Stephanie who I have also mentioned here in my personal story.

Di told me he was so honestly touched by the letter, that he actually kept it on stage with him that night during the first act until his first major costume change, when he instructed someone to put the letter in the costume aside with his personal belongings. I've read that Michael quite often does things like this. He will take pictures of the children he has met in hospitals during his tours on stage with him, so some part of them can remain with him and he can feel them being a part of the experience. There's been a few shows where he has actually pulled photos out and held them up to the camera on stage with him to show and share with the audience. I've always thought that was a pretty special thing for him to do, even if it is to help his energy and help him get through the show. I never in a million years thought he would take my letter on stage with him. That was really special to find out he appreciated it so much. I was informed by Di a few days after Michael left Perth that

215

he actually read it several more times on the ride home from the concert hall that night and also took it onboard the plane with him on his way to Manila, as a reminder of how much these shows meant to the world, as hard as it may get for him at times, travelling so much, being away from family and friends, the lack of sleep; it meant more than anything else in this world to us fans.

So to Mr. Michael Jackson, once more, even though you are so sadly no longer with us to hear it directly from us: Thank you so much for your kindness, generosity and love. For giving up your childhood and so many more years of your life so we may be entertained. For sharing your beautiful soul, amazing music and movies with us. For showing us all how we should respect, love and care for each other and the world that we live in. You were an amazing musician, singer, actor and dancer! But most importantly, what you were most proud of, the one thing you wanted to be remembered for more than any of your other life works, you were an incredible humanitarian. We can never repay your kindness or thank you enough for giving so much of yourself to us. You are greatly cherished, loved and missed. This world will never be quite the same again without you in it, but we are most thankful that we got the chance to share this world with you, to live during your lifetime, Michael Jackson. The world is all the better for having had you in it. Thank You!

Written with much love, respect and gratitude not only for Michael but everyone who made my dreams in meeting Michael a realization! Whoever that wonderful person was from PMH who submitted my information to "Starlight" and "Make A Wish Foundation", to "Linneys Jewelers", especially Mr. Linney, and to all my friends and family that helped make this happen, I thank you!

by Julie Windsor

Most importantly a huge thank you to Mrs. Katherine and Mr. Joseph Jackson because without the two of you, without your dreams and willingness to share your children with the world, wanting the best for them all, we never would have had the "Jackson 5", let alone a Michael Jackson! You gave us the greatest gift of all!

Finally, this is also written for Stephanie, Alicia and in memory of Casey, who were all a big part of Michael's final trip to Perth and shared these experiences with me. I hope your memories remain as rich as mine for many years to come.

Mike,
Be nice!

by Michael La Perruque, USA

Michael La Perruque (= Mike) was Michael Jackson's personal security from 2000 through 2004. He stopped working for Michael before the last allegations by the Arvizo family because he needed to spend more time with his two children, which Michael completely understood. Michael asked Mike to come back to work for him in 2007. Mike worked again with Michael into 2008.

Michael and I crossed ways in the summer of 2000, when I worked as a Deputy Sheriff (police officer) in charge of a small police station at Universal Studios-Hollywood in Los Angeles. Michael was filming his short film "You Rock My World" there and as it happens, an acquaintance of mine worked on Michael's security team. They had problems with people being on the film set without permission and fans trying to sneak in all the time, so one day he asked me if I could help out with providing security. I agreed and once off duty from my police job, I went over to the film set. One day when they had finished a shooting, I was asked to escort Michael over to his trailer and this was actually the first time Michael acknowledged me and we said "Hi" to each other. Although I appreciated his kind gesture, it was no big thing for me because I had to deal with many celebrities on a daily basis. I was not a fan of Michael Jackson, had no album of him and paid no attention to the tabloid crap in the news about him. For me, he was just another artist filming there and I was doing my job. A few days later my acquaintance asked me if

218

I would also help provide security for Michael's children at the hotel they were staying at and help out if anything was needed.

I got to know Michael and his life a little in these days and since everything had worked fine, they thought of me again when they prepared for the "30th Anniversary Concert" Michael gave in New York in September of that same year. On the evening of the first show, Michael was supposed to walk the red carpet at Madison Square Garden together with Elizabeth Taylor. As the limousine with her arrived at Michael's hotel and backed up to the VIP door where Michael came out, all fans at the other side of the street were screaming and waving at him excitedly. Michael, as usual, took his time to happily respond to them, even though he knew Elizabeth Taylor waited for him in the car. I stood right next to him and watched the scene when suddenly a voice from inside the car shouted: "Michael, Michael, what the fuck are you doing? Get your ass inside the car, we have to go!" I knew he heard it and he knew I heard it, having a smirk on my face. So he looked at me with this stunned expression on his face, saying "Oh my gosh, did you hear that?". I replied amused: "I guess we better go!" and he added: "Yeah, I guess so!". From that day on, this memory was a private joke between the two of us and we laughed each time we remembered it.

Michael's second show at Madison Square Garden was on the evening of September 10th, 2001. We all know what terrible events the following morning brought. As soon as we realized what had happened with the "World Trade Center" and how dangerous the situation obviously was, we immediately got Michael out of town. We managed to bring him and his family to a safe house somewhere in New Jersey. However Michael's instructions for us, his security, were to get back to the hotel in New York City and watch out if any of his fans were in need of help and support. He knew they were stuck since no flights

219

went out for days. And indeed, some of them had hotels in lower Manhattan, close to the "World Trade Center" and lost their place to stay due to the horrible events. So we managed for them to stay in Michael's suite at the "New York Palace" hotel, which he paid for until flights went out again. During those two weeks in New York and later New Jersey, I got to know Michael better each day, because I was with him almost every day.

Around two months later, I received a phone call from his executive assistant who asked me if I could help provide security for Michael at the KIIS-FM (a Los Angeles based radio station) "Jingle Ball" in Los Angeles, where Michael would accept an award at the "Staples Center". She told me: "Michael said that he would like to have you and nobody else!" Of course I was very surprised and happy to hear that, so I answered: "Oh! OK if that is what Michael wants, I am happy to do it!". And so I had another security job besides my career as a police officer.

Michael drove to Los Angeles a few days before the event and we met at the "Beverly Hills Hotel". During those days, I stayed with him 24/7 and we started to have many conversations. The next thing I remember was taking him to an appointment and while I was waiting for him, I got a call from his executive assistant again, saying: "I heard you had a nice conversation with Michael. Did you understand what he was asking you?" I remembered the conversation we just had almost word for word, but I did not understand what she meant, so I said: "I am sorry, but I think I am at a loss here." So she continued: "Oh! Well, Michael was wondering if you would like to take over as his head of security and become his main person to provide protection for him and his family!" I was so stunned that I could not believe it at first and answered that I would need to think about it, because after all I still had my career as a police officer and this decision would drastically change everything for me. However,

by Michael La Perruque

not long after I went to his assistant's office and talked with her. She laid out for me what my responsibilities would be. By that time Michael and I had really started a kind of relationship with one another. I had seen a bit of his world and knew that I wanted to be a part of it. So I took the job.

But I still had to learn a lot about and from him. My first lesson was about the relationship with his fans.

During a stay in New York City we were being chased by fans from place to place, the whole day. Everywhere we went they were already there and soon I became kind of frustrated with these kids. So I thought about what I could do to make it easier for us and came up with an excellent plan, in my opinion. When we went to the next meeting, I made arrangements with the driver to get to the back door of the building unnoticed. This way we would not have to get out through the waiting crowd again and I was sure that this was something Michael would be happy about, because I believed he was getting tired of all the commotion, too. So when the time came, I picked him up from his meeting, sneaked him through corridors and staff entrances towards the waiting car. We managed to get away from the building without being seen by one single fan and I felt really great and proud of myself. Suddenly Michael asked me: "Mike, did all the fans leave?" and I proudly told him: "No, Sir, I brought you out at the back of the building to avoid the crowd." But he continued: "But why did you do that?" and I answered: "Well, I thought they were bothering you!" But what he told me then really made me think: "Mike, these people are my fans! They are the ones who buy my albums, come to my concerts and I truly love them! You should never ever, ever, ever try to sneak off from them because I appreciate my fans and if that means that I am slowed down a bit or be inconvenienced, it is OK for me. They are the ones that care about me, buy my music and sup-

221

port me and I would not be here today without my fans!"

I must confess this was not the kind of reaction I had in mind, when I had made my plan to get him out the backdoor. However, this was sort of my "pinch me moment" and I began to understand what he meant when talking about appreciation and tolerance and that it did not matter what social status, nationality or race you are. He taught me to accept and care for all his fans - and not only fans but all people we came across. He wanted them all treated nicely and with respect all of the time. I began to understand that those 22 years of being a police officer had made me hard and jaded my view about other people's problems or misfortunes, their state of health or their educational level. Many times I was very biased and one-sided. When I started to work for Michael, he really taught me to become more tolerant, giving and accepting of people from all different classes and colors. And, that one should not look down upon another or be prejudiced about others. Other people may be less fortunate than I am but most of the time people try the best they can. All this was very important to Michael and through him I was getting a new philosophy and view of life.

Michael would give in big and small ways and wherever we went, he never forgot the people who had less than he did. However, Michael did not want publicity when he gave. There are countless stories of Michael helping other people, countless times he was giving, for example to homeless people he saw on the way; like in London, when he wanted me to go over to a homeless man on the street and give him 100 dollars. Or around Christmas time in Florida, Michael knew about a shelter for abused women where they could find a safe place for themselves and their children. He wanted me to go to a big toy store and buy presents for every range and for every age of kids - from babies to teenagers. I spent thousands of dollars and when everything

222

was ready, Michael and I were going to go to the shelter to give the presents to the children there. However, at the last moment he decided not to be present there himself. He did not want the press to know because they would concentrate all the attention on him. He wanted to make it a special day for all the children there. So I made sure the people at that shelter at least knew from whom those presents came.

I remember another story most people would not believe about Michael. I was told he was driving down a street one day with his driver, when he saw a man standing at the roadside with a flat tire that needed to be changed. Michael asked his driver to pull in to help this man change his tire. Once they got home, he asked his driver to show him how to change a tire, so he could do it himself next time. And, so his driver showed him how to raise up a car, loosen the screws, and so on. A while later he was on the road again when he saw another person on the roadside with the same problem. This time Michael asked his driver to pull in again, however this time he wanted to help changing the tire himself. The driver replied something like: "Oh Michael, I think this is probably not the best idea…". But Michael responded: "No, I really want to help him…". And so they pulled in and Michael himself helped the stunned man change his tire.

I believe Michael got that charitableness from his mother. He always said that Kat (his nickname for his mother) taught him that and mentioned that he remembered driving in the car with her as a kid and as his mother saw a homeless person, she went over and gave that person some money. So he learned at a very young age to always give back a little to people in need.

Michael also had a way of disarming people, of making people comfortable around him. He did not like people being ner-

223

vous because of him because, being a shy individual, that made him nervous, too. I remember one time when we were about to leave for London. He had a very important meeting at the "House of Commons". So he asked me if I could organize wardrobes for such an event be delivered to his hotel. And so a young man and woman from a notable store brought all those things to his hotel and set them up in a room. Those people had no clue who their customer was, as I did not want to tell them beforehand. When I walked in the room together with Michael, they both just froze, wide-eyed and could not speak except for "Oh my God!" But Michael, being the person that he was, kindly said "Hi, how are you?" to them and after not more than a few minutes they all talked like old friends with one another. As much as he was surrounded by thousands of fans and everything, most people were amazed how down to earth he really was once they met him. By being this "normal guy" he had taken the tension away from those two young people and put them at ease.

However, the media never portrayed him the way he really was. They wanted to report on their "Wacko Jacko" type of stuff. Sensationalism that brought them money was their goal, not writing about Michael, the human being. Even though he knew that even negative publicity is important publicity in some way, there were times when it went too far. He became really frustrated with the media, especially when they took pictures of his children, printed terrible lies or took pictures of him and amended those to make him look strange. He found that very frustrating and often said: "Why don't they leave me alone?" As a security agent, especially when you really like your client, you not only want to protect him physically but I found myself wanting to protect his feelings from being hurt. You want to protect him from certain jealous people, bad business people and from the media. I often found myself wanting to kick someone's ass

224

for looking down on him or belittling him, knowing he would have never judged them the way they judged him. Never.

When the accusations against him came up in 2003 and the investigators came to my house, I told them: "Look guys, the charges are fake! I know this, because I was with him 24/7. And with my experience, having been a police officer for 22 years, I certainly would know if any of this occurred!" I was one of the first people who publicly stated in the press that Michael was innocent of the charges against him. Standing up for the truth bartered me a lot of criticism but I knew this was the right thing to do and upfront I let them know that I would fight for Michael and would do anything I could possibly do to help defend him.

It speaks for itself that the Prosecution did not let me testify for him. I believe the Santa Barbara District Attorney had a personal vendetta against Michael. I told them that all he was doing is nothing but waste the tax payer's money and that he would not win the case. And that is what happened because it was all based on lies.

But this terrible time haunted Michael because he knew there were still people out there that thought: "Oh, just because he was not found guilty does not mean he did not do it" or that he has paid himself out of it. But these people did not see and get to know the person I knew. They were not with him 24/7. They did not see all the people and children he helped. They did not know his heart.

Already prior to those accusations, during the time when his "Invincible" album came out, one of his biggest fears was that he would get up on stage and people would not love him or look at him with some kind of doubt and say: "You aren't the Michael

225

Jackson we love!" We can only imagine how bad this must have been for him after the trial. He was deeply scared that even his fans would question him and I think that is the reason why he avoided the public eye for so long. He was scared that he had lost people's confidence and was worried that they would not love him anymore. Two weeks before he died, when I last saw him, he was still scared of that.

When I heard the terrible news about his death I was deeply shocked, to say the least. Not a single day goes by without me thinking of him. I miss him very much and I felt that I finally needed to download Michael's albums, to hear his music. Because of my children, I used to listen to "alternative rock" type of music back then. I remember one time when I stayed with Michael in a hotel, I had this great stereo unit in my room. Suddenly he came in to ask me something but when he heard the music playing, he asked: "Mike, what are you listening to? What is that?" He was very puzzled to say the least about the kind of music I listened to. Michael himself mostly listened to classical music when he was in the car or at home. This music helped him to relax and he needed it to drown out the music and soothe the creating force he always had in his head, which he could not switch off. It often kept him awake during the night and one could say that his biggest asset was somehow also his biggest curse. So his music is now on my playlist and whenever I hear a song of him, I always think back to the time I was privileged to work for him, the time we spent together, being up all night with him and having all those private conversations. But one of my dearest memories is of simply sitting in a van at a parking lot with him, eating hot wings and having hot wing sauce all over our faces and just talk what two normal guys would talk about.

If I could tell him something now, I would say to him: "Thank

226

you Michael, for everything you gave me, for the opportunity to see the world, to do things that I never ever would have been able to do, for letting me fly on the supersonic plane to London roundtrip, for letting me stay at the finest hotels, introducing me to people like Elizabeth Taylor and President Clinton, and so many other celebrities and stars and especially for allowing me to get to know you and your family, Prince, Paris and Blanket. And, thank you for introducing me to Grace and your Executive Assistant, who are two of the finest people. Thank you for those life-enriching moments that gave me more good memories in such a short period of time, than I could have ever made in my whole life. But most of all, thank you for molding me into the person that I am today, so I can exemplify my children and other people what you taught me about tolerance and being charitable."

Now, I am the one when I see someone needing help, I stop, or give a bit of change to a homeless person begging for money. I always feel Michael's spirit whispering in my ear saying: "Mike, be nice!"

INSPIRED BY MICHAEL

by Clair, UK

I became a Michael Jackson fan in 1983 during the "Thriller" era, but it wasn't until 1987 (when I became a teenager) that I wanted to actually go and see him. I went and saw him live in concert two times at his "BAD"-Tour and stood outside his London hotel every day during the summer of 1988.

After Michael's visit to London in 1988, my friend and I really wanted to meet him, so we had the idea to make a book for him. It consisted of the word PLEASE written 500,000 times, lots of poems, songs, paintings and drawings plus photos of fans. We knew his sister Janet´s assistant who was kind enough to help us get the book to Michael in the end. So we knew he got it and were very happy. Of course we also put our contact details in the book.

Only a few months later, in 1989 (I was 15 years old then), I received an amazing phone call from Michael. The phone call lasted about 30 minutes. We talked about many things, but one thing in particular stayed with me. He told me: "I want to go on a tour, not a musical tour, a tour all over the world visiting the sick and homeless children, all my children". He wanted to make a difference. He spoke about his visits to the "Great Ormond Street"-Children's hospital in

228

London and how wonderful it is and they really take care of the children there.

His words about caring for children made a difference in my life. He encouraged me to at least try to make a difference. I worked and still work with children and young people for 10 years now and I know that my inspiration was Michael. While I also have two children of my own now, I still aspire to help all children and I hope to make a difference to at least one child.

Being a fan of Michael has been the majority of my life and I am so happy about that. Over the years I was lucky enough to meet Michael many times and also spoke to him on the phone a few more times. I always felt tongue tied whenever he was in front of me, like I was in the presence of greatness but he always made me feel so comfortable. For me Michael was many things - escapism by listening to his music and rushing to go see him if he turned up somewhere, a role model and an inspiration. I feel very lucky to have had him in my life and that I understood what he meant. He just wanted to help children and make the world a better place. Through him I also made many great friends from around the world. He definitely inspired me to see the world in a different way, he made me want to be a better person, a kinder person and he definitely made me want to make a difference, to somehow help and support children.

Michael's message is simple and one the whole world should know: "Heal the world, make it a better place". I try to live my life that way as much as I can, I have worked with underprivileged children and I have done some charity work. I also make a point of recycling and as strange as that may seem I think of Michael when doing it, he wanted to save our planet. Currently I'm doing some work encouraging people to reuse and recycle.

by Clair

What I want the world to know about Michael is that he was the kindest and most caring person I have ever met. That is why I miss him so deeply, I miss his smile, his laughter and his kindness.

Clair and other fans set up signs along Figueroa Mointain Road, the street leading to Neverland, to show Michael their support during the last days of the 2005 trial.

On the 'Dangerous Tour':

I'm looking forward to this tour, because
it will allow me to devote time to visiting children all around the world, as well as to spread
the message of global love, in the hopes that
others too will be moved to do their share to
help heal the world.

A TRIP OF A LIFETIME

by Heike Arbter, Lisa Hochmuth, Miriam Lohr & Alice Oderinde
The team of the former German MJ-magazine "M-files" had been invited to do an interview with the Wolf family in the summer of 2004 and gave their permission for a publication of a translation of their report in this book.

When in the summer of 2002 a massive flood destroyed count-less cities in Eastern Germany, the incredible story of the Wolf family and Michael Jackson began. In their home town, a city called Meissen, the river Elbe overflew its banks. The water flooded their house meters high, tearing down everything they had. To outsiders this may be an unimaginable scale of disaster, but the Wolfs experienced it firsthand and were suddenly left with nothing. At a charity event organized by the television station MDR, which took place some weeks later in Dresden, the family was suddenly presented with a very special message. It was a fax from the U.S. with the signature of Michael Jackson. It turned out to be an invitation. When Michael had learned of the disaster, he had recorded a video message to all afflicted and had sent signed CD's and towels to be auctioned off for charity. But that was not all: He had decided to invite an affected family to his Neverland Ranch to give them a couple of nice days to recover from the disaster. More precisely: It should be a fam-ily with two children aged 6-10 years, and the Wolfs were the chosen ones.

by Family Wolf

First meeting in Berlin

We sit in the cozy living room of the Wolfs and cannot imagine that two years ago we would have been underwater right in this place. In the meantime the house has been completely renovated and redecorated, and the terrible flood exists only in their memories. The family has mastered the beginning well and now we're all together lively chattering. From Heiko (37) and Susan (33), the parents, we learn that they had never concerned themselves with Michael Jackson before the MDR event. The two sisters Saskia (10) and Sabrina (8) had no idea who he was until they were told that he was a famous singer. When they first saw a photo of him, they were a bit surprised, because they had imagined him quite differently.

After receiving the fax, the family stayed in contact with Michael's management and in the winter of that year, they were already granted a huge surprise. Michael had flown to Germany in November to attend the annual "Bambi" awards ceremony in Berlin. He resided in the hotel "Adlon", which was besieged by his fans day and night. He also had a very special date: the Wolfs had been invited to meet him there. They felt a little queasy, recount the parents. They had seen pictures of a recent court hearing in which Michael had turned up with a three-day beard and plaster on his nose. They wondered what would await them in Berlin...

Once there, they waited in front of the "Adlon" for their meeting in the midst of Michael Jackson's fans. "Why do they all scream like that? There's no one coming out!" was the first thought of the two children. Heiko continues, "At 3 o'clock we were at the 'Adlon', but we did not see Michael before 5 o'clock. All together we went up to a room in the hotel and waited some time with Markus Thiele and his team. The jacket, which was later being auctioned off at the 'Tribute to Bambi', was in that room as well. We have tried it on and it was so heavy, maybe about 10 kilos." When Michael returned from his trip to the Berlin Zoo, the big moment arrived and the Wolfs entered his suite. All doubts were erased when Michael came over to them, says Susan. And continues, "He was very down to earth and not arrogant or conceited, quiet, reserved, he didn't want to be the center of attention and was very normal, like everyone else really should be." Michael was very interested in the flood and listened carefully to what Dieter Wiesner translated for him. He looked at the book about the flood, which the Wolfs had brought him as a gift and had tears in his eyes. "It really upset him a lot but he also wanted to know everything," says Susan. We ask who had the idea to go to the window together. "That was Michael. He said, 'Come on' and took us by

Autographed books to the two Wolf girls

234

the hand", elate the children. Heiko adds: "We were sitting at the table and were talking. Downstairs on the street, fans loudly sang a song. Michael listened and said, 'Aw, this is such and such a song.' He hummed along and sang a bit and then he took the girls to the window. He has thus responded to the fans downstairs." Sabrina remembers: "It was great that the fans cheered for us. Michael made the victory sign and we simply imitated him. We looked down and Saskia wanted to return, because she is a little bit afraid of heights."

In Berlin the Wolfs received CD's and two books with autographs. The Wolfs keep the books "flood proof" on the top of the cabinet, packed in plastic bags. It takes a while before they are unpacked and we can admire them.

Complications on the way

The arrangement for the U.S. - visit was in the hands of Michael's management. It was not easy to find a date as appointments of Michael and the Wolfs had to be coordinated. Originally they were to visit him a week in Las Vegas, but then Michael proposed to change the place to Neverland when they met in Berlin, because he seemed to trust the family. Susan supports Michael's decision: "For the children it was much better. What should they do in Las Vegas? Neverland is a paradise for them!"

For Heiko, who works as a sound engineer in the theater of Meissen, it was difficult to get off from work, because the final date was really on short notice and they were supposed to fly over to California head over heels. He almost had not gotten the days off. An additional problem were their passports that had been washed away by the flood and they had to re-apply for this travel. As the negotiations regarding a date went on and on, the passes expired and they had to apply again. Michael, of course, knew nothing of such problems. In response to our question of how their friends and family responded to the planned trip, Heiko says: "At first it was rather seen like kind of a publicity stunt. But when Markus Thiele told us that the U.S. trip was on, most friends and relatives have commented positively about it."

On departure day - a Sunday - the family began the long journey by car to Dresden, from where they flew to Frankfurt. From Frankfurt they flew to Toronto, where they had a half hour stop. The long journey, however, began to become difficult when the officer at the immigration did not want to believe that the reason for their journey was to visit Michael Jackson at his Neverland Ranch. It had been difficult enough to get through without knowing English, but this was too much. The Wolfs discussed with the woman using hands and feet for fifteen minutes, during which the departure of their connecting flight to Los Angeles moved closer and closer. They even showed the woman Michael's fax, but once she finally believed them, their plane was already gone. So the family had to wait for the next plane, which finally brought them to LA at midnight. Susan admits in retrospect that she was devastated several times during the trip and she was just happy when she arrived in a hotel somewhere and could sleep. Well, one thing they all had already learned before they were even close to Michael: Never write "Michael Jackson" as your destination on an immigration form!

Recreation for the stressed nerves

If you ask the sisters today, what they liked best at Neverland, so many things come to their minds that they can not answer

236

the question and when they see videos they shout excitedly, "I wanna ride one more time, one more time!!!" Even the parents become enthusiastic, "For me it felt really good, because I could completely relax. I forgot about the flood and all the other worries. I did not even have to worry about the kids, because they were all well looked after everywhere. And this wonderful peacefulness ...," says Susan.

What the four Wolfs exactly experienced in their three days behind the magical gates of Michael's home? Heiko begins: "When you enter Neverland, you have to sign an agreement on the first gate that you agree not to film or take photographs on the ranch. Or you simply leave your film and photo cameras behind. And that's what we have done so that we are not even tempted. We thought, this is his privacy and we accept that. The main thing is that we saw it and that's ok then. And we have at least the films of Markus Thiele as a memory. Otherwise there were no controls, it was all based on trust!" It takes a full five minutes by car to reach the next gate.

To welcome the family, Michael greeted them in his library. The kids had stuffed animals with them, which they then gave to Prince and Paris, Blanket got a teddy bear. They also brought a china plate from Meissen, which is famous for its porcelain, on which was written "Thank you for inviting us, Saskia and Sabrina". After about quarter an hour, Michael's son Prince wanted to show Saskia and Sabrina Neverland and so the kids left excitedly. From the main house it's a 15-minutes-walk to the amusement park, to the zoo even three quarters of an hour. So the children went on small electric cars to the park, accompanied by two nannies and a bodyguard. We want to know how Saskia and Sabrina have communicated with Michael's children. "We only said 'yes' and 'nope' if we understood something. They have always shown us where they wanted to go and

Family Wolf entering "Neverland" © Markus Thiele

Bine and I have just nodded. We have also talked by using our hands and feet," explains Saskia. And so Prince and Paris show their German visitors around the fairgrounds. Little Blanket was there, too, but he preferred to stay back in the safe stroller or on the arm of the nanny, while the others frolicked wildly. Sabrina continues, "We went on the bumper cars and Prince was sad because no one drove with him. He went back to the bodyguard, and I drove with a nanny." But later a true friendship developed between the kids – or even more? "Bine and Prince Michael, Bine and Prince Michael", shouts Saskia at the top of her voice and explains that Prince always took her sister by the hand. When Sabrina bashfully gives her sister a punch in her side, she says snippy: "Be happy! Not everyone can be on Prince Michael's side!"

Meanwhile Heiko and Susan continued to talk to Michael, of course with Dieter Wiesner as an interpreter. Michael proved to be a generous host and invited both parents to move around freely. They should take advantage of everything and do what they wanted, that was his most important wish. He said if they wanted to eat something, then they should tell the cook. It was really his greatest joy when they moved freely and did not ask for everything. "Do not ask, just take it. No matter where, "said Michael. "And wherever you went, somebody was there imme-diately to help you, that was no problem," says Heiko.

After settling in the guesthouse and unpacking their luggage, they went back to Michael's house. Michael had to leave and drove away with Dieter Wiesner. He drove the Bentley himself and steered very slowly through his neatly landscaped beds. "We asked where the children are and the staff told us to go up to the station. We went one station by train, got out there and they told us we should go down the valley, past Peter Pan and the cinema where we met the children. The communica-

240

NEVERLAND VALLEY

DINNER MENU

SOUP or SALAD

SWEET & SOUR CHICKEN
Served With
FRIED RICE with CHICKEN
or
FRIED RICE with SHRIMP
or
FRIED RICE with CHICKEN & SHRIMP

EGG ROLLS

FRIED ICECREAM

Michael's signature for Sabrina on a Neverland Dinner Menu

241

by Family Wolf

tion luckily works on this huge property. At the time there was also another family there: the son of Marlon Brando with his children and a friend who came from Germany. He has also translated for us from time to time", says Susan.

In the evening the family had dinner with Michael. They had beans, potatoes and steak. Saskia: "I didn't like the beans, but there was enough candy in our room, from which I ate until I was full."

Michael's house and the attractions

The Wolfs were housed in the guesthouse, which lies directly opposite the main house. The main house, Michael's house, remained in their memories like this: on the lower floor there are a lot of playful things, but not as exaggerated as Martin Bashir wanted to represent it. Especially Susan felt really comfortable there. They were also free to go upstairs to Michael's private rooms, but they didn't do it out of respect. In the living room there is the expensive chess board, which we know from the media, and the Bambi Award together with a Grammy Award sits on a turntable by the fireplace in the library. Michael has all kinds of gifts laying around, although the Wolfs did not see any fan-banners. He has many pictures on the walls, including many photos with celebrities such as Princess Diana, Nelson Mandela and Bill Clinton. It seems like having his picture taken with celebrities is also a little hobby of Michael's. The entire Jackson family is also present in photographs. In one corner stands an old film machine, which can show the film "How the first film was made." There is also a wing, an angel made of glass, a fairy and a lot of valuable vases.

Susan: "What fascinated me was that he had a lot of self-cre-

242

ated images on the walls. He does the sketches himself and has professional painters paint his ideas. If you look at the painted faces, you know exactly who it is. He is always in the pictures as well. He has a picture of a tree, a kind of 'family tree'. His head is in the center and around it are the heads of others like Lady Diana, Bill Clinton and of course his children. Probably those represented there with him are his best friends. There is also a big picture of Michael with two children on his hands, and somewhere behind him more children as well as Janet and his brothers. You have to look at it intensely to find out everything. It is not visible at first glance. He was also depicted as an angel in one picture and in another as Peter Pan."

The famous "Giving Tree" is near the main house, from which one can look at the flamingo pond. But the Wolfs did not dare to climb up. The central area of Neverland is green. Only because it is sprinkled all day this oasis in the otherwise rocky desert can exist.

There are two trains, which can be used to move through the huge estate. But not only that, there are also electric cars available, bicycles, motorcycles, and quads. Heiko and Susan went on a joyride with them once. But just outside the green part of Neverland, where the land is desert-like, Susan got constantly stuck in holes of gophers because her tires were too narrow for such a runway. Heiko drove with Michael's big quad, which had larger tires and a protective shield at the front, so he had no problem.

You can go to the movies and get popcorn everywhere, ice cream or drinks. There is a cook, to whom one can turn with his wishes upon which he creates a meal, for example fruit salad, french fries and hamburgers. In the cinema, there is soft serve, at the station you can find additional chests with packed ice cream, from which one can help oneself freely. Sauces of all kinds are also nearby. In the cinema there are also chocolate bars, chewing gum, M & Ms, Coke, Fanta (with or without caffeine), 7up and other varieties that are available in the U.S.. Every day new popcorn and soft ice cream is made and is constantly refilled. There is a different flavor of ice available every day. Sometimes the Wolfs could not eat any more for supper, because they were already so full.

The lobby of the cinema does not only contain candy. There is also a life-size figure of "ET" and a special display case. Inside it is a figure of "Cinderella" as well as "Pinocchio". If you push a button, Pinocchio starts to dance and once he is finished, next to him is a light and you see a carved wooden figure of Michael Jackson dance. Really funny! In the cinema hall itself there are two separate rooms for very sick children. From their beds they can watch the movies. Everything is wheelchair friendly. One floor higher Michael has his own private cinema box with a couch, from which he can watch. Sabrina recounts, "Once Michael's children were allowed to watch 'Finding Nemo', but unfortunately we were already in bed and therefore could not join them." But on the next day they were allowed to as well, long before the movie was in German cinemas.

"Once when we were in the pool, we did not want to get out anymore. There was a little frog in the pool that I wanted to have as a pet. I took it out with my hands", says Saskia still enthusiastic. The two kids would have loved to flounder about in the water with Michael, but this wish could not be fulfilled, unfortunately.

It seems as if one could endlessly enumerate things you can do and see at Neverland: a Batman car, a park with water pistols, a huge screen from the "HIStory" Tour, a video library, a

244

game room filled from top to bottom with games, including one where you are a taxi driver and have to bring a man to the airport, or a basketball - console with three balls and Djini of "Aladdin." There is a playground, where Prince and Paris have a small house with a kitchenette and a sleeping room, a rocking horse, a tennis court, table tennis and of course the zoo. It consists of a couple of compounds, including two very large enclosures for the giraffe and the elephant, the petting zoo, the snake home and the parrot house. There are two tigers, two monkeys, llamas, horses and more. The horses have their own paddock and a Mexican takes care of them. He's the one you must contact if you want to ride. The Wolfs were told that Michael is a very good rider and often gallops over his meadows. There is a spectacular story regarding the crocodile that also lives there: One day Michael went into the cage to play with the crocodile, but he teased it too much so that it snapped. Michael was so frightened that he leaped over the six-foot fence to escape.

Michael

And Michael himself? Heiko starts off: "When there was no camera, Michael did not hide his children and there was always a very different atmosphere than when a camera was rolling. He is really quite different without the camera. We sat together, hugged him and greeted each other. We were not controlled, or even disinfected, nothing like that. He moved around the ranch very normally. He's also no linnet. He has pretty big hands and a firm handshake. He only speaks calmly." Susan adds: "When we said goodbye, he had a bandage on his nose and told us he had hay fever. We were very close to him and his nose was not falling off, that's ridiculous. Heiko even almost collided with Michael's nose, but of course nothing happened! He wore very little make-up, maybe even nothing at all. He had no eye-make-up and was not as white – he looked much more beautiful without it! Although one could see the dark spots from his skin disease we thought he looked really nice. He had a red shirt, a red jacket, black high water pants, white socks and a hat – just like he is known. The hair was straight and not as long as in Berlin."

But there's one thing the Wolfs regret: They did not take a photo together with Michael at Neverland, as they had left their cameras at the entrance. The children also had especially practiced the "Moonwalk" and had wanted to show it to Michael, but with all the excitement they had forgotten.

Funny is the following anecdote: the Wolfs asked Michael to sign a ticket from the Meissen Theater for a neighbor in Meissen. Michael liked the ticket so much that he wanted to keep it. He did not get it though...

It was a pity that the Wolfs could not speak English, because that way parts of the communication were probably lost in the process of translating. Otherwise it would have been easier to talk about more personal things.

MJ's autograph on the program of the theatre Meissen

246

Prince, Paris and Blanket

Of course we are also interested in Michael's three children. "He has very pretty children and Blanket is a real bundle of joy," enthuses the family.

We want to know if the kids are very spoiled by Michael, and to answer the question Heiko has a story to tell: "In Berlin, Prince's jacket was on the floor. Michael asked Prince to pick the jacket up, but he did not want to do it. Michael stood up and asked him again until he did. So they are not spoiled at all and the nanny does not do everything for them. They have manners and are very polite." And Susan remembers: "Prince sat next to Michael and said to us: 'This is my dad. It's Michael Jackson'. I thought it was so cute, because he was so proud of his father. And he also has a character like his father." They assess Paris as calmer than Prince. She is not as lively as Prince, but yet does her thing.

With all the candy at Neverland it seems easy to raise concerns regarding the nutrition of the Jackson children. "Prince and Paris are not allowed to eat everything, Michael is very meticulous about that. They did not drink juice, but water. And he peels of the skin of the chicken before they eat. However, they have eaten popcorn", remembers Susan.

Once Michael went for a pizza with Dieter Wiesner in the next village. And once a month he and his kids go to McDonald's.

The schedule and the farewell

On Monday morning, Michael went to the funeral of Gregory Peck shortly after eight o'clock, after that Dieter Wiesner

247

showed the family the ranch. On Tuesday the Wolfs had to do some shooting, after all a short film of their visit was to be prepared for German television. Markus Thiele and his team had traveled along, but they were quartered outside of Neverland and were admitted only for the shooting. The cinema, the zoo, the main house, the bedroom in the guesthouse and the Indian village with a real Indian were off limits, therefore the filming was limited to certain selected places.

On Wednesday the Wolfs were picked up by Michael's huge sedan, which is already known from various media reports. They were brought to LA, where they spent an hour with Michael in the studio. When they arrived, there were also local fans who had probably been attracted by the sedan. In the studio itself they talked to Michael. Prince, who was present as well as Paris, pulled out all the colored wires from the mixers and said to Saskia and Sabrina: "Come on, let us build the biggest rainbow of the world." He had a huge pile of cables in his hands. The four children sat down on the studio floor and started to build the rainbow. Michael stood by with tears in his eyes. Unfortunately the work of art could not be finished, there was too little time. When the family finally said goodbye to Michael, they were in his bedroom, which could also be found in the recording studio. If Michael has a creative phase and gets tired in between, he lies down there.

On Thursday Dieter Wiesner showed the family LA, the Sunset Boulevard, the Walk of Fame and famous department stores. On Friday they were free to do whatever they liked before they had to return to their home in Germany.

by Family Wolf

Personal Conclusion

That the family enjoyed the stay at Neverland to the fullest, is beyond question. Today it is a concern to them to talk about the trip as it really was. They want to get their story across as real as possible and not engage in sleazy stories, because that would not be fair towards Michael. They have already made negative experiences with the press and have become cautious. The insight into Michael's life has impressed them deeply, and when they hear a song from him today on the radio, they can't help but smile. They were also impressed by the sympathy on the part of Michael Jackson's fans who have sent them CDs, videos, photos and books of Michael when they learned about the fate of the Wolfs.

The family is glad they were able to experience Neverland in a peaceful atmosphere. The allegations of child abuse distressed them deeply. They vehemently agree upon the fact that they cannot image any of the allegations to be true. They have already discovered flaws in the reports from the media when they compare them to their own experiences. They have also never seen alcohol anywhere on the ranch. Marlon Brando's son wanted to have a beer once, but he was told "No". They were never offered something alcoholic anywhere.

Meanwhile, they have repeatedly tried to contact Michael in order to thank him - so far unsuccessfully, unfortunately, because he has changed his management. It is important to them that Michael knows how thankful they are for what he has done for them. Therefore, we publish a brief message to Michael in "M-files" which he will hopefully read this way. Last but not least we ourselves would like to thank the Wolf family for the beautiful day and the great interview!

249

Message to Michael:

Hello Mr. Jackson, we would like to express our warmest thank you's for the invitation to Neverland and the hospitality at your home! We tried several times to send you and your children our best wishes and the finished rainbow. We all, but especially Saskia and Sabrina, love to remember the wonderful time spent with Paris, Prince and Blanket. We wish you and your family a lot of strength and power to endure the forthcoming events! Best wishes to all of you, yours family Wolf.

Michael's Thank you letter to the Wolfs saying: "I will never forget how Prince pulled out all the cables from the mixers in the studio to create the biggest rainbow in the world together with you. I hope that you, Heiko, Susann, Sabrina und Saskia, have moments that you will keep in your hearts forever as well. Thank you for the joy you have given my children and me. With love, Michael Jackson"

by Family Wolf

My
Michael

by Maria Crawford, UK

It was in a children's hospital near Cape Town during the South Africa leg of the History tour in 1997.

On that same day, Michael had also visited an orphanage where many of the kids had lost their parents to HIV/Aids. South Africa clearly touched his heart, as it did mine. During the weeks there, he was even more open and affectionate than usual, had a lot of fun and received a warm welcome everywhere he went.

I saw him both before and after the hospital visit but I didn't want to intrude by going into the wards with him. What happened inside, however, summed up why Michael was a soul of the dearest kind. He was accompanied by his cinematographer, a wonderful warm and gentle man named Joe Wilcots, who later recounted the following to me.

Michael was being shown through the hospital by doctors and nurses. They were doing the usual things – greeting children on the wards, giving them presents, spending some time with them. Then, they walked along a corridor between wards and there was a separate room with one child in it. Michael asked why the child was alone and what the room was. The doctors told him it was a quarantine room – that they had to restrict who could

251

go in there because the child was seriously ill and they didn't know what was wrong with him or whether the boy's illness was contagious.

The doctors carried on walking. Michael hung back, and when they had gone ahead a little, he ducked into the room. All hell broke loose. The doctors and nurses panicked but none of them wanted to follow Michael into the room unprotected. Joe told me they watched through the window as Michael sat on the bed with the child, spoke to him and kissed him on the forehead. Then Michael just calmly came out of the room and of course the doctors didn't want to scold him – he was Michael Jackson, after all. But they were clearly anxious.

Afterwards, Joe asked Michael why he had done it – what on earth he had been thinking to take what could have been such a serious risk with his own health. Michael replied very simply: "I wanted to do what the child's mother would, if she was here." He knew no danger would keep a parent from their child. No risk would stop a mother reaching her child and making sure he knew he was loved.

This has always epitomised, to me, Michael's relationship with children. He seemed to feel a parent's love and a parent's responsibility for every child in the world. It is so hard for the rest of us to imagine the scale of such love, such worry, such pain. Most new parents are overwhelmed by the emotions they feel for a single child. Who can possibly cope with that intensity multiplied by hundreds of millions?

The privilege of being there with Michael was a journey that began for me when I was eight years old. I had been flicking through a magazine in the Irish seaside town where I then lived, when a warm, benevolent, glowing smile brought an instant halt

252

to my page-turning. It was a small poster with a few lines of publicity beneath (Michael Jackson's Thriller album was about to be launched, he loved animals, he lived on fruit and vegetables... All written by marketing people of course, but adorable all the same). I recognised his name from episodes of Top of the Pops and some clips of the Jacksons TV show that I had seen a couple of years earlier when I was really very little. And for reasons that I now choose to simply accept rather than analyse, looking at that magazine, I was instantly smitten. I knew – I remember consciously thinking – that this man would always be important in my life.

Shortly afterwards came all the hype of Thriller and the Victory Tour, heavily covered in the media even in Ireland. I was glued unblinkingly to MTV when his videos came on; I pored over every printed report. And all I wanted was to be in the US to see him. I had to wait a few more years (which felt as long as they could only to a child) when I lived in the UK and the Bad Tour came to London. Still young, I was only allowed to see a couple of shows, with a chaperone of course. But it was enough to make me yearn for more, to realise this was a real person, not a mere image or phenomenon, but flesh, blood and, above all, a magical soul.

In the years between the Bad and Dangerous tours I worked more hours than any school-age teenager probably should, and saved my money with a discipline I can barely imagine now. By the time the Dangerous Tour premiered in Europe, just days after I completed my school-leaving exams, I was able to attend every show until my cash ran dry a few shows from the end. Aged 17 but with the appearance and heart of a kid, a few friends and I were everywhere Michael was, on front row at the shows, sleeping under his hotel windows - and, to many people's surprise I'm sure - he loved it. Back then, he commu-

253

nicated with us through members of his entourage; he seemed to see us as adventurous little characters and he conveyed his love, warmth and amazing acceptance of us throughout that magical, innocent summer.

Over the following years I travelled to see Michael whenever I could, while trying never to be a bother or burden on him - I pursued my education, career and relationships because it seemed unfair to expect him to provide all sense of happiness and achievement. He faced painful, unjust challenges from the second year of the Dangerous Tour onwards and I was lucky enough to be in a position to be physically there for him, to visibly demonstrate my love and support. And Michael gave me more of his time, energy and love for those 17 years than I could ever have dreamt of when I was a little girl captivated by his picture in a magazine.

There are many memories and stories like the one from South Africa. Remembering and writing about him now also brings no small measure of pain at what we have lost.

Nonetheless, a second and very telling story I want to share here illustrates how far Michael's benevolence extended – beyond children, beyond hospital visits, or any specific 'cause'.

In late May 2009 I was with Michael when he was leaving Arnold Klein's office in Beverly Hills. The hype was building about the This Is It shows and there was a swarm of paparazzi outside the building. I was nervous about him being able to leave – the previous day had been a nasty experience both emotionally and physically: one photographer had shouted a question at him that was designed to be hurtful; then another had audibly banged Michael's head with his oversized camera. It had been truly unpleasant and Michael had no reason to be in a good

254

mood after that.

Today, a woman Michael didn't know had got into the doctor's office. She was older, and although I'd never seen her before it seems she had a habit of chasing away paparazzi whenever she saw them near celebrities in LA. When she met Michael, obviously for the first time, she was in tears, almost hysterical, was ranting to him incoherently, and for no apparent reason kept saying 'please' as if asking for his help.

I'm a little ashamed to say, she was getting on my nerves. I could see he was tired and, after the events of the day before, I was worried about him exiting the building safely. I hadn't

Maria and Michael

even really spoken to him for that reason: I just wanted him to get out of there and be safe. And looking at this woman hugging him and ranting in his face, I wished he would say 'I'm sorry, I have to go', put his own wellbeing first, and walk away.

255

Not Michael. He stood in complete peace, stooped a little to look this older lady in the eyes and said in that low, kind voice that I remember too clearly, 'Tell me what you need. What is it that you need? How can I help you?' She still couldn't answer, so he asked again. Calmly, slowly, as if trying to instil her with some of his equilibrium. And still she couldn't answer. She was just rambling because she couldn't believe that she had really met Michael Jackson, who most people saw as an untouchable icon; the greatest entertainer of all time, who had broken so many boundaries in a stellar career over the past four decades. She couldn't believe that this man, who symbolised so much to her, had hugged her when she asked for a hug. And when she pleaded aimlessly for something she couldn't even identify, he gave her everything a person could ask for. He treated her with love, dignity and respect. He lowered his head, gave her his time and offered of himself, even though he had no idea who this hysterical person was or what she wanted.

He hadn't dismissed her. He hadn't thought of himself or how badly his bodyguards needed to get him out of that building and away from the throng of photographers. He was Michael.

We want to make the World Children's Day a world holiday...worldwide, so we always take the day off. It can't be in the summer, it can't be a weekend. It will have to be a day where people stop and say, "Oh yes, we can't go to work tomorrow, or school tomorrow, because I have to be with my children and give them the whole uninterrupted day". It has to be like that or else it won't be important. It would be the love of my life to have a World Children's Day.

A GIFT
FROM GOD

by Dieter Wiesner, Germany

I was lucky enough to get to know Michael Jackson during the HIStory Tour (1996) and to travel with him throughout the world. At first it was a business relationship, a collaboration to develop new licensing and merchandise ideas, but soon I started working for him as his manager, accompanied him to concerts, performances and award shows and over time gained so much of his trust that he gave me his "power of attorney". Together we restructured his business environment, including lawyers and partners and made concrete plans for his so called "second life" that would lead him towards the film and enter-tainment industry but also to a topic that was very dear to his heart - charity.

Michael was a genius in many fields - fantasy, creating enter-tainment, music and business - but what always gave him most joy was to help other people. Michael did small and big acts of charity all the time, most of them unknown to the public and media.

Of course, we all know about projects like "We are the world", that saved children from starving in Africa, and his later founded "Heal the World Foundation", which ran for many years and donated hundreds of millions to causes all over the world. Mi-

258

chael knew that a lot of money unfortunately gets lost in big organizations due to things like administrational and logistic costs and not all reaches the ones in need. That is why, later on, Michael decided to help more locally and directly.

Whenever he heard or read about something that happened or someone who needed help, be it in his direct neighbourhood or somewhere else in the world, he tried to get in touch and help personally. Michael often just sent the urgently required money or cheque for things like medical operations or equipment. Sometimes he even drove to a family's house himself to bring them things they were in need of. Usually he stayed in the van behind blacked-out windows and just watched how his driver or someone else working for him delivered the goods to these people. It was important to him to personally make sure that the needed things were actually bought and delivered and reached those in need. Michael did not want any publicity or anything in return for that. Most people never knew where the money or the gifts came from. Michael was the kind of person who was happy when he could make other people happy.

His Neverland Ranch was a wonderful home for him and his family but he did not keep this paradise to himself. Regularly he shared it with other people or used it to raise money for charity like he did in September 2003, when he hosted a big fundraising party at Neverland. He supported organizations such as "Make-A-Wish" or other local ones from the Los Angeles area, which came in twice a week, even when Michael was not at home, with busloads of children from underprivileged families. The kids could enjoy an all for free day, enjoy the rides of his amusement park, watch movies in the cinema, visit his zoo and have candies, food and drinks as they wished. They could just be kids for a day or two, having fun in a safe and beautifully inspiring surrounding. Ironically even police officers from that area,

259

who were later part of the raid, sent their kids to Neverland to enjoy Michael's hospitality.

The staff working at Neverland Ranch were mostly people from the area and often people who really needed a job and the money badly. He not only employed them but wanted to help them and paid a lot of extra costs. Whenever there was a medical bill too high for them to manage, either for the workers themselves or one of their family members, Michael would pay for it.

The first time I took my own two children, Jerry and Daniel, whom I adopted, with me to Neverland, Michael asked me to go and buy them presents as a welcome gift. I thought this was not necessary and declined. Michael, however, insisted that he wanted to give something to my children and so he went to buy some things himself. He even wrapped them up himself and added little cards. In the end, he came back with about ten packages of gifts and said, "Dieter give these to them, please!" I said, "No, these gifts are from you, so you should give them to my kids". Michael argued that I should do it but I didn't. He actually blushed and felt embarrassed to give his presents to my kids. This was so typical for him. He did not want to be seen as the "big benefactor", he simply wanted to make others happy and preferred to stay in the background and only watch their reactions. He simply loved to give and see the joy of other people, because their joy made him happy.

Besides his small acts of charity, whenever some tragedy or disaster occurred, Michael's biggest wish was to help as much as he could. After the terrible events of September 11th, 2001, he immediately tried to help raise funds and planned a charity concert, which was held only a few weeks later in Washington D.C., called "United we stand". There, he presented his new charity song "What more can I give" for the first time. Michael's working title for it was "We are the world part 2" and like the original, it was a potpourri of the finest contemporary artists of popular music, like Celine Dion, N*Sync, Carlos Santana, Gloria Estefan, Luther Vandross, Mariah Carey, Beyoncé, Shakira, Boyz II Men and many more. Michael´s record company Sony, however, refused to release the song as a single, a decision that obviously had to do with a dispute between Michael and the company.

Michael himself, was as a very private person, however, contrary to what the media reported, a very down-to-earth, modest and humble man. You can see that in the way he raised his own children. He knew it was very important not to spoil kids and even though his children had of course all they needed, he did not want them to have too many toys and presents. For their birthdays they would usually just get little gifts and a self-baked carrot cake with candles. Michael also made them breakfast himself. He knew that material things are not important, but the time you spend with your children. I believe most children would be overjoyed if they only had half as much time together with their parents as Michael spent with his kids.

Michael, himself, had the most fun, not with material things, but to see happy faces of people especially children. I remember once we were in Las Vegas and Michael spontaneously asked a bunch of kids to come with him. I didn´t have a clue what his plans were when he went straight into a candy store with all of them. Once inside, Michael shouted "It´s candy time!" and of course all the kids had a blast and went through the store grabbing as much candy as they liked and immediately started to eat it! The shop owner and I were in shock, but Michael loved it and could not stop laughing. He was so happy to just see the kids having so much fun. While I was still talking to the owner to find a solution concerning the bill, Michael already wanted

261

to leave the store. But I shouted "Wait!" and Michael was just laughing. In the end, I agreed upon a sum of money with the shop owner to cover the costs of the eaten candies. On our way home Michael was still laughing, he loved those moments. More important than buying big cars or houses, the little things that brought joy and good to the world - that is what Michael loved the most.

This attitude of Michael also showed at his house at Neverland, which was very small and modest compared to other celebrities' homes. Of course, people will say that having a whole amusement park and zoo in the backyard can't be called modest, but these places were mainly for other people and guests, for needy children and families to enjoy. Already in his plans for the park and cinema, Michael had thought of facilities for sick children who could not leave their beds anymore - so Neverland was built from scratch to become a place that could be shared with other people. It was not a place only for himself, but thoughtfully designed to share. That is what Michael was like as a person and as a father, too, thoughtful and down to earth.

I visited Neverland once more after Michael´s death with a German TV reporter who later told me that he needs to revise everything he ever said and thought about Neverland and Michael. He had imagined it to be like Disneyland, very trashy or with a golden palace, but to the contrary it was a very beautiful and dignified place with a calm and relaxing atmosphere surrounded by the most wonderful nature. I, myself, always felt very much at ease when I was at Neverland, it was a very quiet, relaxing and simply wonderful place to be.

262

In 2002 a British journalist called Martin Bashir was introduced to Michael and entered his world. He convinced him that a documentary about his life would be a unique opportunity to finally show the world his true self and stop all the crazy lies in the press about him or his lifestyle at the Neverland Ranch. So the filming for "Living with Michael Jackson" began. To me Mr. Bashir soon lost his trustworthiness when we caught him searching through Michael's private bags in a hotel bathroom and saw him filming Michael's children, which was something Michael never allowed under any circumstances. But Michael was too kind and too trustful to stop it all at that point. However, when Bashir turned up in Miami where Michael stayed in February 2003 and wanted to shoot the final cut of the documentary, which would have been to film Michael's reaction while watching the documentary Bashir had produced so far (the same version that was aired on TV), we at least could prevent that from happening. After that, Mr. Bashir quickly left, taking all film material with him. Already the next day the documentary was aired on British TV - without Michael's consent, of course.

Michael was very angry and highly disappointed that this guy had betrayed him. But he was also ready to fight for the truth and wanted to clarify all the misconceptions people got from watching Bashir's film. We decided to do our own rebuttal documentary called "Take Two – the footage you were never meant to see", which included outtakes from Michael's own cameraman that clearly show how manipulating Mr. Bashir was and how he had twisted the truth and lied to Michael in order to gain his trust. In our rebuttal we also published more detailed facts about the boy Gavin, who attracted the most attention after his appearance in the Bashir documentary. After all these efforts and after preventing the documentary from being released as a DVD, we were sure things would be fine and Michael and me went back to concentrate on his future business projects and ideas again.

263

Among these was the "Number Ones" album, which included the single "One more chance", due to be released in November 2003, and was the last project Michael needed to finish to fulfil his contract with Sony Music. After that, he wanted to explore other areas of film, entertainment and charity. He called this his "second life", after his first life of being a musical megastar. He always said, he didn´t want to end up as an old man on stage. He wanted to continue giving some concerts every few years in spectacular places like at the pyramids in Egypt or somewhere else around the world. This he would do for his fans.

But mainly he intended to invest and go into the film business, buy the rights to parts of Universal films that were on the market and use them to do theme parks and merchandising. Another already very concrete business step was to buy the rights to the Marvel catalogue to turn comics like "Superman" into motion picture films.

Secondly, Michael also wanted to continue creating family entertainment. What most people don't know is that Michael worked with a lot of people in Las Vegas and helped creating new attractions, music, designs and family entertainment, like the trick fountains at the "Bellagio" hotel, the roller coaster in "New York, New York", the volcano at the "Mirage", the "Treasure Island" pirate ship, the "Siegfried & Roy" show or the "Secret Garden". Many years ago, when Las Vegas was still known to be a gambler's paradise, Michael already knew that family entertainment would be a branch worthwhile to invest in and rebuild. And he was right. Nowadays Las Vegas' visitors consist of 75% families, coming mostly to enjoy the great entertainment, not so much the gambling.

(Michael himself loved Las Vegas a lot. I remember once Michael had the idea to go to the "Secret Garden" at the "Mirage Hotel" and invite some kids to come with him and his own three children to swim with the dolphins there. He laughed so much seeing the kids having fun playing with the dolphins when they jumped out of the water and splashed them all. It was a wonderful time for everyone. That day his little son Blanket swam there for the first time in such a big pool.)

Being the artist that he was, Michael very much concentrated on family entertainment that would deliver values and was good and suitable for the whole family, kids and parents alike, so that they can spend valuable time together. On his priority list was the idea to reinstall the family unit again. However imperfect his own relationship with his father may have been, his own family always came first for him and Michael always appreciated and loved both of his parents and wanted them to be well-cared for. That was very important to him! Michael always had a good feeling about where future developments will lead to and he loved creating fun and magical things for kids and families to enjoy. He provided ideas for companies like Disney, too, but gave all of his ideas for free, without getting any money or credit for it.

He was a real visionary in those regards and had great ideas which later on were used to make big money. I believe Michael was so good in creating family entertainment, because he understood and appreciated children very much. He loved to see their reactions to things and knew they would always tell the truth. He always said: "Children don't have prefabricated judgements or opinions, like 'this has to be good because it came from Michael Jackson', children tell you right away if they like or don't like something." And Michael loved their unbiased attitude. That is why Michael liked to be around children so much.

Thirdly, of course Michael wanted to continue doing charity. But

265

not only in his own country but worldwide. Especially he loved and adored Africa and the people there. Quite early on, before "Facebook" and other networks appeared, Michael already had visionary ideas to use the new media, the internet, to create a worldwide social network, via "Ichat" and other new programs. Through them it would have been possible to teach children in Africa or other disadvantaged areas of the world for free. Michael called it "Schools of America" and wanted to provide the computers and all the hardware, organize teachers and professors who could give lessons via video stream and chat.

Another one of Michael's charity projects was to concentrate on young artists who under regular circumstances would never get a chance at record labels or would only be exploited by them as it often happens nowadays. He wanted to give those unknown talents a real chance, wanted to be their mentor, help them financially and business wise. He wanted to encourage young people to go for their dreams and help them achieve their dreams. He always told me, "I am just a tool, the gift comes from God". That is why he felt that he should pass his success along to others, pass on the gift of talent he had received. Michael started this project with a young girl called Nisha from India with whom he recorded three songs in 2003.

So towards the end of 2003 we were in the final stages regarding the deal with Marvel. Financing was set, contracts were made and only in a few days the transaction would have been perfect and Michael's step into the film industry would have been set. In October 2003 the video for "What more can I give" was finally presented at the Radio Music Awards in Las Vegas and the charity song was close to being released as a single independently from Sony. "Clear Channel Radio" supported us and made the song available for download via internet. It was bound to be a success and raise a lot of money for charity, as "We are the World" did almost 20 years before. Other projects, like a cooperation with "Apple" in which Steve Jobs wanted Michael's silhouette as the design for the new iPod, were also starting to be realized. So especially after our efforts, none of us wasted another thought on the Bashir debacle anymore. We were just working on the very last video Michael had to deliver to Sony Music, called "One more chance", in Las Vegas, when all hell broke loose.

November 18th, 2003 was a day I will never forget. Over 70 police officers raided Michael's beloved home and left no stone unturned. Knowing Michael for many years, I knew that this would rip his heart apart. The hardest thing I ever had to do in my life was to bring him this terrible message. I had to tell him what happened and that Gavin and his family had brought these allegations against him. I will never forget how he looked at me! Never! He completely broke down and just cried.

To him this was the most terrible slander that one can ever imagine. When he got to know Gavin almost two years earlier, he had been terminally ill with cancer and doctors gave the boy not very much longer to live. Michael invited Gavin and his family to Neverland, paid for his medical bills, cared for him but most importantly gave him hope and something to look forward to.

I am quite a rational thinking person and don't believe in such things as miracles. However, during the time I was with Michael I saw several things with my own eyes that came very close to miracles. Michael didn't see himself as a healer or some kind of magician, but he knew about the power of the mind and that it can have tremendous effects on a human being's body. In Gavin's case Michael always told him before he went to bed, "Imagine to eat your cancer, you have to believe you can do it!" At the

267

beginning Gavin was thin, pale, didn't have any hair because of the chemotherapies and Michael had to drive him around in a wheelchair. But after some time with Michael at Neverland, Gavin began to recover and regained strength until his health was fully restored and he remains to be a healthy young man still today.

Gavin's whole family were guests at Michael's home and lived there for months. They had access to the whole property and soon took full advantage of it all. After Gavin was better, him and his family, first and foremost his mother Janet Arvizo, took advantage of Michael's hospitality and finally went over the top with their behaviour. In the end it got so bad that I, as Michael's manager, had to tell them to leave. Of course they were not happy about that. Only later we found out that not only were they unhappy, but tried to take advantage of the whole situation to gain more for themselves. Instead of being happy that her son was healthy again and Michael had paid everything for them, she went to the very attorney who had formerly represented Jordan Chandler in his 1993 accusation against Michael. This attorney declined to take her case, but she was advised to go to the "Child Protective Services", a governmental agency, which forwarded the accusations to the Santa Barbara Sheriff's department, where then district attorney Tom Sneddon happily took the case.

Of course we did not know about all this on November 18th. For us it all came out of the blue, totally unexpected and ripped us out of our future plans completely. Some artists who participated on "What more can I give" no longer wanted to be associated with Michael after the allegations came out. Within moments all charity plans, contracts and business contacts broke apart. Everything came to a halt. Michael's life broke apart. The timing could not have been more destructive!

For about a week Michael was hardly getting out of bed. He

268

was so deeply hurt that he could not find the energy to get up. But after that week his fighting spirit came back. He knew all this was not Gavin's fault, but must have been his mother's idea seeking a way to get money. He knew the boy too well and was sure that once he would look him in the eyes, he would tell the truth. But this moment never happened.

You can not imagine how much Michael had to endure throughout his life. But what always gave him hope and faith in such times were the people who loved and stood behind him and who fought with and for him. Those people were mainly his fans. As he heard about candle vigils in Europe for him, he asked me if I could e.g. fly to Paris and take pictures of the fans there. He drew hope and strength from their love and support, things he so desperately needed then. And that is why he was so thankful to the fans who were always there for him, no matter what happened to him during his life.

After those terrible years, when the trial was finally over, Michael needed time away from where it all happened. So he left Neverland and travelled all over the world to find a place he could call home again, where he could truly relax, have fun and just be himself. He desperately needed such a place but did not find it. So in the end he had plans to return to Neverland after some time of healing. Sadly his manager at that time, Thome Thome, had sold Neverland which made a return for him impossible.

One can say Michael was broken inside, his visions and ideas were shattered and his belief in humanity destroyed through the events. But though they took away what was most important to him, to freely help and give to children, his idea of a "World Children's Day" still was most important to him and remained so till the end.

269

It is sure to say that Michael was a genius, not only in music but in fantasy and creating. Many, especially the media, however, always reported about Michael Jackson being that strange and weird person with crazy ideas. In fact, his ideas were all very ground-breaking and visionary, some might have seemed over the top for people like you and me but they made sense and were all feasible for someone with the outreach he had.

Sadly Michael never got to realize all the wonderful plans he still had for humanity, but he inspired many to follow in his footsteps and continue his work of giving, loving and creating. Michael inspired me so much that today I try to continue his "Go for your Dreams" project by supporting young talents. Like Michael said, so many artists are cheated by the record companies. Once they have a big hit, they are sent around the world to dance and sing and advertise their song, but in the end they only get a very small percentage of the money of the record sale. Once the record companies made enough profit off of them, they drop the artist and find someone new. It's a throw-away mentality. And that was something Michael wanted to avoid and change. So right now I am trying to continue what Michael started and help young talents, e.g. a young singer called "Lucenzo".

I am also working on creating a "World Children´s Day" that Michael always dreamt of and hopefully we can soon start with the project in an African country, namely Kongo.

I will never forget one evening when Michael and I were sitting by the fireplace in the library at Neverland when he told me: "Dieter, it has to be possible that all people on this planet live together in peace and love each other". He often pondered why there were wars and conflicts all over the world and how to stop them. That was his biggest dream, his goal and what he

270

was working and creating for. And one can truly say that he did achieve his goal, he changed the world for the better. That's what visionaries have always done.

Ever After

By Brenda Jenkyns

Illustrated by Kathy Garren

Cover of Brenda's and Kathy's first book "Ever After", which tells Michael's life story

272

FOLLOWING IN HIS LIGHT

by Brenda Jenkyns, Canada

"Did you hear the news? Michael Jackson died today."
I had no idea that this moment would be the beginning of a new life for me. How can a person dying, someone that I didn't know, didn't follow, knew nothing about other than news stories, change my life? I don't know exactly how it happened, but this is what I experienced.

I felt a physical opening of my heart. It was as though I had been struck by love. From that moment on, Michael Jackson was my best friend who I had lost, and I cried for months. During that time I learned everything I could about him, to try to understand who he was and to find out what had happened to me. The more I learned, the more I grew to understand that he WAS love. He had given all he had to give to the world, never holding back, never saying no, and never settling for less than he knew he was capable of. In looking at my own life, I knew that I could not say the same for myself.

Michael cared about people, he cared about the world, and he did everything he could to make a difference and inspire others to do whatever they are here to do as well. I wanted to be a writer, and for the first time in a long time, I started writing. Before I knew it I had written a children's book about Michael

273

to inspire them to do what he had done, and be the best they can be at whatever they love to do.

I met Kathy Garren online and she immediately agreed to illustrate the story. We have become close friends, communicating by email between Canada and the U.S. We have devoted many hours perfecting the story and the pictures in hopes that they will be treasured by Michael's friends, fans and family. The book now can be ordered on Amazon.

I am proud of this accomplishment, because I did it by following my heart and trusting, as Michael showed us in his life. It was scary, but I felt like I was doing what I was meant to do.

Sharing Michael's story, and his message of love with future generations through "Ever After" is the most rewarding thing I have ever done. I now feel that I have done something that will make a difference in the world. Michael loved children, and he wanted every child to have hope and love in their lives, and the story of his life can inspire children to go for their dreams and believe in themselves.

Michael Jackson donated hundreds of millions of dollars to charity during his lifetime. In addition to financial donations, he gave of his time by visiting orphanages and hospitals all over the world. These efforts were not often noticed or mentioned by the media. It is now up to us to carry on his mission to heal the world and do our part by giving of ourselves and our resources. That's why twenty percent of the selling price of our book "Ever After" is donated to children's charities in Michael's name. This is another way that the book is helping to continue Michael's legacy and help children. As of December 31, 2012 we have donated $3,700 from the sales of "Ever After" to charities such as "Free the Children", "Room to Read" and "Dream

274

Street Foundation". I get a lot of joy from donating books to schools, libraries, orphanages and charity organizations as well.

"Ever After" is one of the ways my life has been changed by Michael. He has given my life new meaning and purpose in so many areas. I am willing to say 'yes' to my heart and do and be what I am here to do and be in the world. This has led me to many new and wonderful experiences, new friends, as well as many life lessons that help me to be a better, more loving and compassionate person. I truly care about other people, the planet, the animals, the children in a much bigger way than I thought was possible. Michael's music, lyrics, dance, writing, and the way he lived his life are a basis for a way of looking at life that truly can heal the world, as Michael was determined to do. Now it is up to us to continue his work, and I will spend my life doing whatever I can to help his dreams to come true.

http://www.michaeljacksoneverafter.com
Brenda's and Kathy's new book "Forever Loved" can be ordered via amazon.

ONSTAGE WITH MICHAEL

by Andrew Hudson, USA

In 1996 I was 15 years old and living with my aunt and uncle in Bangkok, Thailand. When the dates for the "HIStory World Tour" were announced, I was first in line for tickets. I had seen Michael previously on the "Dangerous Tour" and had been waiting every day since for him to come back.

Through a friend I knew in Hong Kong, I was introduced to a guy who worked for "Tero Promotions". They were promoting the show in Thailand, and at each stop of the tour, Michael wanted 30 native kids to be a part of the "Heal The World"- and "Earth Song"-performance, and lucky me I was added to the list! It was the most amazing day of my life! Being backstage for that show was mind-blowing and awe-inspiring. I got to see the tank that rolls up onstage during "Earth Song" up-close. It was a real tank (looked very real to me at least) and it sat directly behind the stage in the center, and I believe there was a ramp that it climbed.

I was actually a little older than they usually cast for, but thankfully I was able to convince the promoter guy to give me the spot. I told him I'm a little short for my age anyway, and that it would mean everything to me to have this opportunity. I really sold him on how big a fan I was, and how much of a dream

276

come true this would be for me.

A couple of days before the show I was scheduled to meet up with him at the "Central Plaza Hotel", where Michael and his tour staff were staying. We went over exactly how it would take place, what our part would be and when and where to check in on the day of the show.

In the days leading up to the show, after Michael had already arrived in the country, I joined in on all the hysteria and craziness that happened wherever he goes. All the footage of fans mobbing his motorcade, and waiting for him outside of the hotel, and chasing him around the city. Yeah, we did all that. It was fun, and something that really has to be experienced to understand. Michael drew really big crowds wherever he went. Thousands of people. It was nuts.

"Tower Records" was one of the places he visited, and at one point he went to visit a school for the blind, and we were able to convince a taxi to jump behind the motorcade and pretend like we were part of it, which got us out of traffic (MJ had a police escort everywhere he went) and helped us keep up, since we did not know exactly where he would be going next. I really miss those days, that feeling of getting caught up in the craziness with other fans. I always thought I'd get another chance to be part of that again.

When the day of the show arrived, my dad and I arrived at the venue and checked in where we were told. I met all the other kids who were also going to be a part of this special experience. I think my dad was enjoying this whole thing almost as much as I was. It was definitely a privileged sort of feeling to be there.

We were introduced to a choreographer, I don't recall his name,

277

Michael visiting "Tower Records" at Siam Center, Bangkok

Andrew and other children watching a video from a previous show to learn their parts

but I believe he had a German accent. He lead us all to a large practice room in one of the buildings behind the stage, and he showed us video footage of "Heal The World" and "Earth Song" from previous shows, and explained what our parts would be. At some point, we were split into two groups. The smaller one would be part of "Earth Song" and the larger group would be part of "Heal The World". I was part of the bigger group.

After that we practiced the performance a few times. We had our left and right person who we would be holding hands with during the show, and we all knew the words. After that was done, it was still hours before the show. We were given our backstage passes, which was actually a fabric-like sticker, that we wore on our chests (you can see it in the pictures). And we were allowed to leave for a bit, to eat or whatever.

And then came showtime! Backstage again, we met up with another member of Michael's staff and a few minutes before the show, we were all lead out to the press/security pit where we got to watch the first half of the show. HOLY GEEZ! We're so close, and there's Michael! RIGHT THERE! I can't explain what it feels like to be that close, and seeing this enormous production come to life.

A-M-A-Z-I-N-G

Towards the end of "Thriller," we were told we needed to head back, so we all followed the staff member to the gate that lead backstage. I remember clearly that it was the end of "Thriller", because by the time we got behind the stage, the shadow puppeteers and their skeleton puppets were coming down.

We were lead to one of the wings (I believe it was stage right), and told to stay there until our choreographer (who was actu-

279

ally one of the backup dancers) came and got us. I remember we were right next to a big wall of big foam blocks that looked like speakers. We had a clear view of what was happening on-stage from where we were, and there is nothing, NOTHING like seeing choreography for "Beat It" being performed in-real-life right in front of you. By Michael Jackson. This was unreal. Completely surreal. Needless to say, it was an emotional moment for me. There may have been tears. Tears of joy.

And then it was time for "Earth Song". We watched the tank roll on to the stage, and the scene with the soldier and the little girl play out. Then Michael returned and sang. Beautiful.

And then it was time for the big ender, "Heal The World". You can imagine, I was beyond excited. Probably shaking a bit. I've had a smile on my face this whole time thinking 'Is this real life??'

Our choreographer returned, told us we were on next and to get ready. We formed a line and prepared ourselves. He then came over and grabbed my hand and began leading us out on-stage. I was the first kid out! This was towards the end of the song, so Michael was already out there center stage. He reached out his hand and joined us in a circle as we sang our hearts out, smiles so big across our faces. This was incredible!

We sang as we all walked around the giant earth being shown on the giant screen that was in the middle of the stage. I could see my friends from Hong Kong singing along from the first row.

As the song came to an end, we were lead backstage once again. Stage left this time. It was at this point that the music kicked back in and the refrain from "Heal The World" started

280

Andrew in his Mickey Mouse shirt and other children rehearse "Heal the world"

On stage with Michael

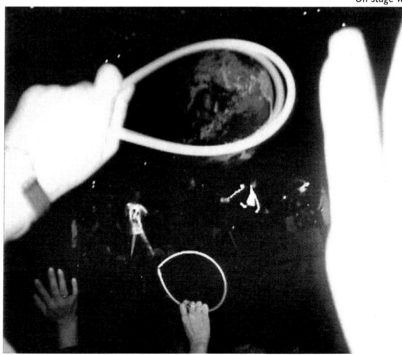

again. Michael was still on stage singing alone. Once we were out of sight, our choreographer friend told us we could run freely back on stage and join Michael in the big finale. We ran back on that stage so fast! We surrounded him, and sang and swayed and danced. And he was right there, singing with us! The King of Pop! This was insanity! Not many people get to experience being next to their idol in this capacity. It was like we were all hanging out, and there just happened to be 100,000 people in the audience watching us.

Michael was happy. He smiled, he laughed, he clapped his hands and gave some of us high-fives or a pat on the head. He was also a lot taller in real life than I though he'd be, and just looked so vibrant and healthy. Most of us (myself included) found it hard to not just stare at him at this point. I was definitely awe-struck, or star-struck, or whatever you want to call it. It was unbelievable.

As the song closed, we all walked back towards stage left, still completely surrounding MJ. Once back there, I'll never forget this, he turned around and looked at us all and he clapped, laughed and smiled and he said "Great job! Great job!". I didn't want any of this to end, but almost as soon as he started clapping for us, someone with a headset and a gray beard came and took Michael by the arm (as there was a show still going on), and ushered him away. He did wave bye to us though as he disappeared in the depths of the mammoth stage.

After that, we were free to go. My dad was waiting backstage for me. He told me he had talked the person who was manning the gate into letting him run out and take a few pictures with the disposable camera he had. They didn't come out that great, but you can definitely make out the big Mickey Mouse shirt I was wearing.

282

I've tried for years to find any video footage from this concert, but this was one of the many shows that were recorded but never released. I'll bet the tape still exists somewhere in his personal archives. I can only hope one day his estate releases it.

Anyway, I wrote all this down after Michael passed away. I miss him a lot, and it feels like a family member has died. I dunno why, but the world feels a little lonelier to me, knowing Michael's not in it anymore.

Be my Guest

by Stephanie Große, Germany

When it comes to Michael Jackson people always think about unbelievable stories and incredible stuff to happen. The public mostly thought of those stories as made up myths for it was too unbelievable to have really happened. That might be the public opinion about Michael, but being a fan of his for many years, seeing him many times on and backstage, travelling and supporting him all over the world, you get to know that things – unbelievable to others - can happen to you from one moment to another. Like this…

I had just come back to Germany from the last trip seeing Michael in Los Angeles for his 45th birthday bash when, after a two-day-recovery from jet-lag, I got a surprising call.

Before I can tell you what was talked about on the phone I have to say that while being in L.A. for Michael´s birthday party, there was the opportunity to participate in a painting contest. All fans could hand in their "artwork" and Michael would choose five lucky winners himself who would be invited as VIP guests (along with people like Nick and Aaron Carter, Ashanti or Mike Tyson) to a charity "Once in a lifetime" event on September 13th, 2003 to take place at his home, the Neverland Valley Ranch.

284

by Stephanie Große

So, back to where I left you… picture me standing in the middle of a copy-shop organizing stuff for my studies while ten other people doing copies next to me - an ordinary day at university. Suddenly my phone rang, showing an anonymous number calling. I answered, "Hallo!?" - of course I answered the phone in German, but somebody replied in English to me: "Congratulations, you are one of the chosen winners of Mr. Michael Jackson´s Artwork-Contest and we would like to invite you to the 'Once in a Lifetime-Event' at the Neverland Ranch, California."

Well, what??? Stop for a moment: Can someone pinch me please? I fell on my knees immediately and tried to sort my thoughts as I finally recognized everybody in the shop was staring at me… embarrassing situation, isn't it? Picking myself up from the floor and coming back to my senses, all I could say was: "Thank you so much, I would love to accept the invitation and I will be there!"

A Once in a Lifetime Event
at
Michael Jackson's
Neverland Valley Ranch

N E V E R L A N D   V A L L E Y

My Dearest Guests,

Welcome to Neverland Valley Ranch. I'm so happy you could all be here today.

I am proud to be involved with events such as this, which bring so much good into this world. I am happy you have come, joining me in hosting this tribute for Romero Britto. Romero is a talented individual, with great reach and a huge heart.

Charities dedicated to helping children in need, uniting diverse groups of people, and those helping impoverished countries, will benefit from your gracious generosity.

Today, you will experience, first-hand, that Neverland is an incredible place. Neverland is much more than my home; it is also the source for much of my inspiration. I am confident that your experience here today will be one you never forget.

Sincerely,

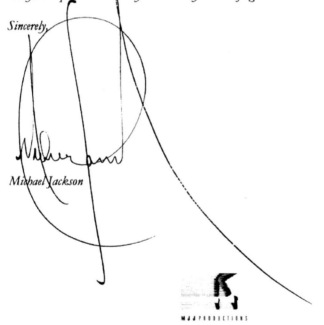

Michael Jackson

MJJ PRODUCTIONS

P.O. Box 6034, Sherman Oaks, California 91413   (818) 905-0386   FAX (818) 905-0389

by Stephanie Große

So here we were, back in L.A. again. It was the day of the party and I was standing in front of the gates of Neverland after getting my Golden Ticket for the event, standing in a row with all the other guests, as they checked everybody via guest list. When it was my turn they couldn't find my name on it. WHAT?!? 'This must be a joke', I thought, 'I travelled all the way and now they can not find me on the list?' I was starting to get desperate. I showed my ticket and tried to explain the situation and begged the man to check again. I even spelled my name: G R O ß E .

I must explain that in the German alphabet we have a letter which is a special form of "S". It is unknown in English spelling and is part of my last name. So they thought "ß" would be a "B". Finally, we cleared up that misunderstanding and I was allowed to enter Neverland through the amazing entrance gate.

It was a beautiful and warm day at Neverland Valley Ranch, which was amazingly decorated for the big charity-event benefitting three different organizations: the "Make a wish-Foundation", the "Oneness-Organization" as well as "E Ai Como E Que Fica", a Brazilian charity chosen by the internationally re-

287

nowned Brazilian artist Romero Britto.

Highlights of the event were the "Songs of Oneness-Concert",
a tribute to Mr. Britto and his art (therefore the Artwork-Contest had taken place), an auction and the assignment of donations to the three foundations.
We also learned about the work of all the foundations:

"Oneness" is an US-American organization fighting against racism, social justice and for a peaceful living together through the
influence of music, art and education. Projects include multicul-
tural concerts and activities after school. Oneness also honors
the work of people that support their goals - especially Michael
Jackson for his countless efforts to unite people of all kinds. The
original members are: Carlos Santana, Sarah McLachlan, Michael
Jackson, Common, Chaka Khan, Brian McKnight and B.B. King.

The "Make-A-Wish-Foundation" fulfils the dreams and wishes
of children with life-threatening diseases. Once again Michael
Jackson was named as an original member.

"E Ai Como E Que Fica" is a charity-organization that works
directly in the slums of Rio de Janeiro to give medical care,
clothing and nutrition to kids living in poverty. Mr. Britto, himself descending from Brazil, was moved to tears by this charity-
event at Neverland Ranch.

It was an amazing experience to join everybody for this important occasion and in this wonderful place full of loving people.
We enjoyed a fun-filled day at one of the most magical places
on earth. We were allowed to roam around freely and enjoy all
food, sweets and drinks as we liked. There was music and entertainment all day long as well as clowns for the little ones. You
could even take a ride in a rollercoaster of Michael's amusement

288

park or take a look at the giraffes and all the other exotic animals at his zoo. By the time it got dark, Neverland really came to life. This place being lit up by lights is simply wonderful.

Late at night Michael entered the little stage and presented the cheque of 250.000 dollars raised by the event to the charities. After that he thanked everyone for coming and said: "In my opinion this is a very special cause, and the cause is our future and the future is our children. I will continue to fight for them for the rest of my life." That was the main reason he hosted that event, to help the children of the world who were always close to his heart.

But that was not the end of this awesome day at Neverland, Michael and us had some more fun. Since Michael's 45th birthday had just been two weeks earlier everybody wanted to celebrate it once more, so to end the day Michael got a "late" birthday cake. Michael, selfless as he always is, wanted to share it with everybody. And while they were trying to figure out how to cut the big cake, someone started shouting "food fight" (I believe it could have been Michael himself *lol*) which in the end turned out to become the biggest "cake fight" I have ever seen. Michael started and smashed a handful of cake right into Aaron Carter's face, he returned the favour and in the end everyone, including Michael of course, was full of cream and cake all over. It was incredible fun. I saw Michael walk past me at the end with still half a cake in his face. It was awesome and the perfect ending for a perfect day for all of the guests, for Michael and the charities who benefitted from the event.

This day leaves me richer with one more experience that I will never forget. Thank you, Michael for making this planet a better place.

by Stephanie Große

My fondest memory here was one night when we had a houseful of bald-headed children. They all had cancer. And one little boy turned to me and said, "This is the best day of my life." You had to just hold back the tears.

How Michael Really Was

by Jacqueline Tas, Holland

During the HIStory Tour in 1996 and 1997 I was lucky enough to become Michael Jackson's personal assistant during his stay in Amsterdam/Holland.

Looking back at it today, it was an extreme time, the whole city of Amsterdam was head over heels. Michael resided at a hotel in the town center. One day we drove, at walking pace, to see the "Dam", the famous town square with its historical buildings. When we arrived there after only five minutes, the security got noticed that Michael wanted to get out for a walk. Seconds later, he indeed got out of his car in the middle of the "Dam Square" and chaos broke loose. But as we were assisted by police and security the situation was under control.

I arranged everything for him, everything that he needed during the period that he stayed in the Netherlands. He came to play three concerts at the Amsterdam Arena in 1996 (and again some concerts in 1997) and the rest of the time I showed him around town.

Many people have asked me, „How is he? Does he always have his mask over his mouth?" No, of course not, he is not wearing it all the time. When you are close to him, you don´t realize that he is such a well-known or famous person. I came to know him as a very nice guy. Very lovely, kind and very considerate.

For example, when he would see a small boy or a girl or parents with kids in the crowd who were in trouble, he wanted to get them out and see that they are alright. Or when parents knocked at the window saying their kid is a huge fan, I knew I only had to ask him and he would love to let a mother and her child in quickly and give them an autograph. He actually, contrary to media reports, was very approachable and open.

A highlight for Michael and for me was the visit at the VU University Medical Center and the Ronald McDonald House in Amsterdam, which was expanding and attaching new buildings at that time and even named a room after Mr. Jackson.

Michael Jackson's management informed me to go and buy toys and presents for a few thousand Netherland Gulden (a few thousand dollars), which I did. Michael then wanted to hand out the presents personally to the sick children at a hospital. Originally he wanted to go there incognito, he didn't want to show off as the big spender, he definitely did not want that.

That is what I really want the world to know. Most people expect celebrities to do those things only for publicity, but that was not the case with Michael Jackson. Actually, I was asked by the director of the Ronald McDonald House if I could get Michael to allow press. For them it is always good to have extra publicity. When I asked MJ's manager he said I should ask Michael myself and try to convince him of this. After my explanation he then decided it was ok to have just one photographer and one camera crew – as long as it was for a children's TV program and as long as I would be able to stop them if it was getting too much. Also we had to make sure that the parents,

292

the hospital and the children would be ok with the pictures and filming.

The children reacted in different ways to him. Some were very shy, which is understandable since they unexpectedly saw someone right in front of them whom they had only seen on TV before. Some of the kids, however, shouted and screamed excitedly, they were just happy and enthusiastic. It was fantastic to be there to watch that. It was so wonderful and touching and one could sense that Michael had a lot of experience in doing things like that. The way he connected to the kids immediately – it all happened in such a beautiful and natural way. One could definitely see and feel his love for children, it was his motivation to do such things.

Beforehand I had promised Michael to quickly ask the mother or the father of each child or the child him- or herself for their name. That way, once Michael came to their bed, I whispered him the child's name into his ear and he would say, e.g. "Hello Johnny, this is for you". That was wonderful for the kids and they felt uplifted and special that someone so famous knew their name. This made the atmosphere very warm and comfortable and there was a feeling of closeness and familiarity instantly.

In general, many always saw Michael Jackson as an unworldly boy who didn't want to be touched or bothered by people. What I witnessed in these days was completely the opposite.

What I will always remember was the last day of his last visit to Holland. The final hours at the airport were extremely hectic and after these last ten days of closely working together Michael ran up the stairways to his plane in a hurry. However, before reaching the top, he stopped, turned around and I saw his eyes were searching through the people standing down on the airfield. After a while his eyes found me and he pointed his finger at me. I was thinking "huh" (in disbelief) while he ran down the stairs again. He came straight towards me and said: "Sorry Jacque", he gave me a big hug and continued: "Thank you so much for everything and see you next year." Then he went up into his plane and flew away. I think that says a lot about how Michael Jackson really was.

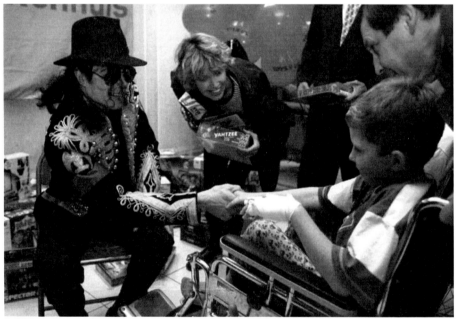

Michael and Jacqueline greeting a boy in a wheelchair at the Ronald McDonald House in Amsterdam.
© Paul Bergen

by Jacqueline Tas

Michael hands out presents and greets children and their families.

© Paul Bergen

Magic echoes over Prague

by Julia, Germany

My story takes place in Prague: It was September 1996 when I decided to attend the world premiere of the "HIStory World Tour" 1996/1997. I took a train from Munich to Prague, where I met some of my friends who had come to the Czech capital a few days before to catch a glimpse of Michael Jackson, who had already arrived to rehearse for the gigantic "HIStory" show.

Michael and his crew stayed at the luxurious "Intercontinental Hotel" in the center of Prague and I was totally excited to see the thousands of fans waiting for Michael outside the hotel screeming and shouting his name to come down and meet them. Some of the fans had wonderful presents like collages, paintings, letters and also flowers to show their love and respect for him, because we all knew that Michael always loved presents and sometimes even came down to collect them with his bodyguards. Suddenly, Michael appeared at the hotel entrance and the well-known Michael HIStery started. He was overwhelmed to see all the fans and their presents, looked at them with fascination and started to collect them. Unfortunately I was too far away to be able to give him my birthday card (it was one week after his birthday) and a present that I wanted to hand over to him, but I was happy to see the smile on his face when he returned to the hotel, carrying lots of presents and looking like a

296

very happy little boy. That was typically Michael, a superstar that could sometimes be so happy about simple things.

After these exciting moments we went to an Italian restaurant at the next corner to have some pizza for lunch and returned to the hotel after a short time, because we didn't want to miss any of Michael's actions. There were rumours that he would do a shopping tour or sightseeing and it was also suggested that he would visit a hospital to meet sick children. As we knew that children were so important to him - and he had asked to visit hospitals in each city on his tour - we believed that he would go to a hospital to meet sick children and bring a smile to their faces. Therefore we asked some native people to tell us the name of a nearby hospital and we took a taxi to the "Motol" hospital before Michael left the hotel.

When we arrived at the huge hospital, it was very quiet and there were no signs that they were expecting Michael. After 30 minutes we were really disappointed and decided to change our plans and take a taxi to the castle to check if Michael was there. While waiting for the taxi, suddenly a van arrived out of nowhere and stopped directly in front of us. Michael jumped out of the car and we were just shocked and paralyzed for a few seconds, and couldn't say anything but "hi". Then we started running after him after we realized what had happened and that it was reality and not our fantasy.

Inside the hospital we asked his bodyguards if it was possible to talk to Michael for a moment, and when they agreed we told Michael that we all came from different countries to see the show, wished him a happy belated birthday, a successful world premiere and shook his hand. Michael said "thank you so much" and "I love you more" with his soft voice, took a bow and walked along the long corridor. As we were at a hospital,

297

A dream came true - Julia met Michael in 1998

we couldn't scream, but we went to a corner to hug each other after these very special moments.

The bodyguards told us that Michael would now visit sick children and that he was very emotional. They also said that if we liked we could follow him through the hospital to give him strength during these difficult moments. We were unimaginably

298

happy to be able to support Michael and to walk along the corridors with him side by side.

Before he entered to sickrooms he took a deep breath, removed his mask and went inside. After a while he came out with tears in his eyes and sadness on his face . He brought some presents for the children and some of them had presents for Michael as well. Meanwhile, outside the hospital hundreds of patients, doctors and nurses wearing their white working coats had gathered to see Michael leave. When he finally stepped out of the hospital they started to call his name and Michael waved before his van drove away. We all knew how difficult it was for Michael to see these kids suffer, but he wanted to give them hope and make them happy just for a short time. We were all very emotional and couldn't believe that we were able to experience something that was so important to him and one of the greatest goals of his life.

Years later, I found some pictures of Michael on the internet that were taken on this special day at the hospital. They showed Michael inside the sickrooms, playing with the kids, singing with them and drawing pictures with a smile on their faces, and I know that I was a part of some very special moments. That makes me very fortunate and proud, and I will never forget any of them.

The night before the "HIStory" concert took place we went to "Letna Park" to experience the soundcheck. It was so amazing to hear Michael's voice during the rehearsals and all the songs he would perform on the next day.

Unfortunately it started to rain later that night and it was getting stormy and cold. So even though it was difficult to leave we decided to return to the warm hostel, while Michael was still

299

by Julia

on stage. When we were lying in our beds, we opened the window and could hear the raindrops on the window pane while Michael sang "Stranger in Moscow" and "Earth Song" again and again, the most wonderful lullabies we could imagine, until we fell asleep.

The echo of his unique voice was above the city of Prague that night and there was lots of Michael-magic in the air. We couldn`t believe how lucky we were to experience that.

The concert was fantastic and spectacular, and Michael demonstrated the world that he was still the greatest entertainer, the "King of Pop", and we also knew that he was THE ONE with the biggest heart for other people, for all who need hope, especially the children.

Almost 150.000 fans from all around the world came to see the show, that was a great success for Michael and another amazing exerience for us. Nothing seemed to be impossible, he became ONE with the rythm, he was pure music and soul.

Michael, thank you for being there and for giving me all the unforgettable moments with you. I hope that your beautiful children Paris, Prince and Blanket will continue with your dream to make the world a better place. You really did.
I will always miss you, you`re my inspiration,
Julia

300

by Julia

What I usually do on my off days...I do as many hospitals as I do concerts. I do as many orphanages as I do concerts. But, because it's good news, the press don't cover it. They want bad news. But I do it from the heart. I don't do it to wave a flag and say, look at me! We bring bags of toys and posters and albums, and you should see how it transforms these kids. They jump up and down and they're so happy.

I WANT ALL THAT RACK

by Wayne Galley, USA

My life has always been quite extraordinary but the experiences I made during working for Michael Jackson as his bodyguard, were surely one of a kind. I got to work for him in 2002/2003 and one of the reasons he hired me, was that I was good with children, being a father myself.

I knew how important it was for Michael to have people around him whom he could trust and rely on, however I only fully comprehended and empathized with his extraordinary situation when my colleague and I were offered sums like 300.000 dollars by paparazzi for just one single picture of Michael's children. This happened not just once and it shocked me a lot.

Michael loved his children more than anything and he wanted them to have a childhood as normal as possible under the unique circumstances his family faces. One occasion I will never forget, was on Halloween Eve in 2003 when he asked me if we could go "Trick-or-treating" with his children. We were in Las Vegas during that time and Michael decided to knock on doors for candies in North Las Vegas, one of the most dangerous areas of that city. Everyone knows that one should not be in that area when it gets dark without security, and even with security and during the day, it can be very dangerous at times. But

302

Michael had set his mind and so we went. His children were dressed as Spiderman and Princess but Michael decided to go as Michael Jackson, dressed in a black shirt and black trousers. I never thought that he would get away with it – but he did! The people who gave them candies admired his amazing "Michael Jackson costume" and he and his kids laughed so much and had a great time.

Being hyped up by the success that nobody had discovered him, he then suggested to visit the "Circus Circus" casino, where they have a carnival-like amusement park with many rides inside. When we arrived, the place was already crowded with people and again I was sure that it wouldn't take long until people would recognize him and chaos would break loose. But again I was wrong. Since it was Halloween Eve and everybody was dressed up as someone else, he and his children could mingle with the crowd undiscovered and again they had a great time. In delight, smiling from ear to ear, Michael rode the ferris wheel for almost two hours and again people admired his perfect "Michael Jackson costume". All was fine until a paparazzi began to take photos of him. My colleagues and I were alarmed. We quickly had to get Michael and his children out before other people might have recognized him, too and either he and his children or other people and their kids would have gotten hurt in the chaos. Luckily everything went fine and he was happy that he and his children have had a chance to spend that evening almost like any other children and parents had.

Michael knew that each child has a unique potential within him-/herself, which only needs to be inspired and cultivated. That's why each week he took one day off for each of his children and would spend that day exclusively with that child. He tried to help them develop special interests and skills and hoped to be able to balance out the unique lifestyle they had to live. But Michael was not only concerned for his own children but wanted the best for all people around him.

I remember one occasion when we were shopping in the Venetian in Las Vegas. Once people heard that Michael Jackson was there, a huge crowd gathered and circled the shop which we were in. We needed to notify the hotel security to help us once he wanted to leave the shop, but even those 40 hotel security professionals were unable to cope with this chaos of people pushing each other to catch a glimpse of Michael. However Michael, being his usual self, was not very concerned about the situation. Through all the hundreds of people, he spotted a freshly married couple from Japan riding with one of the gondolas. Instead of getting out of the crowd as quickly as possible, he turned around and went the opposite direction towards the young couple. The whole security team was confused, but he said that he wanted to take a picture with them and said to me: "Wayne, we can do it!" You can imagine what went through my head at that moment! The couple, of course, was overwhelmed by Michael and couldn't believe their luck. It made their special day even more special and Michael was happy to have made them happy.

Another memory from my time with him in Las Vegas is when we were in the "Caesar's Palace", again shopping. This time he went to one of those trendy clothing shops. Michael looked around and then said to the staff that he wanted to buy "the whole rack of this" and "the whole rack of that". I was standing by and wondering all the time what in the world he wanted to do with all those clothes in all those different sizes and colours. In the end he had bought almost the whole shop and spent more than $400.000. To me it just did not make sense at all, until I heard him talk to his assistant. He told her to let the clothes be wrapped up into little presents and gave her an

304

address of an orphanage somewhere at the east coast of the US. Such events happened regularly. Another time he went to a music store where he bought many instruments which were then sent to an address of a school somewhere.

He simply loved to buy things for others, to make people, who could not afford those things, happy by surprising them - even as his own financial situation got more severe. Most of the time those people would not know who the donator of the surprise they got was. Michael did not want that to be known. He simply loved to make others happy and loved to give and help where he could.

In November 2003, when the allegations against him broke, I was with him in Las Vegas. I was also with him on that private jet that flew him to Santa Barbara on the day he got booked by the police. And I was the one who gave him pen and paper, after he got out of the police station, to write down his horrific experience there. Being a musician myself, I understood that it was essential for him, being this sensitive artist, to transform that trauma into lyrics and songs, so he could survive and deal with it.

After those allegations, everything became different. I would have loved to continue working for Michael, to protect this kind and loving man, but soon his brother Jermaine had arranged the "Nation of Islam" to take over his security issues. Everything changed and I simply found it impossible to work under those circumstances. With a heavy heart I quit the job.

The last night I worked for him we embraced to say good-bye and wished each other well, when Michael suddenly asked his manager Dieter Wiesner to go and get a camera. Michael said he wanted to have a picture from the two of us for him to re-

305

member. Mark Lester, who was also present that evening, was the one who eventually took those pictures of us. For me this was really something very special. I had never asked Michael for an autograph or a picture because I did not want to bother him with those kind of things but then HE asked me! That was really something! A little while later he sent them to me - together with a note from him.

When I heard about Michael's death, I was totally shocked and saddened and did not want to believe these terrible news to be true. During that time I wrote a song for Michael – to transform my sadness into lyrics and music, just like he did when I was with him after he got booked by police. I have not made it public yet but maybe one day I will record it.

I would like the world to know that Michael was a very kind and gentle person. At times he was very quiet and reflective – especially when he created, but he also was a very vibrant personality that could light up a room simply by entering it. I remember him as being a very sensitive person who was always very attentive and never missed to consider the people around him. He was very friendly and treated everyone as a friend. Without exception he treated me nicely, and I think this to be extraordinary given the immense pressure and stress he was under most of the time. He maintained morally balanced even in some of the worst situations, and was indeed a "smart cookie" when it came to business decisions. He simply knew when a good chance came up and took advantage of it. I experienced how much his family loved him - especially his children, who simply adored him. I often told him that. And I am happy and thankful that I let him know what I wanted him to know during the time he was alive.

306

HE BELIEVED IN GIVING

by Markus Thiele, Italy

I am in Michael Jackson's living room at Neverland. Michael is sitting on his sofa and is talking to the Wolfs – a family from Meißen, Germany. Prince and Paris are there, too, and they keep asking questions about the great flood which took almost everything the Wolfs had. We have just arrived in a stretch limousine and are about to explore the wonderful place that Michael calls his home. All of this is kind of surreal! I'm a journalist – how did I get here?

Well, I have to go back a bit further to my humble beginnings. After my studies in Dresden, I started to work for a boulevard magazine called "Brisant" broadcasted by the German TV-station ARD. I was responsible for the short news. One day my boss came in with a "BILD"-Newspaper (THE German tabloid), showing me a story about Michael Jackson's nose, which I was supposed to create a news segment about. As I had learned during my studies, journalistic practice asks for clarification of a story from two sides. So I wanted to find out what Jackson's camp had to say about the story. I called Marcel Avram's office. Avram was the head of MAMA concerts at that time, a company which had organized Jackson's tours in Germany. My call was met by astonishment. It turned out I was the first journalist

307

ever to call and check on a story! They happily explained to me that the printed picture was an unfortunate shot with a shadow which made it seem as if there was something wrong with Michael's nose. They assured me that everything was ok. As this sounded credible to me, I decided to present this information in my news segment. From that moment on I had a very good connection to Avram and his team and got several exclusives.

Sometimes, though, it was not easy to detect which information was private and which was intended for the news. I once put my foot in my mouth when I proudly announced that the HIStory Tour would start in Munich! I just hadn't realized that this information was not yet ripe for decision. And it later turned out to be wrong anyway because in the meantime the highly controversial tax for artists had been introduced in Germany and so no concerts were scheduled for the tour in Germany in the beginning. Fortunately, I could win the trust of MAMA concerts again after this disaster.

As a result, when the HIStory Tour finally started, I was one of the few journalists who had a direct connection to Jackson's team. My colleagues and I were on scene in Prague and followed Michael around the city. Due to the fact that Michael's personal videographer, Amid, could not film when MJ got out of the car as he had to help the children getting out, he finally asked us for our material. In exchange he gave us exclusive shots of Michael inside the car. Because of this trade we were able to produce an inside special which portrayed Michael from a completely different perspective than what could usually be found in the media. We were now deeper in Jackson's circle of trust than ever.

But being that close also meant learning how to live in Michael's environment. First of all there were the car rides. We were

308

inside his convoy now and it felt like being in a conflict zone. Of course MJ's drivers where professionals who could make sure that nobody got in-between the cars or was run over. But there was no professional driver in our team at that time. So it was just a matter of time before the inevitable happened: we knocked someone over. The story was all over the news in no time, having been twisted to suggest that it was Michael's own van that caused the accident. Fortunately, Michael did not blame us for the event and was even nice enough to visit the young man in hospital, where he lay with several broken bones. From that moment on we always hired a professional driver when we were en route with Michael.

Another time, when we were in Monaco, Michael called me up to his room after his security had confiscated all of our tapes. I was a bit worried, but then Michael told me that there was nothing wrong with the tapes but asked me to be more careful with them. That was because in the meantime we had our cutting room always with us to be able to cut videos right on the spot and show them to Jackson for approval. But by now we did not only film and cut material for the news but also for Michael himself, so we had private recordings of Prince and Paris. Obviously, MJ was worried that these recordings would get into the wrong hands and gave me a lesson on how people used every chance to sell him out to the media.

In August 2002 I got a phone call from Dieter Wiesner, who was Jackson's manager at that time. He said he was watching TV together with Michael at the moment and they had seen a report on the flood in Germany. The river Elbe had overflowed destroying thousands of homes and killing several people. Michael had immediately thought of doing something for the affected people, so he had started to sign whatever he could find in his hotel room. Wiesner now wanted me to help them organize an

by Markus Thiele

auction to fund money for the victims of the catastrophe. I told him, I was not sure whether this was a good idea. I was thinking about the last flood in Germany after which Michael had donated a children's playground to help the reconstruction of the flooded areas. The media had not reacted very well on this nice gesture. On the contrary, they had ridiculed Jackson's effort. I was quite sure that they would do the exact same thing with this new endeavor. For them, no matter how much money or how many material things Michael would give, it would never be enough. Dieter and MJ understood my concerns and together we came up with a new idea, which was something that money can't buy: Michael would invite one of the heavily affected families to his home, Neverland. Which better place in the world to forget all your sorrows and problems than Neverland?

In the following weeks I teamed up with the German local TV station MDR, which was mainly reporting in the affected areas, to look for a family we thought were deserving this kind of special present. Our choice was the Wolf family from Meißen, Saxony: Heiko and Susan with their two children Saskia (8) and Sabrina (6). While the MDR prepared a huge show in which the Wolfs would officially receive their present, we prepared the family for what would happen the following weeks; especially we gave them instructions on how to handle the media. It was a bit strange for me to warn people against my colleagues, but from what I had witnessed in connection with Michael Jackson until now, it was necessary.

Finally, it was the big day of the show, in which the MDR also wanted to collect donations for the victims of the flood, among other things by auctioning off the signed material Michael had sent. In this context the Wolfs were given a letter by Michael with his invitation. He had also recorded a message to the victims of the flood: "To the people of Germany: I send my deep-

310

est concerns and my deepest and most heartfelt condolences. You are not alone, I am here in spirit with you. And you are in my prayers. Remember – God is with you. And have faith in the fact that this, too, shall pass. All my love and caring. I love you forever. Thank you." Heiko and Susan were so moved by Michael's empathy, that they started to cry. They did not know yet, that they would meet the King of Pop sooner than they thought.

In November 2002, the Bambi Awards ceremony took place in Berlin and Michael was invited to be honored with a lifetime achievement award. While hundreds of fans from around the world celebrated MJ in front of the hotel, the Wolfs got the opportunity to say hello to their future host in his private suite in the Adlon hotel. Although it was only a short meeting due to Jackson's other obligations, the family was already amazed how human and uncomplicated Michael was. He told them that he was very much looking forward to welcoming the family to his home. My job was basically to translate as the Wolfs did not speak a lot of English. Of course we also did a few shots, during which Martin Bashir kept a jealous watch over us. On a side note: From what I saw of this guy, I already got a little suspicious. At the end of our Berlin trip, he forced us to hand over all our material to him for review – we never got it back!

A few months later it was finally time for us to leave for Los Angeles together with Heiko, Susan and the kids. We started our tour in a stretch limousine visiting Michael's star on the Hollywood Walk of Fame. Then we took the two and a half hour drive to Neverland. As it was not clear whether we would be allowed to shoot any footage inside, I asked my two colleagues to stay behind in our car and take care of our equipment. Together with the Wolfs I entered the main house. Prince and Paris were already there and after a short introduction we

311

Entrance to the main house

Michael's amusement park with the "Spider" to the left, which he called "Puke Bucket"

entered the kitchen to order our meal. Saskia and Sabrina got exactly what they wanted to eat. After our tasty meal, Mr. Wiesner led us to the living room where Michael was waiting.

And here we are, sitting in the comfortable home of Michael Jackson, talking with the King of Pop and his children. Michael is listening intensely while the family recounts the most horrible days in their lives and shows pictures of the flood and specifically their own house. Prince and Paris are also interested in all the details and look pretty shocked by what has happened to the Wolfs. Despite the language barrier the children quickly make friends and start to play. Of course Prince and Paris want to show their incredible home to their new friends, so after about 20 minutes we make our way outside while Michael has to go back to work. He excuses himself and tells me that we will be able to shoot some footage tomorrow.

My poor colleagues come to my mind and I walk over to our car to see how they are doing. They're gone. After my initial shock one of the park employees tells me where they are: the arcade! Michael has a huge gameroom with a collection of arcade games, pinball machines, fortune telling machines, cotton candy dispensers, air-hockey tables and what not. As I arrive there, I see my colleagues being completely absorbed in gaming. It turns out, Michael had shown up while they were waiting, had provided them with food and drinks and had told them to just relax and feel at home.

As we start to explore the area, it becomes clear what an amazing universe of its own Michael has created here – and what an honor it is that he so freely shares it with people less fortune than himself. Especially it is a paradise for the kids. Prince and Paris are eager to show their new friends around. There is ice

Shooting with the Wolfs: In the chairoplane and the train at Neverland

314

by Markus Thiele

cream everywhere, exciting rides, an Indian Village, the zoo, the Neverland train and the staff is always friendly and helpful. In Jackson's own cinema new movies are shown which are not even in theaters yet. Each part of the ranch is designed with love for detail and especially with regards to future visitors; for example there are special dialysis beds in the cinema so that even very sick children are able to watch a movie. We quickly forget the time and enjoy every moment of the day.

While the Wolfs stay in one of the guesthouses at Neverland, my team and I return the next day, this time to shoot a few scenes of how the Wolfs experience Neverland. We try to keep it as low-key as possible and just follow them around because it was Michael's explicit wish that the family enjoys themselves without having to think about being filmed. That is also the reason why the Wolfs have the next two days only for themselves.

We meet again at a recording studio in Los Angeles. This is the place where the final good-bye between the Wolfs and their host happens. Prince, Paris, Sabrina and Saskia spend their time pulling all the colorful cables from the mixer and making a rainbow out of them. The engineer is not amused but Michael loves it! Heiko and Susan thank Michael for the wonderful time they had at Neverland, where they were able to forget all their sorrows. Michael gives them heartfelt hugs to say good-bye. When I look into the faces of the Wolf family, I see how positive this holiday has affected them. They are all-smiles and look relaxed. I don't think any other holiday anywhere on this world could have done this for them so quickly. At this very moment I am certain that we have done the right thing and I am amazed by the generosity of MJ to invite complete strangers to his home. He opened up the door to his home and his heart for this family without wanting anything in return. He of all people was vulnerable; but that did not stop him from giving.

315

Yet a few months later this vulnerability and his generosity were once again disgustingly exploited. There were people claiming that the only purpose of Neverland was to lure little boys. Nothing could have been further away from the truth! Still the media suspected differently and harassed the Wolfs. They even implied that the children might have been molested. Not for one second did they think about the consequences public statements like this had to the Wolfs.

In my time working with and for Michael, I have experienced a lot of the downsides of journalism: lying and cheating colleagues, unfair practices and methods that go against a journalist's professional honor (at least mine). On the other hand, I have witnessed one of the greatest entertainers that ever lived, a man whose simple presence could make fuses blow and lamps burst, whose aura made everyone stop and stare, whose knowledge of how to set himself in scene amazed me again and again, whose music and dance touched millions. But I guess what I will always admire most will be his will to help, to be there for others. Whenever he saw suffering, he immediately wondered: "What can I do to make it better?" And no matter how many times his generosity backfired, he just kept on believing in giving.

by Markus Thiele

The beauty of Neverland

We've been treating Mother Earth the way some people treat a rental apartment. Just trash it and move on. But there's no place to move on to now. We have brought our garbage and our wars and our racism to every part of the world. We must begin to clean her up, and that means cleaning up our own hearts and minds first, because they led us to poison our dear planet.

A BETTER

PLACE

by Talin Shajanian, USA

We all cope with loss differently. My method of coping with the loss of Michael Jackson is helping those he loved most in this world – children.

Michael came into my life at a very young age. His magic and charisma captured my heart and I was instantly drawn to him. Naturally it was his art that caught my attention. I admired him for many years for his talent but then my love for the man that he was grew stronger than the love for his music. Like all other fans, I spent my childhood and teenage years wishing for the day that I would meet him, hug him, and tell him how much I loved him. I was very fortunate to have this dream come true, over and over again.

I had just started High School in the early 90's when I had a few opportunities to see him in person. Living in Los Angeles, I got invited to the taping of "Will You Be There", "Super Bowl", and a few award shows that took place after the release of "Dangerous". Needless to say these were some of the most memorable experiences of my life. The "Super Bowl" halftime show was the last time I saw Michael, until 10 years later…

It was the unfortunate circumstances of 2003 that brought Mi-

by Talin Shajanian

chael back into my life. My love for him and his art had remained the same over the years but without the opportunity to see or meet him. With absurdly false allegations being thrown his way I felt obligated to stand up and support the man who for decades had given so much to his fans and the world.

I became active, joined discussion forums, went to protests, went to court in Santa Maria and made friends with others who were also eager to support Michael and his innocence. These difficult times of uncertainty were accompanied by memorable experiences of seeing Michael on a regular basis and visiting Neverland on numerous occasions. During this time I began to understand who Michael really was, more than I had before. While the world was busy judging him I was able to see and feel the pureness of his heart. I was able to better understand how much he cared and how much he wanted to help others.

It was not a particular incident, discussion, or event that made me realize this. It was just him. His actions, his touch, the way he talked to people, the way he cared, the honesty in his eyes, and his continuous gratitude and appreciation for every little thing that came his way. And it was also Neverland. The purpose and existence of Neverlnad. The feeling of being at Neverland. Complete and absolute magic. There was a beauty about that place that words cannot describe, synced perfectly with the beauty within Michael himself.

I first visited Neverland in December of 2003. It was the "You Are Not Alone" gathering where Michael's friends and family invited people to support him as he came home and prepared for a hard battle. I visited Neverland a few times after that too. The last visit, while Michael was still living there was on New Year's Eve. Five friends and I decided to go to the gates of Neverland to ring in the New Year. Shortly after midnight, while hav-

320

ing champagne at the gate, Michael's car pulled out. His security appeared to be the only person in the car and he stopped to chat for a while. We thought it was odd how he was asking so many questions. He said goodnight and pulled away only to stop a few feet away, stick his head out and say: "Come back tomorrow". Michael hiding in the back seat had asked security to engage in a conversation with us, and as they were pulling off he told him to invite us into Neverland the next day. We didn't see Michael the next day but it was an amazing and private experience at the ranch as we got on a few rides, went to the arcade, and watched "short films" in the theater.

A few years later I had another magical New Year's Eve. 2008 ended with giving Michael a hug and visiting a bookstore in Santa Monica. My friend and I were at the bookstore with Michael and his two security guards. We said hello, had a short conversation about the Christmas gift we had given him, and then gave him space to shop before people in the store realized who he was and started asking for pictures and autographs.

That coming year was filled with unimaginable experiences. The London concerts were announced. When Michael came back from the press conference in London, a few of us waited for him at the airport with gifts, balloons and flowers. He asked us if we were surprised. He was so excited that he had surprised us. Together we were thrilled for what we were about to experience and what the world was about to see. As rehearsals started, I was very fortunate to see Michael regularly. Many times it was a very private encounter with only a few of us present. Other times there were more people around. I cherished every moment, even the times when only his finger tips made it out the window as the car drove past. I never took any of it for granted because I knew our time was limited. Limited because the concerts were around the corner and I was ex-

Talin meeting Michael in May 2009

This autograph was signed on June 25th, 2009 around 1:30am. It is the very last autograph signed by Michael Jackson.
Talin: "Not many people know this, just the few fans that were there that night. I had never asked for an autograph before. I just wanted one to frame and cherish. It just so happened that I bought this picture that week and asked Michael to autograph it as he left for rehearsals on June 24th. When he returned home that night, his security came out and said: 'He's signing it for you now. He wanted to take his time.' A few minutes later, another security came out and gave it to me."

pecting him to be surrounded by chaos in London.

But instead of London, my fairytale ended as our world came to a complete halt in June of 2009.

A few short weeks after Michael's passing, a friend asked me: "How will we survive his birthday? What are we gonna do on that day?" We wanted to honor him somehow but with our wounds so fresh and our hearts in a million pieces, we knew we would not be able to handle a celebration of any kind. I thought to myself: "Children! We need to have a party for underprivileged children!" I knew it was exactly what Michael would've wanted. I shared this idea with my friend and we got to work immediately and started planning. We emailed a bunch of friends in LA and around the world and with their help "Heal the World For Children" was born and we had our first event, the Children's Festival, on August 29th, 2009.

We tried our best to recreate the Neverland feeling. We invited kids from different local organizations to a day of unlimited fun for free. They ate hot dogs and pizza, ice cream, cotton candy and other treats. They played games, won prizes, did arts & crafts, jumped in the carousel shaped bounce castle, learned how to do the moonwalk, got their faces painted, all while listening to MJ's music being blasted throughout the park. Our hearts filled with joy while tears of pain poured down our faces. It was a torturously emotional day, but in the end we all knew we'd done the right thing. We'd made Michael proud.

After the success of this first event, our friends in other parts of the world decided to join in. We laid down the roots of our organization and began to grow.

Three and half years later I'm inspired by Michael as much as

323

ever. It's a bitter sweet feeling each time we have an event. The smiles on the kids' faces make me want to run and find Michael and tell him all about it. This is when I miss him the most but it's also when I feel his presence around me the most.

I have a few reasons for being involved with "Heal The World For Children". One, I adore kids and love helping people. Second, I think Michael came into my life for a reason and the organization is my way of giving back to him for everything that he did for me. And lastly, I want the general public to know that Michael Jackson was such an amazing human being that he inspired others to care for the world and to help make it a better place.

****

Heal The World For Children

Michael Jackson's musical genius and incomparable dance moves will live forever among the human race, securing his position as one of the greatest entertainers of all time. While it's important to recognize and celebrate the artist that he was, it is also important to carry on his legacy. This is how our organization came about. Driven by Michael's message of love, "Heal The World For Children" is operated by his devoted fans who are dedicated to continuing his humanitarian efforts. We are a registered international charity aiming to bring joy, fun, laughter and relief into the lives of disadvantaged children.

It all started in 2009 when we decided to honor Michael on his birthday by hosting a festival for kids in Los Angeles. Since then, our Children's Festival has been our main annual event; taking place on or close to Michael's birthday in many cities and coun-

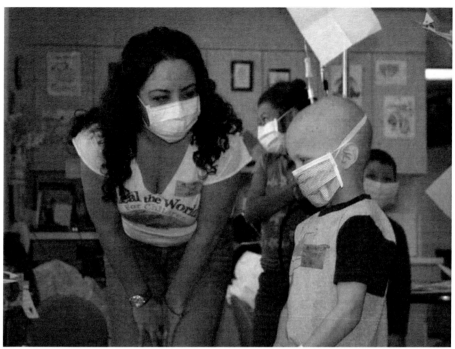

A hospital visit in LA in 2009

An impression of the Children's Festival in 2011

"Earth Day" 2011 - the team of "Heal the world for children" planting a tree

Shipment of goods to Sierra Leone in 2012

tries around the world including Los Angeles, New York, London, Mexico, Romania, France, Italy, Spain and Sweden. At each location we have event organizers who gather up volunteers, raise funds, and invite children with special needs to a day of carefree fun with their families. The kids enjoy Michael's music while indulging in treats, playing games, doing arts & crafts, getting their faces painted, learning how to moonwalk, jumping in a bounce castle along with other fun activities. The Children's Festival is inspired by Neverland - the magical place that Michael created which he often invited children to for the same reasons that we do our events: for a sense of innocent joy and escapism.

We've also visited children in hospitals and brought them toys and gifts; expanding the feel of Neverland to those kids that may not be physically able to come out to our festivals and events. Michael was notorious for his hospital visits and gift-bearing to the children that were sick and shut-in. Mirroring the sentiment of the Children's Festivals, we look for opportunities to reach out to those that often feel left out and left behind by illness.

Michael also cared deeply for our planet, always challenging us to reflect on our own lives so that we may see where we could personally be the spark of change in the world around us. We carry this charge forward with our "Earth Day" Tree Planting events, in which volunteers plant new trees and landscape greenery in various cities around the world. Along with healing our children, we push to heal our planet as well.

In 2012 we started to expand our efforts and reached across the globe to aid Africa. We sent hospital supplies along with some books, clothes and other miscellaneous items to Sierra Leone. Our contacts in Sierra Leone that we partnered with

by Talin Shajanian

for this project received and distributed these much needed items to the hospitals and children of the war torn country. Our global efforts will continue in 2013 as we visit Savong orphanage and student center in Cambodia where we'll provide some living and schooling necessities for the residents as well as throw a party for them in memory of Michael.

Our organization is very unique due to the fact that everyone involved volunteers their time and we have minimal operational expenses each year. This makes it possible for donations to be spent entirely on the children and the events we have for them. We've been very fortune to have great support among the Michael Jackson fan community. The supporting fans, inspired by Michael like we are, provide our main source of funding and have helped make our organization what it is today – an extension and continuation of Michael's efforts to heal the world.

If you want to know more about our charity or you want to help, please go to: http://www.healtheworldforchildren.org

by Talin Shajanian

HE DID NOT HAVE TO DO IT

by Christine Fossemalle, USA

My name is Christine Fossemalle and I own a dance studio in the Santa Ynez Valley. I am a ballet and jazz dancer and teach children. Our dance performance is a non-profit endeavour and we always have to find ways to finance our project.

In the summer of 2003 the time came to plan and prepare for our next dance season and its fundraisers. We decided to dedicate Act II of our performance to Michael Jackson's music as our youngsters – including me – liked his songs, style and rhythm. We chose quite a few of his most beloved songs and created the performance around them. Rehearsals began.

Soon after, the time to plan our auction came. How wonderful would it be to obtain an item from Michael Jackson himself, we thought. So the idea to write him a letter came about. After all, he lived nearby and we chose to honor him, so why not take the chance to try this?

I wrote him about our dance school, our projects and the need to raise funds to make it happen. I did not forget to invite him to attend our performance – just in case – however not really believing that he would consider the idea.

To my greatest surprise, less than a week later, I received a call by a wonderful lady in charge of his scheduling, who told me that Mr. Jackson had gotten my letter and would like to help us raise money by sending us a signed Fedora hat that we could auction off and that last but not least, he would love to come see our performance.

As you can imagine, I got really excited by those news! Knowing that Michael Jackson would come to our performance, it was time to rehearse even more as we wanted to be even better. The kind lady advised me to keep the planned visit private to avoid safety and security issues. A little while prior to our auction, the signed Fedora hat arrived from Neverland and we promptly created a glass case to place it in, to avoid damage, as everybody wanted to touch it.

Sadly, the day prior to Mr. Jackson's planned visit, the lady from his office called again and told us that he unexpectedly had to fly to Florida and was unable to join us as planned. Of course, the disappointment was intense but Michael obviously had thought about everything beforehand. So in the same breath this lady invited all of us, in Mr. Jackson's name, to spend a day

A Special Tribute i

Santa Ynez Valley

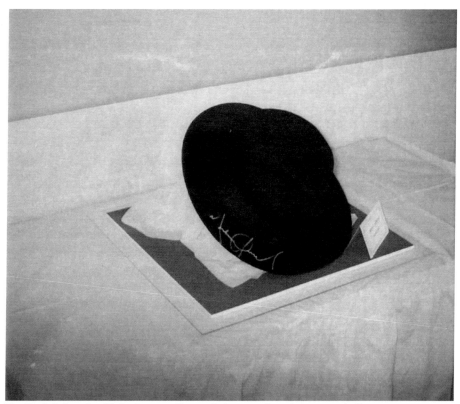

The black Fedora that Michael sent to Christine's dance studio to be auctioned off

MJ letters on stage

ory of Michael Jackson

ing Arts Company 2009

©2009 Christine Photography

at his Neverland Ranch, as a "compensation".

This was unbelievable and we were all so excited! However it took a while to get everything organized, after all more than fifty girls of our dance school wanted to participate. A couple of weeks later, one early morning around 9:00 am, we caravanned out to his ranch and spent the entire day there. We had the time of our life! We visited his zoo and fed his animals. We watched movies in his theatre.

As lunch time approached, we were led to a beautiful spot under magnificent oak trees where beautifully decorated tables were set up for us, each with lovely flowers. An incredibly kind staff served us delicious food with white gloves. While eating, Mr. Jackson came by riding on a Quad, waving at us happily.

We then went on the rides in his amusement park where sweets, popcorn and ice cream awaited us and spent time in his arcade. We were treated like royalties; everything was simply perfect and just for us. It was a visit to remember.

We were all genuinely touched by his kindness. He really did not have to do this, since he had been already so generous in sending his signed hat, for which we managed to get 1200 US Dollars. We were simply overwhelmed and so thankful to him.

During our performance, we had taken pictures of each group performing and so as a token of our appreciation each youngster wrote a few words to Michael and we mailed this huge poster to him.

On June 25th, 2009, I was in rehearsal at the theatre for the whole day. I had not heard any news until some of my dancers came in and told me about Mr. Jackson's death. To put it in a few simple words: We were devastated!

However, soon I felt that I needed to thank him, as he had done so much for us and so we came up with the idea of a tribute for him. The next day we contacted all the dancers to share our plan. We asked anyone willing to participate to join us the next night at the studio. Over fifty youngsters showed up. We only had one week for rehearsal, since the date for our event was previously planned. We worked with dedication and determination to make it as meaningful and special as we possibly could.

"Heal the World" was our chosen song for this tribute. The compassionate lady, who years prior had purchased the Fedora hat at our auction, provided it to us once again. On a stool decorated with dark green silk fabric, here was this glass case with the Fedora hat under the spotlight as everyone could hear the amazing story of our day spent at Neverland. The ambiance was incredible as his presence was felt.

Then "Heal the World" was performed with incredible emotion, there was not a dry eye in the house. At the end, to perfect silence in the audience, the dancers made a procession in the dark, soon they stopped in a shape no one could imagine until suddenly, each individual dancer got a candle out of a glass container and they were lit - the dancers had formed the letters M J. Every evening the whole audience was amazed and many wept. Remembering these facts to write the story bring tears to my eyes all over again.

Michael touched all of our hearts with his kindness and willingness to help. To this day it really upsets me greatly when I witness people talking disrespectfully of Mr. Jackson. Once I tell this story, their outlook changes immediately and I am delighted, I can at least do that for his memory. You know Michael did not need to do all of this for us, the little dance school, but he did it out of kindness and it will never be forgotten.

by Christine Fossemalle

We are Germans. We are Armenians. French, Italian, Russian, American, Asian, African... many other nationalities. We are Christians, Jewish, Muslim and Hindu. We are black, we are white. We are a community of so many differences, so complex and yet so simple. We do not need to have war!!!

SHINING LIKE A BRIGHT STAR

by John Isaac, USA

Back in 1968, when I immigrated to the United States from India with just 75 cents in my pocket to become a folk singer, I would have never imagined that I would one day end up as a photographer working for the United Nations (U.N.).

I travelled to many parts of the world to document wars, famines and all kinds of crisis. Right from the beginning I witnessed unspeakable atrocities. While on my second assignment in Cambodia – covering the slayings of millions in Pol Pot's "Killing Fields" and the Vietnamese boat people – I came across a 13-year-old girl lying on a beach in Southern Thailand having been raped by pirates. All I wanted to do is find a home for her. I met three nuns from California there who were on a rescue mission and asked if they could help. They came with me and took the girl with them.

After returning to the U.S., I told some editors and photographers at a conference about that experience and my desire to help the little girl. They started laughing at me and told me I'd never make it as a photojournalist whose job it was to take pictures, not to intervene.

While covering the famine in Ethiopia in the 1980s, I was travelling in a jeep with my local driver when we came across a starving woman who, unable to make it to a medical facility, had given birth by the side of the road. She lay there naked and helpless, the umbilical cord still attached to her newborn child. I rushed out and covered her with a blanket and ran to a nearby medical unit to get a nurse to help that woman. A television videographer, who had watched everything, had gone back to his jeep to get his camera to video the scene. He was angry that I had covered her, so he confronted me and said, "Why did you ruin my shot?" He really wanted to punch me.

Yet without any doubt I would do the same thing over again. For me, human dignity is more important than making a Pulitzer Prize winning photograph.

In 1994, I was sent to Rwanda to cover the genocide. The Hutu tribe there had been engaged in an organized campaign to wipe out the Tutsi tribe. Between 800,000 and 1 million people were killed. Most were hacked to death with machetes. I first travelled to a refugee camp for the Hutus in Zaire. An orphaned child ran up and hugged me. He told me he had hidden behind a mud pot while watching his parents get killed with machetes. He told me, "You look like my father". He kept telling me that and he wanted me to come back and visit him because he said I looked like his father. In Rwanda, the dead were everywhere. Though I had already seen plenty of death, this was different. I felt I may have reached my limit. I asked myself 'What the heck am I doing?' I was disillusioned. I had been covering one tragedy after another for so many years since 1978.

Once back in my office at the U.N., I couldn't get it all out of my head. My wife had been telling me that I was screaming in my sleep. One day, when I went to work, I had a massive nervous breakdown. I was given medical leave to recuperate. I never

by John Isaac

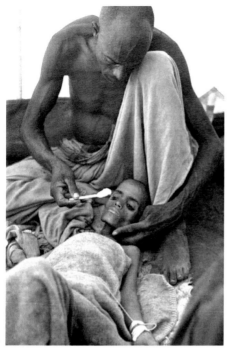
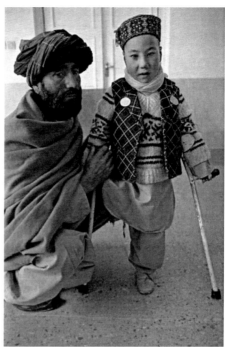

Two of the pictures John took while covering wars and famines. When Michael saw the picture of the Ethiopian father feeding his dying child he started to cry. When he saw the Afghan boy who had lost his limb to land mine he asked, "Why do people do this to little children?"

John in Dogan village, Mali

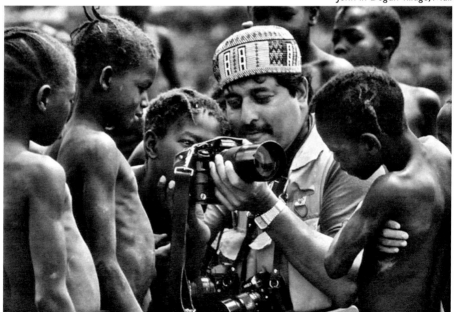

wanted to touch my camera and photograph horrible things again.

A few weeks later I stood on my back porch and saw a large swallowtail butterfly landing on a tall sunflower in my neighbours` garden. I had visited more than 100 countries, including some of the most bio diverse sections of tropical rainforest in the world and had certainly seen butterflies before. But this time, the simple beauty of that scene was especially impactful and it was overwhelming. I ran inside and unpacked my camera and a 300mm lens, and went back out. The butterfly was still there, and it stayed as I shot 36 frames – an entire roll of film. It was like a miracle, like somebody up there healed me this way.

One day in 1996 I received a phone call in New York City (where I live) from a man with a meek, high-pitched voice who asked, "Is that John?". I said, "Yes and who is this?". The voice said, "Michael!". I replied, "Michael who?". "Michael Jackson" was the answer. I was in disbelief and hung up the phone thinking it was a prank call. The phone rang again immediately. This time a deeper voice told me, "I am Bob Jones, manager of Michael Jackson. Why did you hang up on him? He is very upset now." So, I apologized and spoke to Michael. He had bought a poster I created for UNICEF that pictured many children. He loved that poster and wanted me to come to Los Angeles/Neverland and sign it for him. I said, I could sign one and send it to him, but he insisted that I come personally. Three days later, however, Michael and his crew came to the Big Apple to film the "They Don´t Care About Us" short film (prison version) and he invited me and my wife Jeannette to go see the filming of it and sign the poster for him. So we met and I signed the poster for him. I was so embarrassed to sign a poster for him, while he should be signing for me. That's what my wife told him.

338

John with actress Audrey Hepburn. John: "In 1988 one night after dinner Audrey and me were chatting about this and that. I asked her who was her favorite entertainer and without even thinking or pausing she said, 'Michael Jackson of course!' And she asked me, 'Have you seen him live?' I said no.
Little did I know that ten years later I will be photographing the entire 'History Tour'-concerts."

Giving Children a Future

World Summit for Children · 29-30 September 1990 · United Nations · New York

The sunflower and the butterfly that brought John back to life after his breakdown in 1994.

The poster that John did for UNICEF which Michael wanted him to sign.

Some of John Isaac's amazing shots of animals that he showed Michael when he met him in NY and showed him his work.

The next day he asked me to spend the evening with him at his hotel in Manhattan and I showed him my humanitarian photographic work. Michael started to cry when he saw some of the sad pictures. He said he loved my photography and that I should continue to use it to help children around the world. He knew how much I care about children.

After that he took me to Brazil where they were finishing the video "They Don´t Care About Us". It was my first trip with Michael, we were flying on a private jet. It was then that he said something I'll never forget: "John, be my eyes and show me everything that I cannot see". So, while they were filming, I went and made lots of photos of children in the slums of Rio de Janeiro and Salvador.

Michael was very appreciative of my concern about children around the world who needed help. One day he said, "You and I come from the same place".

When the "HIStory Tour" started in Prague, Michael asked me to photograph him on stage while he was singing "Heal the World". He wanted me to go onto the stage with him and the children. My knees were shaking as I stood in front of thousands of people in the spotlight. In the end though, I really enjoyed travelling with him and meeting fans around the world. I must say that I met many fine young men and women and I am still friends with many of them. Michael would not have been who he was, if not for all the wonderful fans who loved him so much.

As exciting as it was to see Michael Jackson on stage, being next to Michael when he visited hospitals and orphanages was something especially touching and meaningful. I remember we were in some Eastern European cities and were visiting many

341

by John Isaac

hospitals with terminally ill patients. One evening, after such a hospital visit, Michael was sobbing in his hotel room feeling sorry for the kids who will die in a short time. I was very touched by his compassion.

When Prince was born, I was asked to photograph him exclusively for magazines. This time I was invited into Neverland. I had the privilege to take pictures of his little baby-son Prince Michael and his father. I´ve been to Neverland twice, drove around in an electric car, saw movies at the theater and rode the train. I felt like a kid myself every time I was there.

One evening we saw a movie together in his private theater. Michael was very philosophical, he often talked about philosophy and life. He asked me to tell him about the children I had photographed around the world while I was working for the United Nations - many stories of pain and suffering and about the different kinds of people and children I have met. Michael was always very compassionate towards the less fortunate children. His message was that children should not suffer. Therefore, we all should get involved in giving to the children of the world who need our help. He said, "John, there are people who get a lot of joy when they get gifts and things from others - and there are people who love to give to others. I want to be the second kind."

Everyone knows Michael Jackson as the superstar, a great singer and performer, but many do not know that he was a very kind man, full of compassion towards humanity, especially the less privileged children.

Michael had the idea of doing a book with me for the children of the world. His wish was that I was involved in this project and took pictures of the children. I accompanied him when he

342

visited several hospitals and child care centers where children were suffering with terminal illnesses. He would actually cry for these children and wanted to help them so badly.

To me, Michael was like my younger brother, I really loved him. I wish he was still here and I would tell him not to worry about what others thought of him and to carry on doing what he does best, to help the children and heal our world. Yet, I know he is still up there, shining like a bright star. Every time I see a clear sky at night I see Michael.

John with Michael

343

He would not hurt a Fly

by Howard McCrary, USA

The first time I met Michael was in the summer of 1979 when my family, "The McCrarys", was on tour with "The Jacksons". My sister Charity introduced me to him with my brothers Alfred and Sam at a swanky Texas house party. Michael asked me if I was married and I told him I was separated from my wife and we were going through a divorce. That's when he folded his hands and said, "I will be praying for you."

I will never forget when I had the joy to work with Andraé and Sandra Crouch on Michael's "Dangerous"-CD at "Westlake Studio". We were recording the background vocals on "Keep the Faith" and as Andraé was conducting, we came to an impasse for over 20 minutes until Andraé turned to me and said, "Howard, fix it!" So I gave out the parts to the ascending figure of the word "faith" leading to the release. And Michael jumped up and down in the control room saying, "I love it!"

Seth Riggs is one of the dearest friends of my life. He was Michael's voice coach for over 31 years. He coached Michael through "Thriller" and toured with him to keep his voice in top condition. I remember one Christmas when Seth called me at Michael's request and asked me to arrange a choir of twelve children to sing at his home on Christmas morning. I

344

Bruce Swedien (left), Michael and The McCrarys

called my sister Charity and we contacted twelve of the best singing kids we knew, of course some of them being our own family members. We had less than 48 hours to rehearse and coordinate this private production before the children got into the limousines from my home in Sherman Oaks to be conveyed to Michael's hotel in Beverly Hills. Seth proudly was there that morning to vocalize all the young ones as I conducted as the children sang "Heal the world", "Silent Night", "Santa Clause is Coming to Town" and other songs on Michael's staircase. He and his children sat in the grand foyer and listened. His children looked like cherubs. Michael was such a loving father. Combined with the Cathedral like acoustics I could hear additional voices of angels that morning. It was a sacred moment for us all.

Michael hugged Charity, Seth and me to thank us and afterwards we enjoyed the Christmas buffet together, which Michael had prepared for all of us. For these children it was a Christmas dream come true. I could never understand how the press could be so ruthless towards him. He was an angel.

When Michael had an audience with Pope Paul, he brought Seth along with him. While they were waiting to meet with his holiness in the outer chamber, a fly came into the room. It skilfully buzzed so freely around them with childlike freedom when Seth was so annoyed that he couldn't take it any more and took a magazine and killed it on the spot. With tears in his eyes Michael asked, "Why did you do that?" Seth retorted," It was just buzzing around here, getting on my nerves!" Michael answered him like a Zen Master and said, "He was enjoying his freedom and living his life, and you ended it!" From that day forward Seth understood, and he took on a deeper appreciation for all life because of Michael's compassion for a fly.

This is the best story that describes the heart of Michael Jackson that I ever heard. If Michael could care for even a fly sympathetically, how much more for a human being, children, animals, the environment, and his fans, friends, and family? This is especially to those who accused him with horrendous allegations that he could never do in a million years.

When he went to trial in Santa Maria and it seemed like the whole world had turned their backs on him, I never stopped believing in Michael and the pure soul that he was. We brought ten busloads of ministers and some of their members to support Michael during his trial at the courthouse. We had singers singing on behalf of his innocence and ministers interceding on his behalf of justice. To thank us, Michael graciously hosted all of us at Neverland.

It is an outrage what some people will do for money. Greed, delusion and anger is something Michael want-

346

ed to see our world healed of. But it's not too late. I know there are others like myself who believe in Michael's dream that we can have a better world if we only keep the faith.

For each of us our life should serve a purpose. I truly believe that Michael Jackson came to teach us how to care. He did with his every breath. This is one man I have met in my life that wouldn't hurt a fly.

Michael, you and your music, your smile, your dance, but most of all your message will live in our hearts forever. You not only are "The King of Pop", you are also "The King of Hearts".

by Howard McCrary

SURPRISE IN THE MORNING

by Nancy Crabtree, USA

My name is Nancy. I live in the Santa Ynez Valley, where Michael Jackson once had his beautiful Neverland Ranch. I'd heard Michael's music, of course, beginning way back when he was part of the Jackson Five, and knew he was a star, knew he lived nearby, but never gave it much more thought than that.

One early morning, while still in bed, my husband and I were awakened by our ringing doorbell. Wrapping myself in my robe, I ran to open the door, presuming to find one of my husband's co-workers. To my shock, there stood Michael Jackson. He smiled broadly, as if I should be expecting him. I said his name aloud, several times, looking at him for verification that he was indeed who I thought he was. He nodded, continuing to smile knowingly at me. Still confused, I looked around. No photographers, no crowd, no commotion. Just a lone vehicle and driver sitting in my driveway. Once more I looked at him, simply asking "Michael Jackson"?

Seeing that I was still confused, Mr. Jackson asked whether he was at a certain home. I said no - realizing though, that I recognized the name, and knew they lived in the neighborhood. He apologized profusely for disturbing me, explaining that he had planned to visit this family whose son was sick with cancer,

348

hoping to cheer him up. He had arranged the visit with the child's mother, but it was to be a surprise for the young man. He applogized again, as obviously he had the wrong address!

I offered to look up the correct address in the phone book, and opened my door widely - not sure whether he would consider coming in. But he did. Meanwhile I rushed back to the bedroom to rouse my husband. I simply told him to "get up now". I didn't tell him that it was Michael Jackson at our door. He ambled to the kitchen to see what was going on. His reaction was much the same as mine. He simply said "Michael Jackson" over and over, in amazement.

While I looked through the phone book for the correct address, Michael walked comfortably around our living room, noticing this and that, running his fingers over a few piano keys and asking about photos of my little daughters (who were by then grown and away at college). I was struck by how graceful - almost cat-like he moved. Then he went into the kitchen where my husband had started the morning coffee. They chatted briefly while my excited fingers finally found the correct address, which I wrote down and gave to him, along with instructions for finding the house. He thanked me again, and again apologized profusely for disturbing us, and then went on his way down the road to bring the surprise of a lifetime to an ill child.

I was very impressed by his politeness, his graciousness, and his grace, and thought how fortunate I was to have had a chance to see Michael Jackson as he took time out of his day to bring hope and excitement to the life of a sick child.

349

Our goal is to change the world and change world consciousness about children, the ecology and the planet, to make it a better place for everybody, starting with the children. That's the future we live, and I'll stick with it forever until it's done. It's forever. It's not a publicity stunt, it's not something that I'm trying to use as a vehicle to launch a single or an album, it's something that's directly from my heart.

HE LOVED MORE

*by Brigitte Bloemen, Marina Dobler, Stephanie Große &
Sonja Winterholler, Germany*

In the beginning we were deeply shocked about everything that
unfolded in front of our eyes and could not believe that Michael
would indeed have to endure such accusations, slander and pain
for a second time in his life!

Although those accusations were ridiculous and obviously fabricated, accusing him of such a terrible crime like hurting a child
and making the whole world believe it, thanks to incompetent
journalists, was the most terrible thing they could have done to
him. We knew it literary ripped Michael's heart apart, especially
when he had to realize that so many of his so-called "friends"
had abandoned him in this time of need and even many fans
were not so sure what to believe and preferred to keep low-
key until things would clear up.

However we knew that we needed to do something - anything
to show him that there are still people out there who do not
believe what was said. So as soon as the date for the first arraignment in January 2004 was set, nothing could hold us back
from traveling to California to support Michael.

Once in Santa Maria we were shocked to see like an army of

by Brigitte, Marina, Stephanie & Sonja

police, helicopters flying above the court building supporting the crazy media circus with about a hundred journalists from all over the world and several hundred onlookers that besieged the place. It was a chaotic scenery, to say the least. We were very relieved as we saw familiar faces of fellow fans standing behind crowd barriers with messages of love and faith to morally support Michael on this terrible day.

When Michael arrived and walked into the building, we thought he looked strong, determined and confident and he even amplified our impressions on his way out by greeting fans along the barrier and finally even jumping on top of his SUV for everyone to see him. To be honest, we were elated to see him like that and it indeed eased our worries for him a little bit. Our hearts, however, knew better, they couldn't be fooled by our eyes' impressions.

After the court proceedings, the crowd headed for Neverland, because word had spread that Michael would open his ranch for the public that day. Thousands of people took the opportunity to finally satisfy their nosiness and enjoyed a day in his amusement park, his zoo, his arcade, they ate and drank as they wished and just took advantage of the opportunity to snoop around Michael's home. Obviously most of them simply had a great time.

However we fans felt very different. Michael once said: "Neverland is me! It represents the totality of who I am", so to us it appeared as if Michael felt that he needed to strip himself naked, to turn his inside out for the public to see and finally understand him. The feeling we had at the ranch that day was a very sad one and to us Neverland had not much to do with the magical place we had experienced before. The fact that the press was besieging the place did not help much either – he-

352

Banners from around the world in front of Michael's home

Stephanie, Sonja, Marina and Gitti (from left to right) in front of Neverland

In the spirit of love and togetherness

Michael Jackson would like to invite his fans and supporters to his Neverland ranch. Please join us Friday, January 16, 2004 from 11am - 2pm. Refreshments will be served. We'll see you there!

Directions:

From Santa Maria. Take Highway 154 east about 4 miles and then turn left on Figueroa Mountain Road and drive 5.25 miles. You will see the grounds gate on your left hand side. You must have your driver's license or some form of official identification (passport) to get onto the ranch.

Invitation to Neverland after the first arraignment

Heart formed by tea candles in front of Neverland

licopters were flying over Neverland all the time and outside waited dozens of cameras as well.

A few days later most fans were on their way home. For some reason that had to do with the prize, we had booked our flight home a couple of days later than the others and so we suddenly were the only ones left. Although we made little trips to nearby sights, we came back to Neverland's gate every day, to at least be closer to Michael for the short remaining time of our stay.

From the outside Neverland was back to normal, however inside the place had been defiled and its spirit destroyed. Like all other fans who cared, we so badly wanted to help Michael - to make it easier, to make him feel better - but we had no idea how to achieve that. We wrote letters of support, made some cheer-up presents and tried to forward those items to him through his security guards.

One afternoon we were sitting in the grass nearby the gate when one of Michael's brothers drove out of Neverland. Since we were eating at that moment, we did not pay too much attention to him, but when he stopped his car and waved to us, we eventually stood up and walked over to him. We said "Hi" to each other and asked him how Michael was doing. He answered that he was "OK" - according to the circumstances, but we did not miss the sad undertone in his voice.

So we asked if he could hand Michael some cheer-up presents from us, but he simply answered that we could do that ourselves. Of course we were confused now, as he quickly continued that Michael would drive out of Neverland the next day, early in the morning, and if we would be there, he would certainly stop for us. We were speechless to say the least and thanked him for his kindness to let us know about it.

by Brigitte, Marina, Stephanie & Sonja

Of course we were very excited now and wracked our brains what we could say or do for him to cheer him up. Needless to say we had an almost sleepless night ahead of us. The alarm clock woke us up in the middle of the night and not much later we were on our way to Neverland. When we arrived there and parked nearby the gate, at our usual parking place, we realized that the security guards were in highest alert at first - because of us arriving there in the middle of the night. They later told us that it was very dangerous out there at that time, especially at night because crazy people, often with racist background or drunk, drove by the gate of Neverland at night and threw or shouted nasty things in their direction. They were scared that one day someone might even shoot at them or try to break through the gate with their cars in order to harm Michael. So it is very understandable that they were very relieved once they recognized us as simply fans.

It was dark and really cold that night and we even had to re-move a layer of ice from the front shield of our car. We had brought many tea candles with which we formed a heart on the side of the driveway, then we prepared our presents, our letter and repeated what we wanted to say to Michael so we wouldn't forget in our nervousness.

Time went by and nothing happened except from us getting frozen. We already thought that Michael's brother had made fun of us, as suddenly headlights of a big vehicle, coming out of Neverland, could be seen coming towards the gate. At first we were unsure what kind of vehicle it was, but soon we recog-nized a big bus slowly rolling closer. Only very slowly it dawned on us that this bus might have something to do with Michael. Absolutely transfixed we stood next to our candle heart and saw the bus stopping for a moment before the gate opened.

356

The two guards walked next to it as the bus rolled through the gate towards us. The next thing we saw was the bus door opened and Michael's assistant walked over to us and asked us if there was anyone from the press here. After we denied, she told us to come with her. Because of our shock and nervousness we hesitated for a moment. Then we saw her going in the bus and as she came back out again, she told us that each one of us could go in – separately.

"Separately!?", we all spoke out loud. We could not believe all this was real. It was, of course, not at all that we did not want to meet Michael, on the contrary, but we had expected a totally different situation, with him driving by and opening a window – something like that. But to walk into a bus, one by one and to have a private moment with him there, was overwhelming for us and each one of us felt unprepared for that.

Our friend Stephanie, who had not heard what Michael's assistant had just told us, came closer to us to hear what was up, and so without a second thought, we told her that she was the first one to go inside to meet Michael. She had no time to disagree…

<u>Stephanie:</u> *So I was the first to enter the bus. I climbed up the stairs and with the last two of them I tumbled to Michael's feet - feeling embarrassed to my bones. While getting up I did not recognize Michael had come closer. When I lifted my eyes, he stood right in my face - nearly tumbling backwards I looked straight into his "eyes" - being in a state of shock all I could say was: "Hi." He replied with a "Hi" as well and kissed me on each cheek. I was trying to remember all these smart sentences we had come up with earlier and even brought to paper, but they didn't come back to my mind. Having this silence around us, Michael frowned his forehead trying to figure out what I might be thinking. Feeling caught, I remembered that a few*

357

b y Brigitte, Marina, Stephanie & Sonja

days ago security guards of Neverland had come out to pick up all the presents that fans had wanted to give to Michael. To support him, me and my siblings, who are hard of hearing, had made a big banner with a sentence in sign language that said "We believe in you". This banner had been among all the presents given to Michael a few days ago. While standing face to face with Michael now, I asked if he had got those presents. He confirmed it and so I asked him if a banner had also caught his attention. He thought about that for a moment and slightly something came to his mind: "Yeees". I jogged his memory by interposing that the banner contained a sentence written in sign language. This made his memory clearer and he re-called: "Oohh yeees!" I asked him if he understood the meaning of the signs. He simply said: "No". Of course I offered him the explanation: "We believe in you!"

He directly fell into my arms and hugged me strongly. I took the opportunity to thank him for being the person he was and being moreover an inspirational influence to so many people, especially to my hard of hearing-siblings. Listening to music is very unusual for them and nothing we can imagine. Everything sounds exotic to them and can not be compared to noises we can differentiate. We are blessed to be able to enjoy Michael's music and all noises around us effortles. Being touched by his art and feeling deep love and admiration for him, they trained very hard by listening to his music over and over, focusing on little details and trying to recognize recurrent elements such as single words. Reaching this level of training, it automatically had an influence on their daily life, for example school-life became much easier for them - still today it helps them to orient themselves better in the world of hearing persons. To hear this, Michael felt overwhelmed and we shared another emotional moment by embracing tightly and for a long time. This was the moment when I felt this is no longer a one-sided support from us fans to Michael – he also needed us around him to take heart from stories such as mine. He supported my feeling continuing with the words: "Tell all the fans that I love

b y Brigitte, Marina, Stephanie & Sonja

them very much and appreciate their support all over the world. You are all very special to me and I need you." Regarding the aggravating circumstances of the time, he added that those responsible for him being in this horrible situation "want to destroy me" and that "it is all a big lie and not true!". He intensively appealed to me to come back and support him. I guess there are no more words required to grasp the deep relationship between Michael and us fans excluding barriers and including an equal status as family to him - having this experience on my back, I left the bus a different person.

As Stephanie climbed down the stairs of the bus again, Sonja was to be the next one of us to meet Michael. Hesitantly she walked up the few stairs...

<u>Sonja:</u> *And there I suddenly stood – right in front of Michael stupidly saying "Hi Michael". I tried so hard to remember the questions we had prepared and I had written down to ask him if possible, but now in this very moment, everything was gone. The only question that came to my mind and that would also make sense in this situation was "How are you?" – and so I asked him that. Michael just stood there and didn´t answer. He didn´t even look at me, but held my left hand with both of his hands very tightly. He then leaned over and kissed me on each cheek, but still he did not say a word. I was a bit confused and didn´t know what to do. So the next thing I asked him was "Are you fine?". He finally looked directly at me and bursted out: "No!" And he continued while squeezing my hand: "I just pretend to be fine, but I´m not – I´m not." In the same second, he hugged me very tightly and I realized that he was crying. Oh my God, now I began to understand why he hadn't said anything before. He had tried not to lose his poise and not to cry, but my questions didn´t help…*

We stood there for quite a while just hugging each other. Michael sobbed a few times and I felt that he was shaking, although it was quite warm inside the bus. It took me at least half a minute to really

359

understand that in this moment Michael was hugging me, crying and just showing and telling me his true feelings. Until this moment I had thought he really would be that strong and positive about the upcoming trial, like he had shown the public at the first arraignment a few days before. How naïve I was! Of course, he was scared and of course he was hurt as much as one can be, facing these terrible allegations, when all he ever wanted to do was to help this kid, as he had helped so many sick children before and after that. Given these thoughts and feeling him shiver, I also had to fight with the tears. But then Michael kept on telling me that the fans' presence at the court helped him so much and that we should tell all the fans to come back to the trial and support him. "It means so much to me!" – and he continued: "Go on the internet and tell all the fans that I love them sooo much!" He said that directly into my ear for we were still hugging each other. Although he was still sobbing between the words, his voice sounded so soft and wonderful. I said to him that we will tell his words to the fans and that many of us would love to be there for him all the time, but live in Europe or somewhere else – I also mentioned that we are from Germany – and that it is hard to make it to all court dates. I only wanted to explain, why we or other fans could not be there every day, although we would so much love to and I think he understood what I meant. He just said "I know" and squeezed me very tightly. In this moment I felt that this was the most emotional hug I´ve ever received or given to someone. Now it really didn´t matter who he was or who I was – it was just two people embracing each other. It was amazing. Overwhelmed by emotions I couldn´t contain myself and said "I love you so much". After holding this BIG hug for a few more seconds, both of us at the same time finally let go.

I was so confused that I almost went out of the bus without saying or doing anything else, when I remembered that I had a little Bavarian flag on which we had written "Munich loves you" for Michael. So I once again turned towards Michael and said "Oh, and this is for you".

360

He took the flag with his big hand so that it almost disappeared in it and answered "thank you". Then I finally turned around and tried to walk down the stairs with very shaky knees.

As white as a wall, Sonja came out of the bus and Marina was the next one to climb up those stairs.

<u>Marina</u>: *The sight of Sonja had made me feel insecure, not about meeting Michael, but about the emotional toll it might take. I stopped when I saw Michael waiting at the top of the stairs, looking towards me.*

Sheepishly I said "Good morning, Michael" to him. At first he just looked at me not moving at all. It seemed he wanted to say something but after a few moments, he suddenly took my hands and pulled me up the two remaining stairs, kissed me on each cheek and embraced me tightly. In that moment all the pent-up tension, all the fear and sorrow for him, all the concern, all the sympathy but mostly all the love for him finally unloaded and tears streamed down my face. "I love you so much, Michael!" were the only words that came out of my mouth. Now Michael could not stay composed either, even though he had tried so hard, and so he broke into tears as well, while saying "I love you so much more". He embraced me even tighter than before, trying to console me by caressing my head and back.

We both couldn't stop crying and it seemed to escalate more and more. I felt and experienced in those moments, how totally upset, deeply hurt and broken Michael was by all the terrible things that went on in his life. He was not at all confident, as he had tried to show the world a few days earlier at the court building in Santa Maria. At some point Michael began to tremble from top till toe. It was so obvious that he desperately needed people in his life that he could lean on and trust and who believed in his innocence. For quite a while we simply held each other sobbingly, when he suddenly with

361

a broken voice said "...you know they hurt me so much with this, they try to destroy me..." His whole body shivered badly as he said those words and I helplessly tried to console him as best as I could by caressing his back, yet found no words of consolation, because I knew the situation he was in was just terrible and to claim anything else would have been a blatant lie. "I know..., I know..." was all I could stammer and again we both had to cry so much, that we could hardly breathe. It felt like Michael was drowning and desperately tried to grasp at straws when he embraced me even tighter, it almost hurt. Yet in this moment of deepest desperation, he now tried to speak again, almost voiceless from all the crying, he croaky whispered in a desperate and beseeching way "...but we must heal the world and help the children". The way he uttered those words worried me more than anything, because they held a feeling of "Goodbye" in them, as if he tried to indicate that he would not be here with us for very much longer and needed us (fans) to fulfill his mission.

Instinctively I answered: "Oh, we will - but we will do it together with you, Michael!", trying to tell him that we all need him so much. By these words he literally broke down again and sobbed so badly that I needed to hold him up, in a way, and keep the balance for us both. Again we cried so much and it took quite a while until Michael suddenly found the strength to pull himself together. I tried to follow his example and both still shaking and our faces wet from each others tears, we finally said Goodbye to one another, before I shakily went down the stairs again, feeling completely worn out, heartbroken and empty.

<u>Brigitte:</u> While Marina had been up there with Michael, I only dared to glance up once briefly to make sure I heard correctly, and indeed Marina and Michael were in each others arms and it sounded as if they were both sobbing. It was dark and quiet piano music was playing in the bus. I was still shaking and freezing because of the cold, but also because of being so nervous and not knowing what to

362

by Brigitte, Marina, Stephanie & Sonja

expect now. So, I continued trying to distract myself and kept talking to Michael´s assistant, who was standing next to the bus driver's place. I told the assistant some stories about why we were still here, that we came for the arraignment, but booked our return flight later since it was almost half as expensive.

While still talking, I heard Marina moving in my direction, trying to get past and down the stairs out of the bus. Without saying a word and looking not like herself, Marina pushed past me and almost tripped and fell down the stairs. The state Marina was in and the sound of sobbing I had heard before scared me a little bit, to be honest. So I tried my best to play for time, but after I held Marina a bit and helped her out of the bus, it was my turn.

Shyly and slowly I climbed up the stairs towards Michael, still avoiding to look up at him. I did not want to look him straight in the eyes, not to embarrass him and myself, so I just held out my hand towards Michael to say "Hi". But before I could say a word, he grabbed my hand and pulled me towards him and immediately hugged me tightly. I was kind of hanging there, about two stairs lower than where Michael was standing while he was pulling me closer and closer. There was a small barrier in the bus to define a place behind the driver and prevent people from falling down which also had a handle for people going up the last stairs to hold on. And since I could not climb up all the stairs for Michael had grabbed me before, I happened to have this barrier directly in my stomach which was not very comfortable, especially since Michael was pulling me against it real hard and was not letting go.

Anyway, so early in the morning, being tired, frozen, nervous and confused, your senses are working quite selectively sometimes — so I managed to forget having this barrier pushed into my stomach after mere seconds. It was only after a while that I realized how warm Michael felt and that he tried to warm me up by rubbing my back with

363

b y Brigitte, Marina, Stephanie & Sonja

his hand. He must have felt me shaking like crazy. The sound that the rubbing on the jacket made finally "woke me up" and I could feel Michael was also shaking a bit and he was weeping on my shoulder. We both stayed like this for at least one or two minutes without saying anything. Then, I heard his voice whispering in my ear: "Go on the internet…". As I said before, I was not completely myself then and there, and I just heard something about the internet, and was wondering, what he is talking about. However, after finally concentrating and probably telling my ear to listen, I could hear him go on: "Go on the internet and tell them all, tell all the fans I love them so much and they should come next time to the court! It´s SO important to me!" Having said that, Michael pulled me even harder towards himself. I could barely breathe, but I responded: "I promise they will come - it meant a lot to us as well" (meaning it made us feel better, too, to be finally able to help and support him and to give back to him after he gave so much to the world for years). After that Michael started to cry again. I felt kind of helpless and confused, I was shaking and sobbing, but could not really cry. It felt more like being in shock, I instinctively started rubbing his back as he did before. He hugged and embraced me tighter for a few moments, I could feel him breathing and sobbing – then he finally let go. He stepped back a bit, held his hands pressed together in front of his face and quietly whispered "I love you". I said "I love you more", turned around in total shock and almost fell down the stairs I was still standing on. Just before going down the stairs further, however, I saw I still had the three postcards from Munich which we had written to Michael last night in one hand. They were a bit bended since they had been stuck somewhere between the barrier, Michael and me, but I turned around once more, said "oh and this is for you" and gave them to him. He said a quiet "oh, thank you" while still wiping away some tears.

I stumbled out of the bus finding the rest of us staring at each other in disbelief, shaking, holding each other…we were simply lost for words.

364

b y Brigitte, Marina, Stephanie & Sonja

The bus kept standing there for another few minutes, the door still open. We all were so exhausted and worn out that we don't remember exactly all that happened then, but what we do remember, is Michael's assistant talking to the security guards about what to "do" with us now and Michael telling them to let us into Neverland, to have something to eat and drink - obviously to make us feel a bit better and calm down our distraught state.

We all went closer to the bus door again as we heard Michael's voice and once he saw all of us again, he immediately walked down to touch each one of us and said "Thank you!". We told him in response to stay strong and keep the faith and that we would be there for him and love him so much. While not letting go of our hands, he said in a very loud and deep voice: "I love you more!". Then the bus door closed and the bus drove off, with him still standing at the window waving to us and us waving to him.

That cold January morning changed all of us. It was the most heart-breaking, most hurting experience of our life to feel that someone you love so much is hurting so bad, yet to understand that you are unable to truly help, besides supporting him with all your heart and by simply being there for him. But what impressed us the most and made us truly understand who Michael really is, was that even in those darkest and most hopeless moments of his life, Michael's heart went out to others, to the ones in need, especially to sick and poor children and to our hurting planet! We understood that this is what Michael really was all about! He was about helping and loving and caring for one another! And no matter how many times people tried to ridicule, belittle and hurt him and even, like in the last years, tried to destroy him, Michael never lost his ability to love and care and his deep desire to help others! He simply loved more!

365

b y Brigitte, Marina, Stephanie & Sonja

HE WAS A GIVER & HELPER

by Curtis Mickey Gordon, USA

I worked for Michael Jackson at his "Neverland Valley Ranch" as a part of his security team for more than 14 years. During that time period I saw several thousand children and grown-ups visiting Neverland, people from all ages and all social backgrounds, from very famous people to underprivileged and sick children.

Neverland was Michael's home and a home for his children. People tend to forget that. For him it was a safe haven, a place where he could be himself. There he could refill his energy after stressful and exhausting concert tours or public appearances and find his peace within to connect with his creativity.

However; throughout the year busloads of kids and adult chaperons from the central coast and the inner-city Los Angeles area, many who have never been out in the countryside before, came to Michael's ranch to enjoy a day full of fun and excitement. Michael hosted such events regularly, usually a few times a month and they were also scheduled during times when Michael himself was not at the ranch.

The buses normally arrived around lunch time and we set up tables with all kinds of food in the garden underneath the old oak trees for them to fortify themselves for the exciting day.

Candies and ice-cream were always available everywhere at Neverland and the kids could take as much as they wanted. After lunch, visits to Michael's amusement park, where they could try all of his fun-rides as often and long as they wanted, followed by visits to his zoo where they could see and pet many of his animals and finally watching a movie at his cinema, made the day unforgettable for them. I have never - and surely will never - see more joy and wonder, then I saw during those years in the faces of children and grown-ups visiting Neverland.

However because of the negative reports by the media, many people had strange attitudes towards Michael and his ranch, so for the adults that came along to supervise the children, it was often like a real shock to see the truth and to realize that they never even heard or read about the fact that Michael hosted all kinds of people regularly at Neverland. Hence those adults gained much respect for Michael when experiencing these events and the real Neverland, which was a beautiful and fun place, designed to host children of all ages.

Only around Christmas time and some weeks in summer, Michael reserved Neverland for his friends and family to visit and not many other events were scheduled during that time. Michael simply loved Christmas and besides a lot of decoration, he had also a huge Christmas tree set up, so huge that it reached right to the ceiling of the room it was in. Around it were more presents than one can image, because he loved to give presents.

Michael also did a lot for the community at Santa Ynez Valley, not just financially, but also by inviting local schools to come to his ranch for their "field day", or to visit his zoo for their biology class. Sometimes some animals of his zoo were even brought to a nearby school for a special biology project.

Occasionally Michael decided to drive to the school right opposite of his ranch personally - on a Quad - to invite them to his ranch. My colleagues and I, as his security team, did of course not like his idea of going there alone, so we tried to convince him, that at least one of us could come with him.

Michael was also very discreet about helping others. When he heard of someone that was in need of something, Michael simply helped. Many of those people have never been told who had helped them because Michael wanted it that way. He did not want to embarrass people; he just liked to help them.

Just like he wanted to help a family that had financial problems and lost their car. For some reason this family was visiting Neverland and as Michael heard about them not having a car anymore, he just gave them one of his SUV's.

Seeing him doing all those things, showed me that even though he was very popular, he wasn't selfish at all. He truly was a giver and helper and that came from the bottom his heart.

Michael also was a very nice boss for all people working at his ranch. He treated everyone kindly and he truly cared for us. Once a year, Neverland was reserved for all the people working for Michael. This day was called "Friends & Family Day" and everyone could invite people to the ranch to have a day full of fun and joy with them. It was a really huge party, because all the people who worked for him, even from Los Angeles, came out to the ranch and brought people with them. Sometimes Neverland almost burst from so many people. Often Michael was at the ranch too when we had the "Friends & Family Day" and he would show up here and there and talk to the people. However word spread really quickly when it came to the whereabouts of Michael and soon he was swarmed by family members and

368

friends of his staff who wanted to say Hi to him.

During all those years of working for Michael and eventually being close to him, I saw and met a lot of celebrities and movie stars coming to the ranch. Many of them tried to find a way to stay in contact with Michael and even tried to give presents and their business card to me for that matter. However I was not impressed or affected by them, because working for Michael was a category of its own.

Michael was the type of person who needed to get to know you first, before he approached. Working for him for so many years, he eventually looked at me more like at a friend than at an employee. He trusted me with a lot of things and often he would call me and say "Hey Curtis, you got my back, right?" And I would say "Sure" and so he would continue "OK, so this is what I need you to do..." Sometimes those things concerned family matters, sometimes some kind of projects he had in his mind or other private things.

From time to time we had our talks and I would tell him my opinion about certain people he called friends and to be careful of them which he did not like to hear because Michael wanted to believe in the good in people. But people tended to act nicely around him, so it was hard for him to see what they really were about. After telling him my opinion on some things, I would ask: "So, do I still have a job?" This question would always make him laugh and things were fine again between us.

Thank you, Michael for really being a friend! I will never forget you!

369

TRUE MIRACLE

by Antonietta Parisi, Daniele's Mother, Latina/Italy

I adopted Daniele from Villa Pamphili Orphanage in Rome on September 13th 1984. Daniele was diagnosed with AIDS after an axillary biopsy when he was only 12 months old. He was the first case in the world of a child who lived, thanks to medical testing treatments, until 15 years old. His biological mother, HIV positive, had transmitted the virus to him as an unborn baby and six months after Daniele's birth she died.

Daniele was a big fan of Michael Jackson and in 1997, when he was 14 years old and the disease inevitably showing its indelible marks, he had the opportunity to attend the concert that Michael Jackson was to hold in Milan/Italy on June 18th.

Some days before the event, when we came back home to Latina, we found a message on the answering machine: Valentino, the famous stylist, wanted to see us in Milan for a surprise. So we went to Milan, but we didn't know what the surprise would be.

A chauffeur picked us up at our home in Latina and took us to the airport, the same happened as we arrived in Milan. There we stayed at the Hotel "Parco dei Principi", thanks to Valentino and his partner Giancarlo Giammetti, who had booked

370

Antonietta and Daniele with ten months and eight days

A picture of Donald Duck that Daniele drew for his Mom in 1997

04/09/97

Per
Mamma

Daniele

the suite for us. Michael Jackson was in the same hotel - you couldn't imagine Daniele's happiness!

When we arrived at San Siro Stadium, before the concert and the real meeting, Daniele was picked up by a member of MJ's staff. They walked behind Michael (who had a foulard around his neck and mouth to protect his voice) and Debbie Rowe; when Daniele saw Michael for the first time, he called: "Michael…Michael!" and Michael answered: "I love you, Dany!".

After this, still before the concert, Daniele and I were allowed to meet Michael in his dressing room. Here Michael greeted Daniele with bows and kisses, thanking him for the gifts we had brought for him and his son Prince. Michael was nothing like I expected him to be, he was kind, open and gentle – I even apologized to him for having been prejudiced by some of the rumours the media spread about him.

The meeting was magic and marvellous; his dressing room was red, with a big mirror and many lights around it. Michael wore a white jacket, black trousers and wavy hair was on his shoulders. He was a vision for Daniele! I still remember Daniele´s lips and eyes: when he got excited his lips and eyes became big, like a fawn!

These are Daniele's words when he told the story of this special meeting to a journalist in Latina: "Michael is the kindest person. I remember he had a particular and sweet scent, so I thought: I don't want to wash myself anymore. I want to wear his scent for the rest of my life! It was like a dream for me. I remember his scent, the flashlights of photographers and my mother with the camera around her neck, so deeply moved that she wasn't able to take a single picture all day!".

372

Daniele onstage with Michael, San Siro Stadium June 18th 1997

MJ & Daniele on stage with other children

Michael's autograph for Daniele

Before the concert Michael also signed some autographs for Daniele and some for his friends, too. At the end of this incredible meeting, we stayed in a big room with other children and some of Michael's relatives. Here some members of Michael's staff gave Daniele some chocolate - still, today I preserve two "Kinder" chocolate bars from that day in the fridge!

Afterwards, Daniele and I were allowed to watch the incredible show from one of the stage sides, together with Debbie Rowe and Luciano Pavarotti. During the show, a member of the staff gave Daniele a gift bag, including the program of the HIStory Tour. They were all very nice to us and some of Michael's dancers even gave Daniele a "high-five" a few times.

Towards the end of the concert, during "Heal the World", Michael came towards us. Daniele was sitting on a chair (unable to walk very well because of the weakness due to his disease), Michael kneeled before him and kissed his right hand several times. Afterwards he picked him up and twirled with him while going towards the center of the stage in front of 40.000 people; there they posed for some photos and then he carried him back behind the scenes before the end of the song. It was an unforgettable concert.

When we came back to the hotel, Daniele was pure happiness! He ate a piece of cake, drunk a glass of milk and said: "How I love life, mum!". That night we left Michael with a promise: we will go and visit him at Neverland as soon as possible!

After this amazing experience, Daniele´s health improved visibly, so quickly that the doctor called it a "true miracle". It was as if Michael had given him some years of life, since Daniele started to walk again (sometimes he got to run, too) and eat (putting on weight), but what was most important of all, he

by Antonietta Parisi

gained self confidence to continue to fight and keep going.

Out of that meeting, also a friendly relationship was born between Daniele and Michael. Sometimes Michael called Daniele by telephone, he always wanted to know about his health. He was so sweet!

These are some words taken from the letter Daniele wrote to thank Valentino and Giancarlo Giammetti: "I liked it very much to travel by plane. Meeting Michael was a great thing and it was exciting for me (my heart was thumping and thumping). He picked me up, gave me a kiss on my head and took me on stage with other children. The hotel was marvellous, it looked like a fairy tale castle. Our room looked like a flat. I know I'm a lucky child, because I have two angels. These two angels make my dreams come true. You are always on my mind and I love you, Daniele".

And this is the letter Daniele wrote on November 9th 1998 to Michael:
"Dear Michael,
thanks for the magic moments I spent with you. I'll never forget it. I was with you on stage in San Siro Stadium in Milan on June 18th 1997, do you remember? It was beautiful when you picked me up and took me on stage. I'm Daniele of Latina (Italy), a friend of the stylist Valentino. I'd like to see you again, even if I know you are busy with your children and your work.
I love you, Daniele".

Unfortunately, Daniele died two years later (on March 4th 1999) from a brain infection due to the influenza and the dream to go to Neverland in the same year of his death never came true. The wonderful memories of Michael, along with my loving care, gave him the strength to keep fighting until the very end.

376

When he knew that Daniele died, Michael sent us the picture of him and Daniele on stage and he gave me his condolences with this e-mail: "It's admirable what you did for an Angel like Daniele".

This is the letter I wrote to him on April 23th 1999:
"Dearest Michael,
I'm Antonietta Parisi, Daniele's mother. I'd like to thank you from the bottom of my heart for everything you've done for my son, for the wonderful moments you gave him that night of June 18th 1997, during your concert in Milan.
Unfortunately, my child died on March 4th because of a bad flu. The virus hit him at the only part of his body doctors couldn't cure: his head and no medical testing treatments could defeat it. It was a bad loss, he was my only reason to live and now that I can't see, hold and care for him, it hurts so much.
I'd like to thank Mr. Valentino and Giancarlo Giammetti for making his dream come true by writing to you.
Michael, I'd love so much to have the pictures and the tape of the concert of June 18th 1997, so that I can relive these moments while my son was in your arms. I was backstage and couldn't see and enjoy it with him and now that Daniele is not here anymore I'd like to feel him close to me through those images. Please, let this dream of mine become a reality, Daniele would have loved it.
Please, find enclosed two pictures of Daniele. One was taken on the occasion of his 15th birthday, the other was taken at the hospital one month before his death.
He was so fine you couldn't expect such a tragedy. I'll keep on fighting against AIDS by gathering money for research, so that other children can be saved. Thanks to those cures, my child could live for 15 years and if it wasn't for the flu, he would be still here with me. Some day, a national project will start named "Project Daniele", thanks to the doctor Mr. Aiuti, thanks

377

to Dott. Vullo (Chief of the Policlinico Umberto I in Rome) and to ANLAIDS.
Thank you for being here! You're a very important figure for all the suffering children of the world.
I love you,
Antonietta Parisi".

Michael Jackson was a very special person with a huge heart, especially for children. Many of the good things he did never made the news. For example, he gave all the revenues of a concert to Ethiopian's children.

I learned that you should never judge another person unless you know him. In Michael´s case, he was very misunderstood by the world when all he wanted to do was to help and he got punished for it.

When he finally was acquitted of these allegations, after the trial in 2005, I sent another message to him:
"Dearest Michael,
I'll never forget what you did for my son, Daniele. After meeting you, the doctors called it a miracle, because for some months it was like he never had AIDS.
Now that justice has been served, I just wanted to express my gratitude and my happiness. Please don't ever let people get at you like that again. I know you are a kind-hearted man and want to help everyone, but not all people deserve so much attention.
My child is not here with us anymore, but I know that from up there he's always watching over you. What you did for him will never be forgotten.
God bless you,
Antonietta"

378

Michael responded: "Thank you for your testimony. May God always bless you and Daniele."

I planned to visit and meet with him at one of his London concerts in 2009, sadly that never happened. The news of Michael Jackson´s death brought my heart back to a pain that has not been soothed yet…the death of my son Daniele. Our meeting at the San Siro Stadium in Milan on June 18th 1997 was magical and absolutely wonderful and knowing that Michael is now up there with my son Daniele eases the pain. We miss Michael Jackson - the artist, but especially the man.

During all these years I have been very active to try to raise awareness about AIDS and to raise funds for AIDS research. I support many charities in Italy that work with AIDS victims and

research, in particular "Anlaids Lazio Onlus".

In 2012, I also published a book called "La forza dell'amore - In ricordo di Daniele" ("The power of love – In memory of Daniele") which you can buy directly from the publishing house, email to: info@cera-1volta.it. In this book you can find Daniele's story and his meeting with some important people like the Italian singer Renato Zero,

379

Luciano Pavarotti, the tenor, Mother Teresa of Calcutta, Dario Argento, the producer, Valentino, the stylist and even the meeting with Michael Jackson and much more. The revenue from book sales and from other charity events will be used to purchase a machine, the hyperthermia, which serves to block tumour metastasis; it would be the second machinery of its kind in Italy.

If you want to help and for more information, please go here: https://www.facebook.com/inricordo.didaniele (also on YouTube; type in "La forza dell'amore. In ricordo di Daniele" to see the video)

Finally I would like to thank, with all my heart, the journalist dott.ssa Roberta Colazingari, who helped me to translate Daniele and Michael meeting's into English for this book. Thanks so much to Team MJJBook who give me the opportunity to show the world Michael's humanity and Daniele's story.

If you would like to know more about ANLAIDS' work for the AIDS research or would like to donate, please go to: http://www.anlaidslazio.it/

If you enter this world knowing you are loved and you leave this world knowing the same, then everything that happens in between can be dealt with.

To be a Father

by Seány O'Kane, Ireland

People have often asked "why do you love Michael Jackson so much?". I immediately think the real question is why don't 'they' love MJ so much, but I would never verbalise that back, because everyone has their passions. Michael Jackson to me however, was like a real-life Super Hero in so many ways, but he didn't come without his flaws.

I am Seány O' Kane, 30-years-old and a father of a 3-year-old son Kuziva-Aodhán. I work as a specialist Young Fathers Practitioner and in 2013 I graduated in a Masters in Child and Family Interprofessional Psychology Practice. Part of my role enables me to connect young fathers from marginalised backgrounds into the lives of their children, something I am extremely passionate about. I have dedicated my life to doing this for the past five years alongside my academia.

When it comes to Michael I would describe myself as a supporter first and a fan second. He himself was a loving and dedicated father, often seen travelling the world with his children in tow. His adoration towards Paris, Prince and Prince II to me was inspiring and it saddened me that his efforts to be the best father he knew to his children always seemed to be overlooked particularly by the world press. That said, I take solace knowing

382

that those three people who benefited from his love and nurturing as a caring dad will always know how magnificent a father he was and that's what is truly important. In some ways I guess sub-consciously Michael's humanitarian efforts have helped to inspire me in carrying out my own professional practice for which I am very grateful.

Many fans may remember me from the trial in 2005. I was the exuberant Irish fellow who would often be seen standing above the fans on a ladder outside the court house with my many banners and placards in support of Michael. It was actually during this period that I was introduced to some of the most colourful, loving and dedicated Michael supporters for which I am eternally grateful to have met and many whom I remain in touch with to this day. We are all one big universal MJ family united because of our love for one man and his art.

I have always been passionate about families and the role and responsibilities a father plays in the lives of their children's upbringing, as well as the abundance of opportunities that is evident when a positive active father is present. You can therefore only imagine how excited I was when I discovered that I was going to be a father for the first time. Our child was due on the 08.07.09 - five days before the start of the 'This Is It' tour. I had tickets for eight shows in total, with a VIP box pre-booked in advance for the opening night. I will admit I was anxious that the expectant mother would go into labour on the day of the opening night (or even worse, during the performance)! I knew how hard this might have been, however, nothing would have stopped me from being present at my child's arrival into this world.

Of course all of this was soon to be circumstantial and never played out to be an actual dilemma I ever had to contend with.

383

by Seány O'Kane

In fact it was much worse than that for the reasons we now are all aware of.

14 days after Michael Joseph Jackson passed my son was born. Yes, I had considered calling him 'Michael' but his mum wanted something that represented his African/Irish heritage instead which was fine with me. Actually that reminds me, a day or so after June 25th 2009, myself along with a few friends felt that the city of London where I reside, really needed some kind of shrine, a place central that was dedicated to the life of Michael Jackson. A place where everyone could gravitate to and share their fondest memories of the impact MJ has had on them. I approached the managers of HMV music store on London Piccadilly and asked if we could start to place pictures of MJ outside of the store. They gave us the go-ahead, and we created the most fantastic and visually stunning memorial wall outside. I found images of the shrine had gone global online hours later. The reason I mention this story particularly was because as I was glazing from afar at the wonderful and heartfelt messages being placed up from passers-by, I noticed one that read "Michael I named my son after you, he was born the day after your death, with Love, PJ". That really touched me, the powerful impact MJ has on people even in the afterlife.

Following Michael's death, I was presented with the chance to climb Kilimanjaro in Tanzania for charity to raise money for a foundation that creates sustainable and ethical projects in Ghana. The M.A.D (Make A Difference) Foundation was founded in 1998 and helps to ensure that children receive an adequate full-time education with the right resources in appropriate sheltered environments. Coincidentally, the day in which the group of us were due to reach the peak of Kilimanjaro was also the 1 year anniversary of Michael's death and I knew that this was something that I just had to do. For Michael, the charity, myself

384

Seány and his son

Seány at the memorial in London shortly after Michael's death

and ultimately for my son, the driving force that also evidently inspires me in every decision that I make.

With the help from friends, family, strangers and many Michael Jackson fans worldwide, I was able to raise double the target amount for the charity for which I was overwhelmed by, with £3,000 donated in six weeks! The love and support from people was heartfelt and it was a great opportunity to really promote the humanitarian efforts of Michael himself and to remind others of the great charitable deeds he too was involved in. I knew then that I also wanted to complete this challenge for every single one of those people who donated and believed that I would achieve it. Luckily I was in good health and had trained well in advance. Of course I reached the summit of the vast mountain, but it was not without its tribulations, that's for sure. It was truly the most horrendous and challenging experience both physically and mentally I have ever endured. That said, I wouldn't take it back for anything. It was worth the pain, the sickness and the blisters.

On the afternoon of June 25th 2010 I reached the peak of Kilimanjaro. I placed a flag of Michael Jackson right at the very top and watched it flutter in the wind. I stood back in my exhausted state, and looked into the sky – space seemed almost within my grasp. As I collapsed onto the snowy terrain I began to weep. I cried tears of joy because the anguish that I held inside of me ever since I learned of his death had somehow vanished. As I smiled with the tears running down my face, I looked up above and took solace knowing that I was closer to Michael on that single occasion more so than any other human being and realised that I was finally at peace with myself over his loss.

386

On June 25th 2010 Seány reached the top of Mount Kilimanjaro

by Seány O'Kane

The Children's Congress

by Maria Drown, UK

It was August 1992 and I'd travelled to Regents College in London to take part in Michael Jackson's European Children's Congress that he had arranged as part of his "Heal the World "-Tour. I was there to represent the County of Avon for 'Youth Clubs UK.' I had been given the honour to attend because I was Chairperson of the Young Leaders committee at a Youth Centre in my home town. Many of the other children had won their place in a competition, or had travelled from Europe as their country's representative. As we arrived on the Saturday, I saw there were children of all ages and backgrounds, but they all had the same excitement about them, something very special was going to happen!

The children were gathered together, and introduced themselves, played games to get to know each other and quickly made friends, all with the same discussion of how much they loved Michael Jackson's songs, and that they couldn't wait to meet him, and was he really coming to see them?

That evening, we went to see Michael in concert at Wembley Stadium - it was incredible. I've always admired him as a dancer, and I soaked up every step he took, it blew me away, there's no doubting he was a musical genius and a fabulous performer. I

388

tried so hard to remember every moment of it, as I knew this was a once in a lifetime event. We were in Wembley Stadium, in VIP seating watching the King of Pop in the most incredible live show.

There was a blacked out van parked next to the coaches when we returned to Regents College. Most of the kids walked right past it, but it made me wonder if it was Michael's and he was sat in it, watching the reactions to the children as they disembarked, practising their moves, chattering away about the concert and singing "Thriller". I could imagine him loving that, seeing how happy he had made the children, the difference that night had made to their lives, just as he wanted to do with his Foundation work. I'm not sure anyone got to sleep easily that night, everyone's heads were buzzing from the concert!

The next morning, the atmosphere was electric - Michael was coming to see us! The smaller children were hyper with excitement and the older ones quite nervous, realising the honour that had been bestowed upon us. We were all split into groups and in different rooms, and each group chose a theme that they felt affected the children of the world, and the future generations, something that was dear to Michael's heart.

Our group had older children and teenagers, and we chose to speak about AIDS. We had a workshop to discuss what we were going to say, and then, we heard something from outside, someone shouted "Oh my God, it's Michael Jackson!" A member of the public walking past had just spotted him climbing out of a van - the one I'd seen parked next to the coach the night before - it WAS his van, and he'd arrived! Room by room, Michael spent time with each group, listening to what they'd thought about the concert and what they'd been doing to prepare for our own performances on stage later that day. Our room was one of the last. We could hear the screams of excitement as he entered each one in turn. Michael was getting closer! Then, there he was, his trademark dark trilby hat and glasses with his tousled hair and a big smile. He came through the door along with a wave and a high pitched whispery "Hi". No one knew what to do, it didn't seem real. We sat down in a circle, and I don't think anyone took their eyes off him. He couldn't say much, the concert had left him with a sore throat, and he whispered his questions to his PA. His presence in the room was huge, but his smile was full of warmth and he seemed genuinely very concerned and wanted to make the "Heal the World"-Foundation a success. We all stood up and got into a group for a photo. I found myself standing next to Michael and was surprised by how tall he was, which made me laugh to myself. Here I am, standing next to the King of Pop, his arm is brushing next to mine and all I can think is "Wow, he's taller than I thought he'd be". He was a very impressive figure, tall, lean but so warm and caring.

Our meeting was over all too soon, he left to visit the next group of excited children. His PA said he was looking forward to our performances later, when we would give a presentation to Michael about our chosen subjects. The door closed, we were all left standing still like statues, their mouths open, did that really just happen?? I sat down on the nearest chair and the room gasped and looked at me - what?? "You've just sat in Michael's chair!", one of the girls said. Which broke the silence and they all laughed, I think all the kids in the room had a go sitting in 'Michaels chair'.

Then it was time for our performance. We made our way to the Auditorium and in the distance we could just see Michael sitting in the audience. Michael Jackson was going to watch US

390

Maria stood next to Michael, leaning on the back of the wheelchair, when the group's picture was taken

on stage! Some of the groups danced, some read poetry, some sang. Michael listened to it all, clapping everyone for their efforts. Then it was our turn. I didn't feel scared, it was dreamlike, too surreal to feel like it was actually happening. Each one of us had a small speech to make, my turn came and I started to say my lines. Then something happened, I made Michael Jackson giggle. In fact, he was giggling so hard his head was on the desk and his shoulders were shaking uncontrollably. I'd just remarked to Michael, that AIDS was a terrible disease, and though the scientists were working hard to find a cure, even HE couldn't perform miracles, referencing his recent work with the magician David Copperfield, but that with his influence and the "Heal the World"-Foundation, he could help to make a change in the world. The leader I had travelled up to London with said it was so

391

by Maria Drown

funny, Michael just couldn't contain his giggles.

At the end of the concert, Michael got up and thanked everyone for coming, and said he'd do his best to help. We were each presented with a "Heal the World"-Tour hat, t-shirt and tour programme. It was over all too soon, we had to say our goodbyes, and travel back home. But it wasn't over!

The press had heard about it and came to interview me and I appeared in the local papers, and to this day, I'm still known by a few people as 'the girl who met Michael Jackson and made him giggle'. It was a once in a lifetime chance and something I will never forget, I hope he remembered that day, too. I didn't stay in touch with anyone who was there that weekend, but I've often wondered if they grew up to be someone to make a change, to make a difference, and if so, was it all down to Michael's Conference that weekend in August '92...

by Maria Drown

The foundation of all human knowledge, the beginning of human consciousness, must be that each and every one of us is an object of love. Before you know if you have red hair or brown, before you know if you are black or white, before you know of what religion you are a part, you have to know that you are loved.

Michael Jackson's Neverland Dream

by Robert E. "Rob" Swinson, MJ's "Maker of Dreams", USA

If you would have told me prior to the summer of 1990 that I would be having dinner with Michael Jackson on Halloween night the following fall at his recently acquired private residence, Neverland Valley Ranch near Los Olivos, California, I would have laughed in your face. But there we were, laughing, telling stories and sharing some very special moments together. It was the night we became close personal friends, but it didn't happen right away.

At the time, I was National Sales Manager for "Chance Rides, Inc." located in Wichita, Kansas, personally specializing in the development of new amusement ride projects, especially those involving our internationally famous product line of carrousels and 1/3 scale C. P. Huntington miniature trains. "Chance Rides" was one of the world's leading and most renown amusement ride manufacturers at that time.

In early June 1990, I received a call from Mr. Brick Price, owner of Wonderworks located in Canoga Park, CA, a company that builds models and special effects. I was informed by Mr. Price he represented a well-known personality whose identity he was not at liberty to disclose. This anonymous client had recently inspected an antique "merry-go-round" in England regarding a

394

possible purchase, and had also viewed others in Western Europe. As an afterthought, Mr. Price mentioned his client owned a ranch north of Santa Barbara and was interested in acquiring a carrousel. I was asked to please forward some information to him, so I sent out a package of literature by express mail that included color brochures and photos, animal selection guides and a wonderful promotional video featuring our classical, custom-made carrousels. When I hung up the phone, I had a "feeling" about the identity of this mystery buyer and remember proclaiming to my peers in the office that I thought I had just received a call from someone representing Michael Jackson!

A couple of days later I received a call from Ms. Norma Staikos, who identified herself as being with MJJ Productions in L.A. and was Michael Jackson's Executive Administrator. Norma acknowledged she was in receipt of my package, and we visited for awhile, just getting acquainted. Before we concluded our conversation, Norma told me she would share the information I had sent with Michael, and the very next day I received a call directly from the "King of Pop" to personally thank me for the product literature - especially the carrousel video!

Michael first explained he was currently in a hospital bed in the L.A area (Santa Monica, I later learned from Brick Price), recovering from a stomach inflammation similar to pleurisy, as I recall. He was very excited and talked about how he had been watching the video over and over from his hospital bed for the past two days and had looked at every photo in our two colorful selection posters of ornate horses, plus numerous real and some fantasy menagerie animals. Michael stated he had fallen in love with our incredible carrousels and was interested in buying one for his 2,700 acre ranch located in the beautiful Santa Ynez Valley, and extended into the San Rafael mountains north of Santa Barbara.

It wasn't long before Michael ordered his "first" custom carrousel. This was our "opening volley" to be followed with numerous discussions in person and by telephone during the next few years about amusement rides and parks, paintings, sculptures, landscaping, and many other subjects pertaining to developing his childhood dream at his private "fantasy island" – Neverland Valley Ranch!

Soon thereafter, this led to Michael's next decision to purchase one of our C. P. Huntington miniature trains. We were visiting on the phone about his order for a new carrousel, when I mentioned to Michael we also built miniature trains for children, which were designed so they could also accommodate their parents. I had previously sent him our full product line catalog, which he soon had in his hands, and upon opening it to pictures of the C. P. Huntington miniature train he immediately exclaimed, "Yes, Rob, I want one of these trains, too!"

Initially, Michael ordered a custom 3-abreast Chance Rides 36' Classical Carrousel with two chariots, one of them to be handicapped accessible, and 30 jumping animals riding on shiny, polished brass poles. He also desired to place one of our large, decorative finials atop the center pole of the carrousel that would tower above the colorful fabric top and the beautiful ornate scenery with its hundreds of lights and antique-style beveled glass mirrors. However, when we were trying to select the thirty individual horses and menagerie animals he wanted, it became clear to me that his "wants and desires" were much larger than this carrousel could accommodate and that he basically wanted everything! It was mentioned that we did have a much larger 50' Grand Carrousel with positions for sixty jumping animals, and Michael immediately proclaimed, "Yes, yes, Rob, I want one of those instead!" So I canceled his first carrousel order, replacing it with his "second" choice—the "granddaddy"

396

of all carrousels.

My first visit to the ranch regarding Michael's acquisition of some amusement rides was in late June 1990 to meet with Norma Staikos and some potential contractors for pending ride installations. I was able to view the area where an amusement park would eventually be built—it was just "bare dirt" surrounded by a ring of magnificent ancient California oak trees. The valley was quiet and peaceful, and the only visible green grass was about one-half mile away behind Michael's 13,000 square-feet residence. That would change rapidly over the next few months, and I was anointed Michael Jackson's personal ride consultant and developer of his dream—"Neverland Valley Amusement Park."

My appreciation and sincerest thanks are extended to Ms. Norma E. Staikos, Michael Jackson's former Executive Administrator at MJJ Productions, Los Angeles, CA, for allowing me during those "early" years of building Neverland Valley Amusement Park to take numerous personal photographs. Following our very first meeting at Neverland Valley Ranch on June 27, 1990, and throughout my period of involvement with Michael, I was allowed to document by photographs the creation of Michael Jackson's dream.

In July of that first summer, I was asked by Norma to contact the surveyor and earth-moving contractor who were trying to assist Michael with a track layout at Neverland. After chatting for a while with the surveyor, I realized then he was somewhat "clueless" about miniature train installations, and the next thing I knew I was on my second flight to Santa Barbara, California, to visit Michael's nearby ranch and meet with Michael's surveyor, dirt contractor and Norma on-site.

397

During one of these first visits to the Neverland Valley Ranch, we were having a morning meeting in Michael's conference room that featured a large full glass window on one wall. Suddenly, Elizabeth Taylor was seen strolling by in her nightgown! Norma quickly excused herself and went outside to inform Liz there were other guests at the ranch, and then Larry Fortensky appeared to escort her away. That afternoon, I again saw Liz Taylor outside Michael's residence, fully clothed this time, and was introduced to her by Norma. She was very gracious and polite, and her violet eyes were stunning! At the time, media were reporting that she and Larry were missing—location unknown. I recall thinking, "I know where they are hiding!" Liz and Larry were frequent ranch guests, and the following year were married at Michael's residence under a white gazebo built for the occasion on the back lawn.

So for the next several months I went back and forth between Kansas and Neverland, overseeing the installation of the train tracks and the pad site and electrical requirements for the carrousel. We found it necessary to install a large, silent-running generator to provide power to the ride area. A plan was devised to install the unit directly underneath one of the magnificent large oak trees surrounding the site. Then a multilevel, well-lit "fantasy tree house" designed like the castle featured at each Disneyland park was constructed so as to completely hide the power unit from view.

Michael enjoyed climbing the stairway to an upper level of his castle, and there we would spread out various brochures on the carpeted floor for his personal review and input, listening to Disney-type music from interior speakers. Michael was eager to actualize his long-time dream into reality and became like a "kid in a candy store" when we reviewed product literature, often proclaiming, "Wow, I want one of those too!"

398

During late summer and into the fall of 1990, Michael assembled a team of trusted creative people and artists that became his "dream team" for what would later grow and expand into an actual amusement park project, complete with large, colorful flower beds with floral butterflies, candy and ice cream carts for the kids, well-lighted potted plants molded into lighted zoomorphic figures of an elephant toting an umbrella in the rain, a caterpillar atop a mushroom, a teddy bear and the Cheshire cat from Alice in Wonderland. What started as a small, two-ride project eventually became the principle showplace at Neverland, and was the primary reason for Michael and his staff bringing bus loads of children from the Los Angeles inner city area to visit—especially those who were underprivileged, handicapped and terminally ill.

Tony Urquidez was selected as the project's general contractor to handle the building construction and some of the ride installations. Artist David Nordahl was there to provide some original artwork and add design and color to some of the park's elements, and Brad Sundberg, another "dream team" member, was brought in to provide music and sound systems. It was my responsibility to select individual rides with Michael, determine their future placement in order to create the amusement park feel he desired, and then obtain the go-ahead approval from Norma Staikos at MJJ Productions. (Michael usually got his way!) The team had their marching orders, and each dove into his area of expertise right away, working hard to give birth, so to say, to "Neverland Valley Amusement Park."

Few construction workers, ranch employees and guests ever realized that Michael had many strategies for making observations without anyone knowing he was even there. He would drive his golf cart down a dirt road through the oak trees along the mountainside behind the theater building and watch the workers below in the park, or he'd park his black SUV at a distance and watch without actually being seen. The most comical method was to "hide" behind the corner of a building and sneak peeks; however, his bright red shirt usually gave him away! His most creative and secretive strategy involved a hilltop retreat that few people even knew existed. It looked like an open air clubhouse-type structure located high atop one of the mountains and had a large deck protruding over the edge of the mountain. On the deck, Michael had installed a couple of high-power commercial-type binoculars like the ones used at various attractions and parks around the country. From there, Michael had a good view of the entire valley below in total secrecy!

Michael and I had many conversations about the topic that was so close to his heart—doing something that benefited the "children of the world," a dream that he had carried within himself - heart, mind and soul - since the age of 17. In his 1988 autobiography, Moonwalk, Michael remarks that his "first real date" was in the 1970s with then child actress Tatum O'Neal. He was 17 at the time and Tatum was 12 and already an Oscar winner for her role in the movie, "Paper Moon". "We exchanged phone numbers and called each other often. I talked to her for hours: from the road, from the studio, from home." Michael called her "my first love – after Diana [Ross]." (Moonwalk, p. 165-166) He told me how they spent many moments talking about finding ways to help the world's children.

In a comical note from page 99 of Tatum O'Neal's book, "A Paper Life", she writes, "Michael was around 17 at the time (I met him), about 5 years older than me, & he seemed very sheltered & fearful & lonely--not at all what you'd expect a world-renowned performer to be. As I recall, he didn't even know how to drive a car. He gave me his number, & we started talking everyday—long, drawn-out conversations that sometimes got so boring I would hand over the receiver to my friend Esme Gray. Michael would just keep on, thinking he was talking to me."

Few people were let in on our project, and those were some of Michael's most trusted personal inner circle of associates and friends, which back then in addition to his "dream team" included Marlon and Miko Brando, Elizabeth Taylor and Norma Staikos. I recall the "National Enquirer" publishing a centerfold color photo that first summer that someone had taken overhead of Michael's Neverland Ranch and proclaimed in the text that Michael was "building a golf course" at his private ranch! These photos were usually snapped by one of the several helicopters that frequently came by to hover above our heads and gawk. Michael seemed to be fresh fodder for our nation's tabloids during the years we worked together, but for the most part it was more humorous than hurtful. However, I do believe stories later published in the tabloids eventually hurt Michael very deeply.

Neverland Valley Ranch soon became a beehive of workers. Tony's team was busy pouring and stamping concrete walking areas, installing fences for rides and erecting the first buildings. David was making numerous drawings and creating fantasy artworks that brought Michael's ranch residence to life in vivid colors of fantastic artwork. Brad was working his magic surrounding the park area in music and designing some amazing systems for both the train and the carrousel.

One of my teams was busily installing a 2 ½ mile track layout that reached the far points of the valley and incorporated a loop for turning around at each end. I personally designed the train's route so it would allow Michael in the future to transport his guests as old-time train passengers riding to various places of interest he would create around the ranch. These later attractions were not yet built nor even conceived for the most part.

The amusement park was definitely a "project in progress" that would eventually expand to include other features, such as swan-themed paddle boats on a small lake adjacent to his home, a "water fight" fortress complete with water cannons and water balloon launchers, a nearby Indian campground with carpeted teepees and music speakers, a petting zoo and a second larger animal zoo, a reptile garden inside an old horse barn, a luxurious 50+ seat theater complete with two "viewing beds" at the rear where special guests like Liz Taylor would come to watch movies and a large concession counter at the entrance well stocked with "Michael Jackson" logo chocolate candy bars, and a train barn for storage and maintenance. Attached to the back of the theater was Michael's personal dance studio.

Of course, the featured center point for the entire miniature train layout was Michael's future amusement park site, with the train passing by on each side as you rode up and down the valley. Meanwhile, a few hundred employees at "Chance Rides" back in Wichita, Kansas, were busy building the new custom train and creating a one-of-a-kind, world-class carrousel for Michael. It was a crazy and exciting summer!

By mid-October, the train was loaded onto our factory truck and trailer, ready for its premier debut as the first on-site phase of Michael's Neverland dream. It was delivered to the ranch and set on the tracks under the personal observation of Marlon and Miko Brando in Michael's absence. Everyone admired how our artists and craftsmen had incorporated Michael's "Blue Boy in the Moon" logo into the train's theme. Marlon informed me he had brought some of his family members up to the ranch for an inaugural train ride the following day. I remember thinking

402

that hopefully all would go well!

That night I was invited to the main house for dinner. Michael was not able to be at the ranch, but Marlon Brando and his son Miko and daughter Rebecca were there. Marlon and Miko were both close friends of Michael, and Miko also worked with Michael in the studio and on tour. Truthfully, I don't even remember what was served, but I do remember Marlon and I sharing two bottles of a delicious white wine while visiting about many different subjects. Indulging in any type of wine was an extremely rare occurrence at Neverland, since Michael rarely would partake of any alcoholic beverage, and when he did it might be one glass of a white or blush wine.

Marlon Brando was one of the most curious, intelligent, well-read, well-spoken, and at-ease individuals I ever had the privilege of meeting, not to mention our sharing a private dinner and conversation at Michael Jackson's home. It developed into an evening laced with many laughs and wonderful stories. Marlon was seated at the head of the dinner table, myself on his left, and other guests seated around the table respectfully listened in. I fondly recall our moment of "bonding" that would occur during that evening.

"Rob, I would like to ask you about Michael's new train."
"Sure, Marlon, what do you want to know?" I politely responded.
We visited for a bit about the C. P. Huntington, then Marlon abruptly turned and leaned directly towards me to ask his next question: "What type of drive system does it have?" he blurted out louder than before.

It took me by surprise, because this was rarely an issue discussed even with knowledgeable train buyers. Michael, for

403

sure, had never bothered to ask me. Obviously, if only to myself, Marlon was asking me about the drive wheel arrangement of the 1/3 scale locomotive.

After absorbing the impact of his question, I replied, "It has a 4-2-4 drive system!"

"Mmmmm..." he paused, almost enjoying the silence. After many seconds he continued. "You know, I bet Rob and I are the only two people at this table that have a clue of what we are talking about right now!" More awkward silence, and then he started to laugh, and I tried to explain to the other guests what we had been talking about, though they really didn't seem to fully understand or care about the topic.

I continued with the following explanation, "There are four small drive wheels in the front, two false drive wheels in the middle, and four more small drive wheels in the rear." This is common language among railroad enthusiasts, but it was so surprising coming from Marlon Brando, one of Hollywood's all-time most talented and famous actors!

This was a very powerful moment for me, and one that I will never forget. Marlon Brando was, like Michael, an avid reader and so very knowledgeable about many different things. He greatly appreciated and enjoyed this kind of stuff. He, like Michael, was a special and unique person, almost a "Renaissance Man," as they say.

Marlon and everyone else at the table seemed to be looking forward to going for a ride the following day on Michael's new train. This was the most popular and desirable of the amusement industry's miniature trains and one that might be found at various theme parks and zoos around the country, as well

404

as several international locations. About 1960, the company's founder, Mr. Harold Chance, designated it the "C. P. Huntington" when he developed a one-third scaled set of drawings and then built the first one based on the original narrow gauge historical locomotive exhibited at the railroad museum in Sacramento, California. The original C. P. Huntington locomotive was used during the construction of our nation's first transcontinental railroad in the late 1860s.

The morning after our delightful dinner, we rendezvoused where the train had been unloaded the previous day and placed onto a new 24" gauge track installation. Everyone ran to a seat in one of the three coaches, except for Marlon who was a bit slower due to his size and the fact that he was still wearing his bedroom slippers. I climbed onto the train's locomotive, and after a few blasts of the whistle and some bell ringing, we were on our way. The train slowly tested its way northeasterly up the valley along the north side of the future amusement park site, past an old red barn that housed some of Michael's pet reptiles, finally reaching the original zoo location near the upper end of the valley. There, a loop had been installed in order to reverse our direction. We returned along a portion of track just traveled until approaching the future park site where we were diverted by a track switch to the opposite side of the valley across from where we had commenced this first of many exploratory rides to be shared by thousands of future ranch guests. It truly became a "train ride of discovery" that Michael greatly enjoyed sharing with guests of all ages who would visit during the coming years.

This next portion of the track had a long straight section where we were able to pick up speed for a bit of a thrill. I was beginning to become overly optimistic about our first train ride. From this point the train chugged past the house, downhill

405

alongside one of two small lakes, thence followed along the paved main entry driveway towards the lower end of the valley where another loop was installed that would allow us to reverse direction again and return back toward the future station site from where we had earlier departed.

I got just a hint of nerves as we headed up the valley towards the house. During some of my test runs, the train bogged down just a bit as it climbed a modest grade near the lake. My mind was racing with thoughts of, "Please little train... just this once, get us up that hill... please!" As we approached the steepest portion of the incline, I hit the throttle just a bit, knowing the spot where the wheels had spun during a couple of earlier test runs. Sure enough, I heard the sound of steel wheels spinning on the steel rails and knew it was not going to be a perfect ride. I eased the throttle back a bit and hoped the wheels would bite, but the track was either too damp with dew or had some oily residue on the new rails. We backed up several times, and I throttled the little train forward to no avail. Some passengers even got out and tried pushing. Developing a gradual feeling of panic and exasperation, not to mention embarrassment, I eventually threw some dry dirt onto the track and under the drive wheels to finally get it to pull up the grade.

Upon returning to our place of departure, all the passengers started to climb out of their seats, but Marlon became stuck. This train's coaches were designed primarily for children and normal-size adults. However, Marlon was certainly not an average-sized man by this time in his life. He heaved and struggled. When I observed his left leg and slippered foot flailing away in the air, I rushed over to assist by placing his foot on top of an outside rail near the floor of the coach. I helped pull him out, both of us chuckling at the irony of it all.

406

Rob Swinson, National Sales Manager, Chance Rides, Inc. taking inaugural ride on new C. P. Huntinton miniature train at Neverland Valley Ranch in October 1990

Interior view of 'horse barn' at Chance Rides, Inc., Wichita, KS; Zebra and other animals for Michael Jackson's new 50' Grand Carrousel

Later that month, I was back at the ranch with several "Chance" employees, which included ride installer Bob Boyle and our incredible in-house artist, Robert Nolan Hall. At times I would spend one to two weeks at Neverland, staying in one of four guest quarters near the main house while there visiting or working. This trip I was there to oversee installation of the 50' Grand Carrousel. During my brief absence, Brad Sundberg installed hundreds of feet of hidden wiring on the C. P. Huntington train's coaches, covered them with small white lights and developed a state-of-the-art sound system with music pouring out of countless speakers—all to Michael's specifications. The music (always classical per Michael) played from front to back, and at night the train looked like a 150' Christmas tree on tracks, glistening with lights and beautiful music drifting into the evening air! I had seen, built, ridden, sold and installed a lot of miniature trains in my life, but this one was fantastic. It looked like it jumped right out of a child's storybook!

During the last days of October, the "Chance" crew erected and assembled Michael's carrousel on an elevated pad site with a ramp for the handicapped visitors that Tony's workers had constructed to our specifications prior to its delivery from the factory. The last day of October, two chariots and all sixty animals and horses were finally installed. They worked all day and into the late afternoon, completing the installation on Halloween eve. Tony's team finished some of the site work, Brad had his music system thumping, and everything was ready. None of us had ever seen such attention to detail, such beautiful animals. Robert Hall had gone overboard in creating something so beautiful, and it was easy to see why Robert had designated it "The Magic Carrousel" for Michael.

Norma Staikos made prior arrangements for a special celebration dinner at Neverland on Halloween eve that would include,

408

in addition to Michael, Robert Hall and Bob Boyle with "Chance Rides", David Nordahl, and of course myself. Robert Hall was being recognized by Norma and Michael as the "guest of honor" for his extraordinary efforts in designing and completing the sixty custom animals selected by Michael for his new carrousel. It was late in the day when some of us gathered in the living room before the dinner party, when Michael walked around a corner and into the room directly toward me. Dressed in his traditional style while at home, he was wearing a long sleeve red shirt, white tee-shirt, black slacks, white socks and black loafers. He pulled up in front of me and proclaimed with a very serious look on his face, "Rob, I've been bad!" Needless to say, I was taken by total surprise.

"How so, Michael?" I asked with a puzzled tone.

Maintaining a stoic expression, he began relating an experience the previous night initiated by himself that included David Nordahl as his co-conspirator. Everyone there knew we had intentionally kept Michael from seeing the carrousel animals by leaving them stored in our delivery trailer. Even during the daytime, if we placed them out on the pavement to identify where each was to be installed correctly on the carrousel, we first made sure he was not nearby. However, on the night mentioned, Michael admitted that David Nordahl had helped him sneak out to our trailer, open the back doors and crawl inside with flashlights so he could get a "sneak-peek" at his carrousel horses and menagerie animals. He laughed and I laughed, then we had a good laugh together.

Before we adjourned to the dinning room, Michael presented me with my personal copy of his autobiography, "Moon Walk", which he first inscribed with a red maker pen prior to handing it to me, "To Rob Swinson, Thanx for all your help, Love, Michael Jackson" with his trademark "starburst" below the signature.

(A couple of years later, Michael would pen another personal note to me with a black maker pen on the back of a "Chance Rides" product catalog with a gold color cover, which read: "To Rob. My Maker of Dreams. With Love and Appreciation. Thanx. Michael Jackson."

Unfortunately, this "Chance Rides, Inc." product catalog with gold cover personally signed and given to me by Michael Jackson at Neverland Valley Ranch in May 1992 was stolen from my personal property by another employee after I left "Chance Rides, Inc." in June 1998. The Catalog was discovered missing upon my return to the company soon thereafter to pick up the personal items from my office.)

Everyone there had a very enjoyable evening and a late gourmet dinner with Michael. During dinner, a special plaque decorated with the "Blue Boy" logo and a fairy godmother with her magical wand was presented to Michael from the employees at Chance Rides, Inc. It read:

Michael Jackson,
Neverland Valley
Dreams are living things! They exist outside time & space, yet
they help us understand, & fashion our own worlds. When
carefully nurtured, they have the unlimited capacity for growth
& change. Dreams are generous, forgiving, & life-long compan-
ions. They urge us to reach beyond our very best efforts, to
seize something greater than ourselves. The happiest feeling
imaginable is when a dream embraces reality.
You have shared your dream with us & taken us into its
special world of delight and fulfillment...& happiness. We, too,
have shared our dreams with you...to create one of the most
beautiful carousels ever conceived.
Thank you for enabling us to realize our dreams & may all your

dreams find fulfillment.

Chance Rides Inc.
October 29, 1990

Following dinner, Michael drove me in his "flaming" golf cart out to the carrousel for our inaugural ride. We rode it several times, switching animals and laughing like a couple of kids. Michael's personal video guy was there documenting the event, and some Neverland staff arrived in costumes to join in the fun. It was amazing to see him so at ease—and so happy.

Later in the evening while we were visiting on the carrousel platform, I casually inquired of Michael if he had selected any menagerie animal or horse as his favorite. Instantly Michael began running around the platform inspecting various pieces of incredible carrousel art until he reached the "Butterfly Winged Cherub" horse with flowers woven through its mane, which "Chance" artist Robert Hall had custom designed, fabricated and painted as his special gift to Michael—and had kept it a secret throughout the evening! I was literally blown away when immediately Michael declared loudly with much joy in his voice at his discovery, "This one!" His excitement was infectious— like a kid at Christmas!

I knew Robert Hall had spent many long hours in his shop at the factory, which we affectionately referred to as the "Horse Barn," developing on his own time a unique and very special animal as his personal gift for Michael. As mentioned, it was a secret project, but he shared it with me on occasion as the custom-made and highly decorated animal became a reality. I was impressed with its quality, beauty and style, but nearly all of our custom animals fell into that same category. Robert was truly a professional sculpture and artisan, in both his public and private life. In a lot of ways, his personality, creativeness and

411

Chance Rides, Inc. artist Robert Hall's special beautiful gift for Michael Jackson - 'Butterfly Winged Cherub' horse with flowers woven through mane

Chance Rides, Inc. 50' Grand Carrousel at Neverland Valley Amusement Park; note zoomorphic floral butterfly in flower bed

incredible attention to detail, were some of the same traits I would discover in Michael.

For years after our evening together on the carrousel, I remained overwhelmed at Michael's spontaneous response and then actually selecting the very animal that was Robert Hall's supposed "secret" gift for Michael. It had never even been mentioned to Michael prior to that moment! Finally, on July 4, 2013, David Nordahl disclosed to me in an email, "On that night (Oct. 30 1990) Michael was the one who got a flashlight and coerced me into coming with him to get a sneak preview of the fabulous merry-go-round. He could simply not wait for the official unveiling. That's why he knew exactly which horse he loved the most. Michael always had a difficult time waiting once a project was started."

After several carrousel rides and it getting rather late, most who were sharing this moment with us began departing for the night. Michael and I remained, hanging out by the carrousel, enjoying the moment. Nearby, his miniature train with all the magnificent new custom lighting and music was sitting on the track in full view.

"Michael, would you like to go for a train ride?" I inquired, as an afterthought.
It was getting rather late, but then realizing we were there on "Michael's time," I was pleased when he remarked, "Do you think it would be okay, Rob?"
I think I was roaring with laughter inside as I assured him it would be okay, then reminded him, "Michael, of course! It's your train!"

We walked over to the train, and I recall being a bit disappointed when Michael selected a seat in the second coach, well

413

back behind the engine. I didn't think much about it at the time, so I turned around and hollered to make sure he was ready. He grinned and gave me a thumbs up. After blowing the whistle and ringing the brass bell, I hit the throttle and off we went into the dark of night, racing around the valley. Our way along the track was lit only by the train's headlamp. I must admit, it was a bit spooky!

After some time I slowed the train to a stop and asked him if he wanted to come up and ride on the locomotive next to me.
I will never forget his cautious reply, "Do you think it would be OK?"
I chuckled and said, "Yes, of course it's OK! Michael, it's your train!"
He climbed up on the seat with me, then off we went again into the darkness.

After some more racing along the tracks, I asked him, "Do you want to operate the locomotive?"
Now he was getting very excited.
"Really? Could I? Would it be OK?"
"Of course you can!" I replied, and slowed to another stop for some very basic instructions.
"Just release the air brake here and ease this throttle lever up... that's all there is to it."

He followed my instructions, and it was as if he were eight years old! He laughed and shouted his feelings of great pleasure into the now moonlit crisp night air as his little train chugged around the dark valley at his Neverland Ranch. Lap after lap we rode together. Michael seemed to lose all sense of time; he was just having too much fun.

Then something happened that I will never forget. I remember glancing at my watch, seeing that we were approaching the midnight hour. A gorgeous full moon had peeked up over the top of one of the mountains, coming into our full view. Michael, without warning, suddenly threw his head back and started to howl at the moon! He howled and laughed, and looked over at me. Almost simultaneously, in sync with Michael, I threw my head back and commenced howling with him! Two grown men, riding a miniature train, howling at a full moon! It was an incredible, magical and amazing experience. He knew how to have fun and how to enjoy life.

Then one of the most memorable of my times with Michael occurred next. He turned to me and definitively stated, "I love bringing out the child within each of us! I live for these moments, and wish I could bring out the child that exists within everyone!"

We truly connected on the same level that night and bonded as close friends at that very moment while we were sitting there in the moonlit draped night on his new C. P. Huntington miniature train.

At the end of our Halloween evening together in October 1990, Michael expressed great joy and tremendous appreciation. He was excited that his long-time desire of owning these first two rides and having them installed at his ranch for visitors to enjoy - especially the children - was completed. Our combined success and first-time efforts at his Neverland Ranch would later become the nucleus for fulfilling a very special childhood dream that I believe he rarely shared with others nor talked about openly. Nearly all future plans thereafter revolved around developing and building an actual amusement park at Neverland Valley Ranch for Michael and his guests to enjoy. He had always wished that this dream, as it became a reality, would benefit

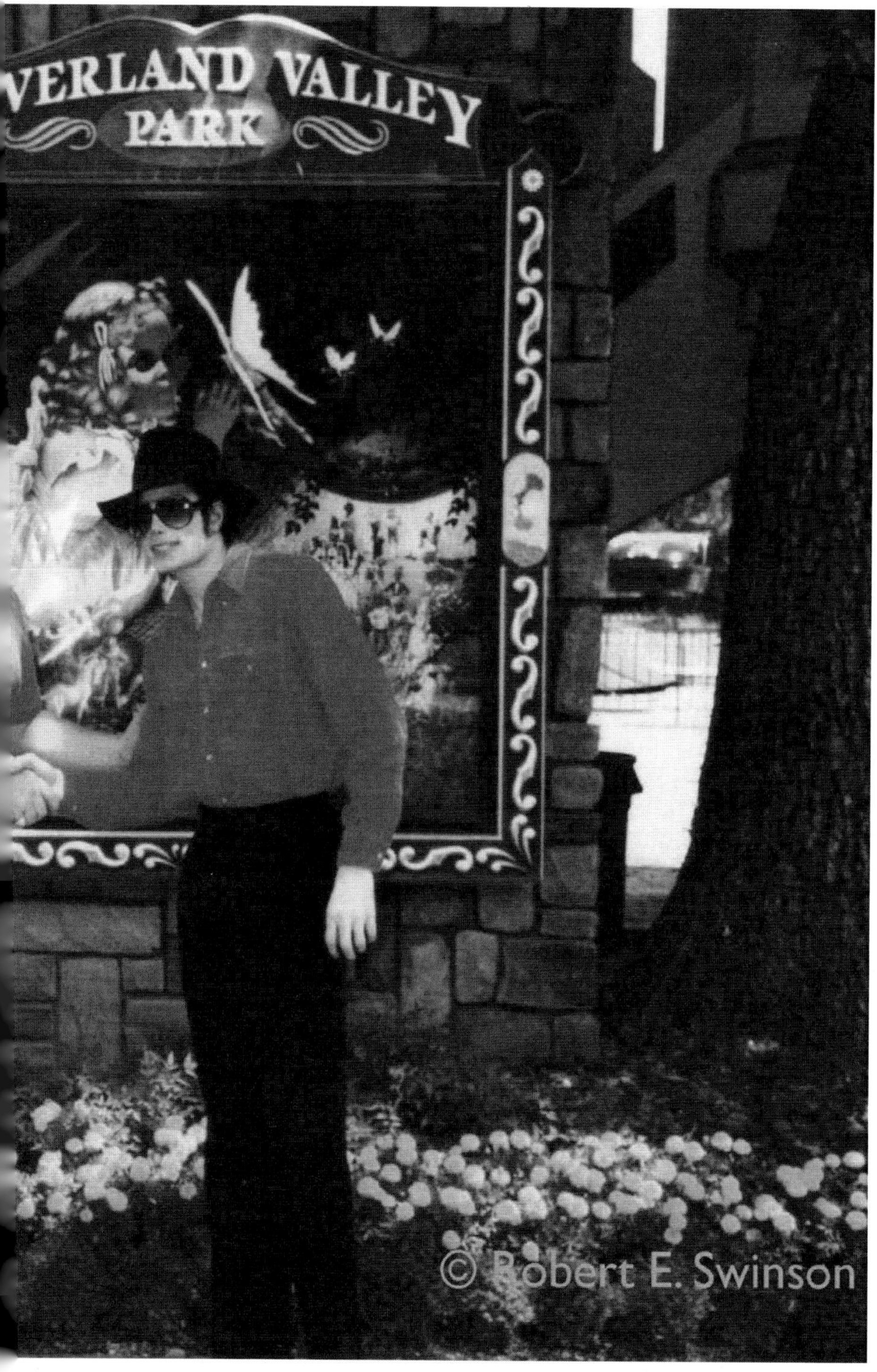
VERLAND VALLEY
PARK

Previous page: Rob Swinson & Michael Jackson in front of Neverland Valley Park sign - sign design copied from David Nordahl's 1989 painting, 'Playmates for a Lonely Child'

David Nordahl, Artist - 'Playmates For A Lonely Child' - 1989; original painting hung in Michael's dining room at Neverland

Delivery of Chance Rides, Inc. Wipeout ride (on padsite in center) being installed in new expansion area of Neverland Valley Amusement Park in May 1992; Ferris Wheel & Sea Dragon far left, theater directly behind Wipeout

and help inspire some of the world's children, and it finally was coming to life.

Michael disappeared into his home and I settled into bed at my guest quarters, although all I could think about that night was riding around on the "Chance Rides" train and carrousel with Michael Jackson! I had never had a client be so genuinely grateful after the delivery and installation of some of our spectacular amusement rides.

The problem with the slipping drive wheels on the train was resolved, and that little train carried thousands of boys, girls, families, friends, celebrities and impoverished kids around Michael's fantasyland - Neverland Valley - for many years. As the amusement park grew, and as bigger and faster rides arrived, I always loved that little train and the beautiful carrousel, and I know Michael did also.

We did our very best to make his dream come true in the form of a special and fun place where he could be a kid and share his dream with children from all walks of life. It was a dream come true not just for him, but for me also.

Every time when a new amusement ride arrived, Michael was as excited as a child having a surprise birthday party. Prior to the delivery of each ride, he would give his input as to where it was to be set up and knew exactly what he wanted. Every detail you saw at Neverland was there because Michael personally wanted it to be there. He literally was Neverland's soul.

I believe one of the reasons why Michael and I bonded so well and enjoyed working together is the fact that we were both perfectionists. This park was very important to him, so important that even after one of his big concerts in Europe, his first

419

thought was to call me at 2 a.m. his time to find out how some new rides were coming along.

Those around Michael were used to his late-night calls and wanting to have a conversation. Norma related to me with a look of exhaustion how Michael would wake her in the middle of the night when she was staying at the ranch and ask if she would meet him at the bottom of the stairway for a "visit" that was never brief. Michael would often call in the middle of a night, and when you answered he would innocently inquire, "Did I wake you?"

Neverland grew constantly, but would never be completed nor fulfill some of his dreams. Many of the huge oak trees found all through the valley of Michael's ranch were filled with thousands twinkling white lights. Disney music could be heard from nearly every part of the valley. Even though it had reached a considerable size over the following years and included over 18 rides by the mid 1990s, Michael's dream had not ended. He had big plans for Neverland because he had dedicated this place to the "children of the world" and especially to the underprivileged, handicapped and terminally ill children. It really was an amazing place and eventually became Michael's personal Fantasyland!

During the development of the park, Michael truly tested the fortitude of county employees with regards to their zoning ordinances that sometimes might slow or restrict the development of this amusement park in his backyard, even though he owned 2,700 acres. The most important ride Michael desired to install as a focal point of his Neverland park project was a thrilling roller coaster, but we were never able to obtain the county's approval. They had been pushed too far!

Regularly he invited bus loads of children, usually arriving on

420

Fridays, from the inner city area of Los Angeles. As I mentioned earlier, those kids who were very sick or came from difficult backgrounds were so special to him, but all the children were warmly welcomed to his ranch to spend a day there, sometimes being there himself in person to share their experience. He wanted them to feel like children and forget whatever problems they had, even if it was just for that one day. He knew about the importance of being a child and understood what it meant to not have a childhood. Michael loved to see those children enjoying his park and zoo and seeing their faces light up with sheer joy and excitement. This was reward enough for him. He was a person who loved to see others happy.

I was witness to Michael welcoming his very special children at the ranch during one of my visits. Before I realized what was happening, he was in the backyard, rolling in the grass with the kids and automatically, like a chameleon, became one of the kids himself. It was a remarkable, instantaneous and almost magical transition.

Michael was deeply committed to helping any child, especially through the Make-A-Wish Foundation. I received a call one day from a lady in Wichita whose daughter was terminally ill, and asked if I could assist her in making arrangements for the daughter to visit Neverland. After discussing the call with Norma at MJJ Productions, I gave her the necessary information about whom to contact, and it was handled from then on by those responsible at Michael's end. On another occasion, Brick Price with "Wonderworks", told me about Michael learning that a female friend of his son Eammon was terminally ill in the hospital and had only one week to live. Almost immediately, the little girl's hospital room was flooded with flowers, dolls and special gifts from Michael. He even called and spoke with her by phone. It lifted her spirits so much that her life was extended for another year. The family credits Michael's intervention, love and inspiration as the reason for their daughter's precious few more months of life. Brick remarked to me, "It was as close to a miracle I have ever witnessed and shows so much of what the mind and a positive attitude can accomplish." Also, others close to Michael have shared stories about witnessing him give unknown needy families large sums of money to try and help them get through difficult situations. Michael was such an unbelievably sharing and giving person, and did so many wonderful things in private of which the general public nor media were ever made aware of. It was never done for publicity!

Neverland's nature was a creative and healing force of its own. You could find your inner peace just by breathing the clear air, taking walks, and admiring some of the hundreds of old oak trees covering the mountains and soft hills. At night time, thousands of stars shone down and you could actually admire the Milky Way from there. Michael would enthusiastically tell me about his future plans for this place, which he already had so clearly created in his mind as it was being developed, and he described it as a place that could bring out the child in everyone, a place of laughing and of healing, a place close to heaven. It indeed was a sacred spiritual place.

On occasion, Michael and I would stroll through the park en route to inspect a recent ride delivery and check out the action with an inaugural ride, which was always fun and entertaining. Sometimes, Michael would suddenly break into a song and dance routine while we were walking. My jaw would drop and a reality check would kick in, reminding me that, "Wow, this really is Michael Jackson, the King of Pop!"

One important fact I have always cherished most about our special relationship, while becoming one of Michael's personal

422

friends and partner in developing his long-time dream, was never placing him on a pedestal - to me has was just Michael being Michael! He was an exceptionally talented individual, loved reading books (voracious reader - 10,000 volume library) and was the most incredible, one-of-a-kind, caring individuals anyone could ever wish to get to know personally. Michael wanted to be remembered primarily as a caring and charitable person – not as a famous personality!

During dinner one evening with Norma and some other guests, Michael really gave me chuckle. We were talking about the 1893 "Chicago World's Fair" when Michael abruptly stood, walked casually behind the chairs, and when he reached the hallway that led back to his library and master bedroom, he took off running down the hall at full speed, unaware that we could still see him! He soon returned carrying a reproduction copy of a book about the Chicago fair, placed it on the table in front of me and started thumbing through the pages to share some pictures, which were of poor quality. When I returned to Wichita, I located an original copy of a book about the same fair, and after inscribing a personal note in the front to Michael, I mailed it to him so he could add it to his own book collection.

We shared many memorable moments and conversations during the coming years. You were truly blessed to be a part of his inner circle of trusted close friends and associates.

Michael and I equally shared what few others could really understand. One thing above all else Michael and I discovered we had in common in our relationship was P-T-T: Performance – Truthfulness – Trust. So many tried, it seemed, to take advantage of him or were involved in some faction of his life primarily for their own personal gain. Never once did I receive any special commission or bonus from MJJ Productions or "Chance

Rides", where I was a salaried employee, for my participation assisting Michael make his dream become reality; nor from any other amusement industry manufacturer I often referred to Michael for their role in helping me develop his Neverland Valley project.

The following is the inspiring forward to "Michael and Norma" copied from the first of three presentation journals by "Chance Rides" artist Robert Nolan Hall, which reads on the inside title page, "THE MAGIC CARROUSEL – Thoughts from the Journal of Robert Nolan Hall , 1990," and was personally inscribed to me in blue ink on the first page of this journal book, hardbound in one of the Neverland Ranch covers titled NEVERLAND VALLEY and features Michael's "Blue Boy in the Moon" logo at the top. The inside first page reads, "8-/6 – 1991 To Rob.... The first copy of the Journal. Robert N. Hall," and was presented to me by the author at that time:

> *MICHAEL AND NORMA*
>
> *My conviction that there is nothing*
> *greater than helping others found its*
> *confirmation during the brief, and yet*
> *timeless moment that you shared your*
> *special world with me.*
>
> *The true magic of Neverland Valley does*
> *not lie only in the beautiful things*
> *to be seen there but radiates from the*
> *inner, quiet understanding that life's*
> *truest fulfillment is bringing joy,*
> *creating peace, and rekindling hope.*
>
> *Being involved with you has left such*

*a strong feeling that this has happened
before.
The inspiration of your Carrousel and
all you are accomplishing has started
my own creativity flowing again as never
before. Thank you for allowing me to
be a part of this.*

May there be magic in all you touch.

Robert Nolan Hall 1/3

If my friend Michael Jackson were still here today, I would tell him, "Thank you, Michael, for allowing me to share some of your footsteps on your path through life... I hope you have found the peacefulness so much desired, and may God bless you for what you were able to accomplish during your too brief of a lifetime here on Earth! Love always - in your name."

Closing Comment

Rob Swinson worked with Michael Jackson during some of the pop star's happiest years and together they built Michael's longtime dream that eventually became a reality at his beloved "Neverland Valley Ranch." Rob, affectionately called "Maker of Dreams" by Michael, is simultaneously publishing a companion photo album book titled "Michael Jackson's Neverland Valley - The Dream Begins!" being released on what would have been his 55th birthday, August 29, 2013. Rob's photo album book illustrates in beautiful color pictures the creation of Michael´s "Neverland" from the very beginning and preserves some wonderful memories he feels are important to share with others, especially Michael's three children. This book will allow its' readers to visually appreciate Michael's dream and enlighten them about his very private life. Together, these two books will forever preserve some wonderful memories in stories and pictures for Michael's many worldwide fans and admirers.

Comments from Friends of Michael

David Nordahl, Michael's personal artist, email July 12, 2013:
Congratulations!...I thought the story was great and it was very well written. Takes me back to a time when Michael was really happy.

Oliver "Brick" Price, owner of "Wonderworks", emails July 13, 2013:
Your story is very well written and thoughtful...You have filled in some major gaps in what I knew about Michael and what we shared...and that between us we brought some joy into Michael's troubled life. I am delighted to see that you feel the same as I about Michael and so glad that I made the introduction to him. A lot of people were simply out to rip off Michael and it was difficult to separate the good from the bad. Unfortunately, Michael was child-like and innocent of the dark side of people.

Brad Sundberg, lights and music for Michael, email July 14, 2013:
Rob, wow...amazing what you have done! Really nice story, great "word-pictures," even brought back several memories of mine... Congrats on a job well-done!

On-line Related Stories

Park World Magazine: "Neverland - Michael Jackson's playground"
http://www.parkworld-online.com/news/fullstory.php/aid/1356/Neverland_-_Michael_Jackson_s_playground.html

www.kwch.com: "Wichitan Talks About Friendship With Michael Jack-

by Robert E. "Rob" Swinson

son"
http://www.kwch.com/kwch-wichitantalksaboutfriendsh-
10673638,0,3977141.story

Youtube: "Neverland ride developer talks about Michael Jackson"
http://www.youtube.com/watch?v=VRucWXcTd44

CNNiReport: "The Maker of Dreams"
http://ireport.cnn.com/docs/DOC-287255

Youtube: "David Nordahl talks Michael Jackson"
http://www.youtube.com/watch?v=RsjVrFBOOto

USA Today: "Michael Jackson's personal artist shared pop king's vision"
http://usatoday30.usatoday.com/life/people/2009-08-20-jackson-paint-
ings_N.htm

www.mjjcommunity.com: "MJJC Exclusive Q&A with Brad Sundberg"
http://www.mjjcommunity.com/forum/threads/129219-MJJC-Exclusive-Q-
amp-A-with-Brad-Sundberg-Read-his-Answers

www.blogtalkradio.com: "Brad Sundberg: In the Studio With Michael"
http://www.blogtalkradio.com/a-place-in-your-heart/2013/06/07/brad-sun-
berg-in-the-studio-with-michael

The Garden Island: "Wailua's Sumi stands by Michael Jackson, his former boss"
http://thegardenisland.com/article_4c82e7c2-26df-52d4-bcb9-
aa04d1e5b620.html

by Robert E. "Rob" Swinson

The Power of Love

by Violet Gaitan-Silva, USA
Neverland Ranch - Head of Security

The most remarkable outcome from working at Neverland is how much we became a family. We all became a team. All ordinary people, none of us "Hollywood", music or celebrity background – we were local. Nevertheless we somehow managed to really embrace what Michael wanted there with his home - to be very welcoming to his guests and treat them with love and affection. Down to earth and family orientated people understood that and were willing to serve. In my experience in working with him, he made me understand that to be of service to people is really a privilege and being able to give to other people from your heart is not something everyone can do. You have a profession, a skill or training, but you cannot train people to be respectful, to love right from your heart, to be caring or to be genuine. The people who worked there were those kinds of people.

We were a very young group of people as far as working together, and we had our growing pains, learning to be around each other, to function as a team and communicate, but we grew together. The events that we did at Neverland were the source of our growth, an opportunity to be creative outside of our normal positions and we were surprised at how cre-

428

ative and well we worked together. Our goal was to present Michael's message in the best way.

Most people don´t know that Michael took so much time to every detail and the purpose of Neverland. The impression and message was "You are very special." From every flower bed, to placement of lights, statues or the music that was played - every little thing was touched by him.

That is what drove Neverland. It was not Michael's intention and he never asked "I want you to do this for me, for my comfort." It was always for each visitor of Neverland. The experience should feel absolutely wonderful and special. We represented him and the love and care that he wanted people to feel. It was even true for every person who came through the gates, even contractors and vendors. We were to mirror his values.

Doing all these events at Neverland was something very special. So many children visited who either had terminal illnesses (i.e. from the Make-A-Wish foundation) or who had disabilities and it was very touching to see them suddenly come to life. They would open up, be happy, their eyes were sparkling, they were smiling, not really knowing or remembering what they were ailing from - they had all this energy! They were really inspirational for us as a staff to continue that work.

In any job you do regularly it eventually becomes routine. Well, it became kind of routine for us to have a wonderful time at these events, however what made it special were the groups were different every time. Each group brought their own energy and left us with a sense of gratitude for spending time with them.

What they shared was very touching, to see them suddenly

by Violet Gaitan-Silva

come to life. No matter how many times we did such events, it was always such a great feeling at the end of the day.

Imagine we were doing big and small events on a weekly basis whether Michael was at home or not. Michael had kids visiting the ranch for six to seven months out of the year. It was amazing to see some of these kids coming in, disadvantaged ones from neighbourhoods without any privileges, and here they were spending the day being able to do whatever they wanted. It was a beautiful thing to see, but on the other hand it was also very sad, because there was this shyness about them when it came to choosing a treat from the snack bar in the theatre and not understanding that they can have whatever they wanted. They would take forever to make a decision about the candy they wanted, because they thought they can only have one. So they were going to pick the very best candy and when we said, "Oh no, you can pick two or three", you could see this relief happen in their little faces. It really took them a little while to adjust to the freedom of choices - that was nice to see.

The kids visiting Neverland came from many places and from all over the world, but Michael also did a lot of good things for the local people in his community. For example, there was a small elementary school across the street and Michael let the trainers of the zoo take animals there, as a show and tell for the kids. They could touch the animals, hands on – snakes or parrots. He also did this for other elementary schools in the Santa Ynez Valley and around Santa Barbara.

Michael also often opened up his home to many local schools or any sort of organization raising money through silent auctions by donating a package for ten people to spend a day at the ranch. The highest bidder and his guests could spend a really nice day at Neverland and it was a win-win situation for all. The

430

cost to host ten people at the ranch takes the same amount of work as if you are going to have hundred people. The staff is on for you that day, the entire staff, and not just a few people. We did a lot of those events, big ones and small intimate ones.

Michael also loved to watch these group events from inside of his home. Very few times did Michael come out to greet event guests, if he did, the day would suddenly become about him and he avoided that attention. He wanted it to be about them, the children. He wanted them to enjoy themselves. Once he came out, it was over. They didn't care about the rides or the animals anymore, they just wanted to be around him. He was so charismatic that he could have had ants following him.

I recall one smaller event when fifty kids and adults were visiting the ranch and Michael came out to greet everyone. He invited all the kids into his house; they were local kids from Lompoc. A friend of mine is a speech therapist chaperoning this group of special kids. Whatever disability they had, it did not seem to affect them because they all knew who he was and they had the time of their life. These kids spent a little time with him, Prince and Paris. Prince was a very good host who welcomed them in and showed them through the whole house. At such a young age he felt the privilege of helping others.

A touching story about Michael and Prince happened on an evening of their return after many weeks of not being home. During that time the "Neverland Gate" was being installed and it was quite a production and so was greeting guests. As I mentioned earlier, Michael was very particular to the effect it would have as guest entered and arrived.

Usually, when guests came in who were driven to the house, the staff would line up at the front walkway. This included the house staff, the cooks, security and fire department - if it was during the daytime we would also bring animals to the house, elephants or parrots. All of that, the music, the staff and animals, as you might imagine, made the arrival at Neverland very special. And for us it was so much fun.

We set up a dry run for him from the perspective of what the guests might experience, when they come in and the gate opens. We practiced it through: when a car pulls up and puts weight on the asphalt before the gate, it would open automatically.

As Michael arrived with his children Prince and Paris, it was around 9pm and already dark. I must add that whenever guests came or events took place, Michael beforehand would specify if the guests would be driven directly to the house or if they were to be dropped off at the parking lot in front of the gate and walk in. It depended on what he wanted his guests to experience. So, that day Michael came in a limousine and he wanted to park at the parking lot and he wanted to walk in through the gate.

We had someone at the gate with a remote because now there was no weight of a car to open the gate automatically and start off the music at the right time. So, to make it all perfect for Michael, someone had to use the remote and press it exactly at the right moment.

On this night, we especially welcomed him home and lined up all along the road from the gate up to the house. The kids, Prince and Paris looked a little sleepy; maybe they had fallen asleep in the car. Prince was walking a bit behind Michael trying to keep up, although Michael walked slowly. He was looking at everything, saying it was beautiful and he stopped and talked

432

to me for a little bit. I welcomed him home and he continued walking. Then Prince walked by, he was still tiny, maybe three or four years old. I said, "Good evening Prince, welcome home, it's nice to see you again." He didn't say anything, but kept on walking.

Then Michael stopped, walked back, took Prince by the hand and said, "Prince, Violet said good evening to you". Of course I am feeling very small and bad at that moment, but I really appreciated that he was teaching his children that everyone was the same. Prince probably knew that I worked there. And as embarrassed as I felt, I also felt quite humbled that Michael took the time to very gently show his son that everyone is important especially when they are greeting you.

I must say that all of the kids, Prince, Paris and Blanket were just so lovely. Every time they came out, they would always acknowledge everyone. I know that could only have come from Michael himself – he was teaching his children what he believed in, his values…and that was done consistently. The children were always very attentive, appreciative of everything you did for them and very polite.

I was very touched by that little exchange between Michael and I - Prince just looked at me, his little face was so sleepy. It was nice and showed what an awesome father he was.

To be a part of providing a safe place to raise his children and seeing him as a parent was just the most amazing thing. That was the first thing I thought of when I heard he had passed away, I just cried and cried for his children. The love that was between them was a thing of beauty. How he cared for them and they loved him so much. It was a privilege to be a part of that, making his home safe for him and his family.

by Violet Gaitan-Silva

My training was in Law Enforcement and before I was hired as security, I went through a very extensive hiring process. Having graduated from the Police Academy I was unsure how my training and skills would be applied in such a setting as Neverland. I was fortunate in many aspects, mainly working with great officers and fire-fighters. The fire and security department ran as one and the "Neverland Valley Ranch Fire Department" was a certified state fire agency. We were dispatched from the ranch to respond and assist the Santa Barbara County Fire Department. We ran many calls off the property, to help with accidents or brushfires and helping people in need. This was Michael's contribution to his community of Los Olivos (the little town nearby Neverland Ranch). He had high regard for his community and simply wanted everyone to be safe. The actual state fire department closest to the area had a response time between twenty and thirty minutes which is precious time for someone injured or in dire need. We responded mostly to calls on Figueroa Mountain Road leading into the ranch.

A few years ago, almost the whole county was on fire with bushfires and every fire department in the area left to fight the fires. In that time we would do little patrols through town every day, so people knew we are there and we would respond if something happens, just to make them feel safe while everybody else is gone. This was our purpose throughout the year whether Michael was at home or not. Our first priority remained at Neverland but more often than not we responded to calls outside of the property.

I would say to him when he returned home after a longer absence, "Welcome home, Neverland missed you!" Neverland wasn´t just a piece of property, it was a living thing that required him, that missed him, needed his touch, his warmth and thoughts…he used to give me a smile then. His vision was our

434

purpose and mission... He was the heartbeat of Neverland and he did breathe life into it.

It would be easy for anyone to assume that Michael Jackson was a demanding boss and working for him required patience. Now that I can look back at that time it was really Michael who was being patient with us. He could see we were trying to do our best to create his vision and we were doing it from our heart - not with the skill he was maybe used to in the show business - we were kind of running off our heart in a willingness to do it. He was so creative, it was just pouring out of him all the time. He wasn´t this extraordinarily eccentric person everybody thought he is. It was never hard working for him, because of his generosity. Mistakes were made but all converted themselves into learning experiences. His influence and kindness worked as a safety net for our growth.

In many ways he was a down to earth, funny, practical and spontaneous person that injected surprise. Michael drove his golf cart or quad runner to one of the two schools that were across the road of Neverland. Michael would play basketball with the students, hang out and all of a sudden he calls us and there is this huge group of kids coming into the ranch, practically the whole school walking across the street, spending a couple of hours at Neverland and having fun.

He would also drive up to the outer gate on a quad with his helmet on and just see what is going on. If there was a family or other people there, he would often go up to them, take off his helmet and after a bit of shock or screaming, he would talk to them. He loved to get to know more about people, he would ask where they are from and often he would say, "Well, just come in" and he invited them into his ranch. People were overwhelmed of course, expecting nothing more than passing

435

by the outside gate of Neverland, maybe taking a quick picture and next thing you know is that Michael Jackson greets you personally and invites you in. It sounds unbelievable, but he did that a lot of times! It was amazing to see how Michael could really touch all kinds of people, even those you would never expect. He was able to do that being himself and make you feel comfortable that way.

Just recently I watched the "This is it" movie and watching how he included and treated people he worked with, reminded me of his generosity. Sure, he had high expectation for us to "perform" because that was what we did, we were performing and it was an honor to represent him. He raised the bar so high, not because he was demanding, but because he believed in us. It became even more clearly at the end of the "This is it" movie, in the credits, he gives thanks to certain people, including about ten people who worked for him at Neverland. I was one of those people. I found out about that only a year ago - I was just overcome, because it made me realize that the credits were published just weeks before his death. For him to be that thoughtful and caring to thank those people, he really must have been in a place where he was lucid and strong and caring - just the person I always knew he was.

I believe there are so many aspects about Michael Jackson, that people will find a connection to him, a comfort or something familiar. Whether it is his music, his dancing, his lyrics or the human person that he was - there are many sides to him that people will identify with and love him for.

His message is timeless I think and will go on forever - there will never be another Michael Jackson. In all he did and achieved, he was always spreading a good message. He could have given up many times, when he was publicly scrutinized, he could have

436

just put his hands up and say "I´m done", "I´m going to retreat and live by myself and mind my own business", but he kept that good fight up which was good even till the end.

I worked for Michael for 16 years, obviously I don´t know how you can ever compare working anywhere else to working at Neverland. Since I left and stopped working for Michael, I have not been back to Neverland. I love the memory I have and want to keep it that way.

I spent my time at Neverland protecting him and trying to understand him, but he has really taught me so much that I feel I have a lifetime of protection by him. It is ironic in a way.

At the time, I was quite busy being very professional and very serious about the job, about him and his family and everyone who was there. Only later, after his passing, I realized how much being around him, being influenced by him and his generosity, just the kind of person that he was, changed me in a profound way. Obviously those lessons are protecting me now in many ways – emotionally and mentally. But it doesn´t make me guarded, it makes me a more open person to everyone. Realizing his message, which was the power of love, is really the only way to get through things. No matter if you are afraid of anything, the truth and love is what rules the world.

I wish I had the chance to thank him for this, but my position did not really allow it. But he respected me; I respected him, in a way that worked for both of us. However, realizing afterwards, what an opportunity I had to be around him for that many years, and all the trust that he had in me, I would like to thank him for that. To let him know that there is a stigma, of being professional and not allowing your emotions to get involved, but working at Neverland, it was impossible to lock out your

by Violet Gaitan-Silva

emotions. You could not come with a resume and bullet point describing yourself as a caring person, it had to be something that he felt in you and that you were able to display in your actions. I am most proud of that...that I worked with outstanding caring people who rose to a challenge, continued working with the best integrity during very difficult times without wavering.

We all showed him in our work, in respecting him and sticking by him, but there was never an opportunity to have a personal exchange to express gratitude and really mean it as an individual - from one person to another. I never had that opportunity, but maybe he did know how I felt – I am sure he did.

If I could say anything now, it would be, "I love you, thank you for being my friend."

© Markus Thiele

by Violet Gaitan-Silva

Neverland appeals to the child inside every man, woman and child. It's a place where I feel that you can return to your childhood. You find grown-ups doing things they haven't done since they were ten years old and it's just a wonderful place to be. There's unlimited space to go on quads, mountains and horse back and all kinds of fun things. I love it and I will always love it. I will never sell Neverland. Neverland is me, you know, it represents the totality of who I am.

I WAS THERE!

by Seth Riggs, USA

I had been a vocal coach for many years already before I met Michael Jackson. I had started to work with Stevie Wonder, later with Ray Charles and many more talented artists. Then came Michael. I became his vocal coach when he was in his early 20s. Of course I knew about him before, but I had never met him. Quincy Jones arranged our meeting.

On "Thriller" I spent two hours a day, six days a week. On his tours I usually vocalized him from noon to 1 pm, 4 to 4:30 pm in the afternoon and 8:15 till 8:30 pm before he went on stage. So I spent a lot of time with Michael and got to know him as a friend.

He had quite a sense of humor. One night he called me over to vocalize him at 10 pm. I got to the studio where he was recording and he was talking on his cell phone. He was just saying: "I don't know what the name of that is..." when I arrived. When he saw me, he immediately called: "Oh, Seth, would you go over into studio A? There is a guy and he knows which song it is that I like." He was obviously looking for the name of a song. So I said: "Sure!".

I went over and the guy who was there played the song for

me that Michael liked. It was "Non piangere Liu". So I said: "Ok, that's the other aria from 'Turandot', 'Nessun dorma' is the one that's known so well."

When I came back, Michael was still on the phone and he said: "Oh, Seth, what was it?" I answered: "Non piangere Liu". He asked: "What?" -"Non piangere, don't cry, don't weep, don't be sad. And her name was Liu. Don't be sad, Liu, it's from 'Turandot', the opera by Puccini." But as he couldn't speak Italian he told me: "I can't say that. I don't know how... here, take the phone!" So I took the phone and I said: "Excuse me, he's talking about..." and then I started singing "Non piangere Liu". On the other end this voice exclaimed with an Italian accent: "Really good voice. Always keep a good line." And then the voice sang the line to me and it just blew me away. So I asked: "Excuse me. Who is this?" And the voice answered: "Luciano Pavarotti". I turned around to where Michael was and he was lying on the floor on his back with his feet up on the couch, holding his stomach, rolling back and forth from laughing so hard. I put my hand over the mouth piece of the cell phone and hissed: "I'm gonna kill you, Michael!" Then I went back on the phone and said: "Oh, I'm so sorry, Maestro. It is 10.20 pm out here and I had no idea Michael would be talking to you because it's twenty minutes after one in the night in New York where you are." And he said: "No, no, it's all right. Always keep a good line." I said: "I'm sorry, Maestro. If I had known I'd say hello to you I would have vocalized for twenty minutes." Michael loved moments like that. He loved to laugh and make other people laugh and see them happy and having fun. As much as laughing, Michael loved to give.

I became very much aware of Michael's charitable side very early. There are many stories that immediately come to my mind when I think about Michael's humanitarian efforts. One of the

441

by Seth Riggs

most amazing stories is this one:

There was a man who put his son in a hotel room and set fire to the room. And the boy was burned very badly. When Michael read about it he immediately chartered a plane and went to see him. As Michael walked into the room, the young man was a whole mess of bandages with little chunks of hair sticking out amongst them on the top of his head and a little hole to talk or breathe through in the very front. They talked together and at one point the young man said in a muffled voice: "I dunno what I'm gonna do." And Michael said: "Don't worry. I'm gonna take care of you for the rest of your life." And he did! He found work for him, supported him and stayed in contact with him until he, Michael, passed away.

Michael was always aware of what was happening around him and tried to help whenever he heard about dramatic events. One time Michael read in the newspaper about a married couple with three kids in Long Beach, California. For some reason the man had walked off and left the family. The wife had no money, was desperate and didn't know what to do. So she went down to a bridge and threw the baby off, then the other kids and then she jumped herself. People saw that and they ran down and fished her out. It was too late for the baby already, it drowned, but the two other kids and the wife were saved. A little time later there was the funeral for the baby and everyone was waiting for the funeral to start. It took some time, so people started asking: "Why hasn't the funeral started?". Someone from the family said: "The person who paid for it is not here." And at that moment a limousine came up and Michael stepped out.

But even without a specific event, Michael just loved to give and make people happy. I remember in London at 10 o'clock

442

at night they would open a toy store for Michael. He would go through with two or three clerks and he'd say: "Oh, look at that doll. Give me ten of those. Oh, look at that truck. The boys will love that. Give me ten of those." and so on…then he would stay up all night long putting batteries into the toys so they worked. The next day security would help him carry all the toys and he'd go to a children's hospital and pass them out and take pictures with them. That is Michael!

We also started a camp together and I would hire a big bus and take parents and their children to Neverland Ranch. Of course the kids just loved it, they ran around while I sat down somewhere and watched. But soon the parents came over with tears in their eyes saying: "Where have you brought us? This is a magical place!" And they were right. Neverland was the most unbelievable place. Unfortunately the media made it into something that it never was. When you were at Neverland, you understood that Michael's was a different existence than that of any person you know. He was always the eternal child.

When we went to Italy once, somebody gave a big party for him. He got there and all of a sudden he disappeared. Security was going crazy. So finally they went to the end of the big room where everyone was meeting, eating and drinking and waiting for Michael and they opened these big doors that went from floor to ceiling – there was Michael sitting on the floor in the midst of little boys and girls and they were playing with dolls.

He worshipped youth. But I've never ever seen him mistreat a child in any way. Never! But after they had raided Neverland, Michael told me: "They have ruined my home. They have gone through it and ripped everything apart looking for something they'll never find because it doesn't exist. I don't think I ever want to go back." They walked into the middle of his dream.

And his dream was real. There was a train that ran around the property, there was one whole building of pinball machines, there was a theatre and you could come out and take as much candy as you wanted - like a miniature Disneyland almost three hours out of L.A.

After the horrible events of 2005, I worked with him on "This is it" as well. Michael was terribly loyal and so we were basically the same old crew: Karen Faye used to do his hair, Michael Bush did his clothing and I worked his voice. But then I left the project. I told Michael: "Mike, they offer me less money than they did twenty years ago. They want me to take less salary that buys two thirds less of what it used to buy. They are doing it with everybody." He said: "I know. They're taking away all the people that I know and that I'm comfortable with. My security blanket is disappearing. I don't know what I'm gonna do. I can't sleep."

When he died, I had known him for 31 years. I have 125 Grammys in my studio and taught over 300 celebrities for over half a century but Michael was the most amazing man that I have ever met. He was such a magnificent, innocent, but very misunderstood man. His message was that we are all one family. I really want people to understand who he was and how marvellous he was – not just as a performer but as a human being. Some people don't choose to believe that. But the thing is that: I was there!

Michael and I used to pray together. One time we were on our knees and we thanked God for our careers. We were arm in arm. And he said: "It's your turn." And I prayed: "Dear Lord, everything Michael has said I agree with, but particularly I'm so happy that you have put me in his life so I can watch all the wonderful things that he does and the way that he does them." That was my prayer.

444

Michael, my dear beloved friend, those of us who knew you will try to carry on in the best Michael Jackson manner. The only problem that we have is that we are not the supreme star and dance and singing genius that you still are somewhere. But we will find you, Michael – sooner or later.

Seth Riggs today

by Seth Riggs

EPILOGUE

by Brigitte Bloemen, Marina Dobler & Miriam Lohr

Michael always emphasized that he cannot heal this world on his own but only WE can do it.

What we are left with is the memory of a good example to inspire us.

He set the spark – let's keep this fire burning!

> *"And in the end the love you take
> Is equal to the love you make"*

Light conjures a heart on Michael's hair in Monaco, 2000 © Kerstin Reinke

  446

I really feel that nature is trying to compensate for man's mismanagement of the planet. The planet is sick, like a fever. If we don't fix it now it is at the point of no return. This is our last chance to fix this problem that we have or it's like a runaway train. The time has come! This is It! People are always saying, "Oh they, they'll take care of it. The government will do it. They will..." They who? It starts with us. It's us, or else it will never be done..

Bibliography

page 9
"Dangerous." in: Upscale Magazine. August/September 1991.

page 31
Piers Morgan. "Edited highlights of the Mirror's world exclusive interview with pop superstar Michael Jackson". April 13, 1999 <http://www.youtube.com/watch?feature=player_detailpage&v=X4BzkoqpHrc> 25.11.2009 [20.07.2013].

page 43
"Michael Jackson talks to Oprah: 90 Minutes with the King of Pop". ABC. 10.02.1993.

page 50
"Private Home Movies". Fox Television Network. 24.04.2003.

page 87
Michael Jackson's address at Oxford University U.K., 06.03.2001.
"The Oxford Union – Videos of Speakers." <http://www.oxford-union.org/about_us/videos_of_speakers> 23.03.2008 [20.07.2013].

page 108
"20th annual American Music Awards from the Shrine Auditorium, Los Angeles, California." ABC. 25.01.1993.

page 127
Michael Jackson's adrdess at Oxford University U.K., 06.03.2001.

page 149
Press conference at Kennedy Airport in New York City, New York, USA. 24.11.1992.
"1992 Michael Jackson Heal the World Conference Sarajevo 2." <http://www.youtube.com/watch?v=AmJaiIUSZvU> 25.02.2010 [20.07.2013].

page 231
News conference at the "Radio City Music Hall" in New York City where Michael announced the "Dangerous Tour" and the creation of his "Heal The World Foundation",. 03.02.1992.
"Michael Jackson - Pepsi Speech 1992 (sottotitoli italiano)" <http://www.youtube.com/watch?v=4u5O71kloRE> 29.01.2011 [20.07.2013].

page 257
Boteach, Shmuley. "Honoring the child spirit". Cds Books, 2011.

page 258 - 271
composed from an interview with Dieter Wiesner on 1st November, 2012
Similar and more information can be found in:
Wiesner, Dieter. *Michael Jackson. Die wahre Geschichte.* (München: Heyne, 2011)

page 290
"Michael's World". in: Who Weekly Magazine, June 1993.

page 301
"Private Home Movies". Fox Television Network. 24.04.2003.

page 318
Jackson, Michael. Dancing the Dream. Poems and reflections

written by Michael Jackson. 1st ed. Doubleday dell Publishing group, New York. July 1992.

page 334
"Bambi Awards". ARD. 01.11.2002
"Michael Jackson Bambi Awards 2002" < http://www.youtube.com/watch?v=z9yo_Z3Lyqk > 23.05.2011 [20.07.2013].

page 350
Jackson, Michael. Heal The World (Spoken Version) Audio - Promo CD Maxi Single "Signature Series" Epic, 1993.

page 381
Michael Jackson's address at Oxford University U.K., 06.03. 2001.

page 393
Michael Jackson's address at Oxford University U.K., 06.03. 2001.

page 439
"Private Home Movies". Fox Television Network. 24.04.2003.

page 447
"This is it". The Michael Jackson Company, LLC/AEG Live. Columbia Pictures. 2010.

page 451
Jackson, Michael. Dancing the Dream. Poems and reflections written by Michael Jackson. 1st ed. Doubleday dell Publishing group, New York. July 1992.

page 446
Lennon, McCartney. "The End". On: Abbey Road, Apple, 1969.

As long as love is in my heart,
it's everywhere.

Thank you's

Alina Arenz
Gina Banic
Jesica Gimenez
Stephanie Große
Claudia Sanchez Maureira
Dr. Karen Moriarty
Chantal Obrist
Vera Serova
William Wagener
Frank Wagner
Sonja Winterholler

Communities
:: Dear Michael... Mensajero de Amor
   (facebook.com/groups/dearmichael.lizjohnson)
:: Jacksonvillage (mjklub.com)
:: King of Pop Fanatics Sweden (kopfsweden.com)
:: Malibu Michael Jackson & Family Fanclub
   (http://malibufanclub.de)
:: Memorial in honour of Michael Jackson in Munich/Germany
   (facebook.com/MichaelJacksonMemorialMunich)
:: Michackson (michackson.com)
:: Michael Jackson World Network (mjworld.net)
:: Reflections on the dance (reflectionsonthedance.com)
:: Team Michael Jackson (teammichaeljackson.com)
:: Vindicating Michael (vindicatemj.wordpress.com)

CREDITS

Cover
Background Picture back: Ramona Lehnerer
Background Picture front: Alan Z. Uster - Fotolia.com
Layout: Olaf Haensch & Miriam Lohr

Layout
Miriam Lohr & Jenny Jo Zimmermann
Brush: Ahmed Galal (Vector Pack 3)

Pictures
All pictures © the authors of the respective stories unless otherwise noted

MESSAGE FROM MAKE-A-WISH

We are really pleased and excited that Make-A-Wish Deutschland e.V. is again the beneficiary charity – a special thanks to Gitti, Marina, Miri and Sonja as well as all authors and supporters for donating their time, individual stories, experiences and pictures to make this project come true. The generous support through the proceeds will help us to grant magical wishes of children with life-threatening medical conditions.

Michael himself believed that a wish experience can be a game-changer. During a wish experience, joy eclipses illness – this one belief guides and inspires us.

Our wishes are truly special. Whether a wish is to be a princess or a policeman for a day, own a special playground, meet a favourite celebrity or just enjoy some special time away from home with their family, a wish come true brings so much to a child's life and provides memories that last a lifetime

Wishes are only made possible through the hard work of supporters like you – thank you!

Laura Eckerl
CEO Make-A-Wish Deutschland e.V. (Germany)

Deutschland

Make-A-Wish® Deutschland e.V., Landwehrstraße 61, 80336 München

To whom it may concern

Munich, July 4 2013

Dear Madam or Sir,

I am happy and pleased to hereby confirm in the name of Make-A-Wish Deutschland e.V. (Germany) that all proceeds of the book

"A life for L.O.V.E. - Michael Jackson stories you should have heard before"

will be generously donated jointly on behalf of all authors.

A special thank to Sonja, Gitti, Marina, Miri, and to all authors and supporters of this project for their generous gift to support Make-A-Wish Deutschland e.V. (Germany) and help us to grant magical wishes of children with life-threatening medical conditions to enrich the human experience with hope, strength and joy.

If you have any questions please do not hesitate to contact us.

Sincerely

Dr. Patrick Ams
Chairman of the Board,
Make-A-Wish Deutschland e.V.

About Make-A-Wish* Deutschland e.V.

Make-A-Wish* Deutschland e.V. grants wishes for children with life-threatening medical conditions to enrich the human experience with hope, strength and joy for the children and their families. The non-profit association was founded in June 2008 in Hamburg. Representing one of more than 35 national affiliates of the Make-A-Wish Foundation* International. Fore more information about Make-A-Wish* Deutschland e.V. please visit www.makeawish.de and discover how you can share the power of a wish*.

About the Make-A-Wish* Foundation International

Make-A-Wish* Foundation International grants the wishes for children with life-threatening medical conditions to enrich the human experience with hope, strength and joy. It is the largest wish-granting organization in the world and can be found in over 36 countries on five continents. Make-A-Wish Foundation* International serves children outside the United States, while the Make-A-Wish* Foundation of America serves children within the United States. Both organizations gave granted more than 300.000 wishes around the world since 1980, giving children hope, strength and joy. For more information about Make-A-Wish* Foundation International, please visit www.worldwish.org and discover how you can share the power of a wish*.

Make-A-Wish® Deutschland e.V.
Landwehrstraße 61, 80336 München
Telefon: +49 (0)89 411123305
Fax: +49 (0)89 420 959 4809
www.makeawish.de

Vorstand:
Dr. Patrick Ams (Vorsitzender),
Gerlinde Henger (stv. Vorsitzende),
Christian Bartsch, Anton Wald,
Petra Pohl-Feuchtinger

Bankverbindung: Deutsche Bank, Hamburg
Konto: 0562266 00
BLZ: 200 700 24
IBAN: DE 84200 700240 056226500
BIC-/SWIFT-Code: DEUTDEDBHAM

Vereinsregisternummer
AG München VR 204561
Steuernummer:
Finanzamt Hamburg-Nord
17/451/07008
Neue Steuernummer ab 2013: Finanzamt
München 143/219/01078